The Trout

A volume in the New Naturalist Series, a survey
of British natural history published by Collins
and edited by John Gilmour, Sir Julian Huxley,
Margaret Davies, and Kenneth Mellanby. The
New Naturalist has been described by the *Listener*
as 'one of the outstanding feats of publishing
since the war', and *The Times Literary Supplement*
as 'a series which has set a new standard in
natural history books'. Founded in 1945, it now
contains more than 50 volumes, of which the
following have already appeared in Fontana:

The Snowdonia National Park WILLIAM CONDRY
The Highlands and Islands
  F. FRASER DARLING & J. MORTON BOYD
The Peak District K. C. EDWARDS
A Natural History of Man in Britain
  H. J. FLEURE & M. DAVIES
Wild Flowers J. GILMOUR & M. WALTERS
The Open Sea – Its Natural History
Part I: The World of Plankton ALISTER HARDY
Insect Natural History A. D. IMMS
The Life of the Robin DAVID LACK
Life in Lakes and Rivers
  T. T. MACAN & E. B. WORTHINGTON
Climate and the British Scene GORDON MANLEY
Pesticides and Pollution KENNETH MELLANBY
Mountains and Moorlands W. H. PEARSALL
The World of the Soil E. JOHN RUSSELL
Britain's Structure and Scenery L. DUDLEY STAMP
The Sea Shore C. M. YONGE

EDITORS

John Gilmour MA VMH
Sir Julian Huxley MA DSc FRS
Margaret Davies MA PhD
Kenneth Mellanby ScD CBE

PHOTOGRAPHIC EDITOR

Eric Hosking FRPS

The Trout

The Natural History of the Brown Trout
in the British Isles

W. E. Frost and M. E. Brown

Collins
The Fontana New Naturalist

First published in the New Naturalist Series 1967
First published in Fontana 1970
Second Impression April 1973
Copyright © W. E. Frost and M. E. Brown, 1967

CONDITIONS OF SALE: This book is sold subject
to the condition that it shall not, by way of trade
or otherwise, be lent, re-sold, hired out or
otherwise circulated without the publisher's prior
consent in any form of binding or cover other than
that in which it is published and without a
similar condition including this condition being
imposed on the subsequent purchaser

Printed in Great Britain
Collins Clear-Type Press: London and Glasgow

Contents

Editors' Preface   11

Authors' Preface   13

Introduction   15

1 Anatomy and Physiology   21

2 Taxonomy   42

3 Distribution   57

4 Life History   65

5 Age and Growth   85

6 Heredity   109

7 The Physical Environment   124

8 The Trout's Food   176

9 The Biological Environment   218

10 Trout and Man   241

  Appendix

   I *The routine examination of trout*   270

   II *Age and growth determination from trout
    scales*   272

   III *Rivers*   278

   IV *Lakes*   280

   V *How to calculate specific growth rates*   283

VI *Specific growth rates* 285

VII *Examination of stomach contents of brown trout* 286

VIII *List of waters for which we have data on total hardness* 290

List of References 292

Index 305

Plates

1. Female trout excavating her nest (*T. A. Stuart*)

2. Brown trout spawning (*T. A. Stuart*)

3. Early stages in a brown trout's development
    (*A. E. Ramsbottom*)

4. Alevin (*A. E. Ramsbottom*)
    Trout fry (*A. E. Ramsbottom*)
    Adult brown trout and rainbow trout (*John Tarlton*)

5. Wastwater (*Sanderson & Dixon*)
    Small Water (*T. Parker*)

6. Scales from trout in rivers (*A. E. Ramsbottom*)

7. Scales from trout in lakes (*A. E. Ramsbottom*)

8. Scales of brown trout, sea trout, rainbow trout and
    salmon (*A. E. Ramsbottom* and *J. A. Hutton*)

9. Windermere (*C. H. Wood (Bradford) Ltd.*)
    Lough Derg (*Bord Faillte*)

10. Filby Broad, Norfolk (*J. Allan Cash*)
    Eye Brook Reservoir (*Stewarts & Lloyds Ltd.*)

11. Mossburn, a tributary of the River Tees (*K. Parkes*)
    Upper River Liffey (*J. R. Harris*)

12. River Swale (*Kenneth Scowen*)
    River Wharfe (*G. Douglas Bolton*)

13. River Tweed (*Kenneth Scowen*)
    River Barle (*G. Douglas Bolton*)

14. River Dove (*G. Douglas Bolton*)

15. River Itchen (*Mustograph*)

16. River Avon (*Mustograph*)
    River Arun (*Kenneth Scowen*)

Maps

I Distribution of brown trout in the world   51

II Orography of the British Isles   153

III Average temperatures of the British Isles   154

IV Geology showing lime-bearing rocks   156

V Growth of trout   158

VI Total hardness of various waters   159

VII Distribution of coarse fish   161

Figures

1. Internal structure   27

2. Brain   36

3. Eye   37

4. Vision under water   39

5. Ear   40

6. Hypothetical phylogeny of salmonids   45

7. Palatine and vomerine teeth of salmonids   47

8. Trout and salmon parr compared   49

9. Stages of development of the ovary   67

10. Structure of a redd   73

11. Cycle of survival of a typical trout brood   80

12. Survival in Three Dubs Tarn   81

13. Petersen method for ageing fish   87

14. Trout scales   89

15. Annual growth in length for three rivers   97

16. Length/age data expressed in three different ways   101

17. Diagrammatic growth curves   117

18. Maintenance requirements against temperature   145

19. Some larval aquatic insects eaten by trout   179

20. Some aquatic insects eaten by trout   180

21. Some invertebrates eaten by trout   181

22. Food of young trout   183

23. Food of young trout and salmon compared   226

24. Stock, production and crop   249

25. Allen's picture of the angler's crop   264, 265

Editors' Preface

The two distinguished scholars and highly experienced field workers who have written this monograph for the *New Naturalist* are not primarily anglers: Dr. Frost admits (with some pleasure) that she learned the art of fly fishing, to collect research material, from one of the greatest biologists who ever studied the trout, the late Rowland Southern. Dr. Brown admits (with some candour) that she started her study of the trout as part of wartime work on fish production; her interest in the most popular of our fresh water fishes stems from that, and she has not become an angler in the strict sense.

These two biologists are masters of the general natural history of the trout—its anatomy, physiology, taxonomy, geography, life history, ontogeny, heredity and ecology. These are their prime occupations, and have been the subjects of what, in man-years (or rather, woman-years) has been a combined half-century and more of published researches. This work has brought them to eminence in their profession: Dr. Frost has been, since 1939, a member of the staff of the Freshwater Biological Association at Windermere; and Dr. Brown, who started research on trout physiology at Cambridge and has been for the last decade Consultant Biologist to the Salmon and Trout Association, is a Fellow of St. Hilda's College, Oxford, a Lecturer in that University's Department of Zoology—and wife to fellow-zoologist Professor George Varley.

The Trout, as a monograph, gives as fine a conspectus of existing knowledge of an animal species as any in our present series. Anglers will welcome it for a legion of reasons—perhaps most of all for its careful and deep analysis of all aspects of the great fish's environment. Biologists will welcome it because, of all the fresh water fishes of the world, it is the most deeply researched in both field and laboratory. Though the trout has been known as an angler's fish for nearly five hundred years, and appears, as *sceota* and *truht*, in Old English essays and glossaries of a millenium past, and was doubtless widely hunted and eaten in Stone Age times, its truly scientific days are rather new, virtually of the last hundred years and important only of the present century. When Winifred Frost and Margaret Brown write that "there remain considerable gaps in our knowledge" they are being scientifically scrupulous. This goes for every best-known animal, including man. The fact that emerges is that the trout *is* now probably the world's best-known fish in the general natural history sense. Drs. Frost and Brown, in their modesty, ascribe this to formidable pioneers, among them Knut Dahl, Rowland Southern, and Kenneth Radway Allen. But with their experience, not only in England but in Ireland, continental Europe, Africa, North America and the laboratory, our authors have firmly established themselves (also with economy and clarity) as the reigning experts on *Salmo trutta*.

We count it a privilege to publish what is, in effect, not only the natural history of the trout, but also the present state of knowledge and wisdom on the most pressing problems of its culture, angling "exploitation," cropping, nurture, management and conservation.

THE EDITORS

Authors' Preface

We have talked about the brown trout to all sorts of people—anglers, fishery scientists, fishery officers, fish farmers and naturalists. Although it is impossible to name them all, we are deeply aware of our debt to them for much of the information in this book.

Both of us are fortunate in having colleagues and friends who are interested in fish so we have had many opportunities to discuss the trout and its habits and to obtain expert knowledge on particular aspects of its life. All this has helped us greatly in writing this book. Among the friends, we cannot forbear to mention Dr. E. B. Worthington and the late Cecil Myers. Professor G. C. Varley has shown great patience in listening to many of our discussions. We thank Dr. T. A. Stuart for reading chapter 4, Dr. T. T. Macan for reading chapters 7 and 8, and Mr. E. D. Le Cren for reading chapters 9 and 10. We thank Mr. R. C. S. Walters, B.SC., M.I.C.E., for providing many of the figures and checking the list of references.

We are much indebted to Dr. T. A. Stuart for plates 1 and 2 and to Mr. A. E. Ramsbottom for the photographs on plates 3, 4 (above and centre), 6, 7 and 8 (except 8b and 8c which were taken by the late Mr. J. Arthur Hutton). Photograph 11a is by the late Mr. K. Parkes of the Nature Conservancy by whose courtesy it is reproduced here. In plate 5 of this edition the photograph of Small Water, which replaces Goat's Water in the earlier edition, is by Mr. T. Parker. Figures 24 and 25 are reproduced by permission of Mr. K. Radway Allen.

We have tried to avoid the angler's approach and equally

that of the experimentalist and to present a true picture of the brown trout and how it lives in its complex environment. We would like to be able to say, as Izaak Walton did in his Epistle to the Reader: "And though this discourse may be liable to some exceptions, yet I cannot doubt but that most Readers may receive so much pleasure or profit by it, as may make it worthy the time of their perusal, if they be not too grave or too busy men."

W.E.F.
M.E.B.

Introduction

PISCATOR. The Trout is a fish highly valued, both in this and foreign nations. *Izaak Walton, 1653*

The brown trout, which we associate with the more beautiful of the lakes and rivers of our islands, also lives in the highlands of Africa, in the lakes and rivers of the Antipodes and in the hills of Kashmir. This diverse and curious distribution is explained by the passion for angling displayed by the British, who have introduced this favourite sporting fish wherever they felt it could survive to provide them with familiar sport and pleasure.

Probably more is known about the life of the brown trout than about any other freshwater fish because for centuries anglers and others interested in the trout as a sporting fish have observed its habits and thus amassed a store of general knowledge. Much of this has been recorded, so that ever since Dame Juliana Berners described in 1496 how "ye may angle to hym" there has been a steady flow of writings. Much of this extensive literature deals, directly or indirectly, with methods of capture since "if the angler take fysshe surely thenne is noo man merier in his spryte." A great deal of information about the life of trout was incorporated into books about angling since it was soon realised that knowledge of the fish's habits was necessary for success. Some of this information is merely reiteration of "an old truth" and is of little value but there is much that is based on careful observation, sound deduction and long experience.

The centuries-old interest in the trout as a sporting fish, which incited the study of its natural history, is also the basis of many of the present-day investigations for, as demand for fishing grows greater, management of trout waters based on knowledge of the trout and its environment becomes imperative. Thus it is that owners of fisheries, river keepers, River Board officials, water undertakers and, of course, trout "farmers," all of them concerned with the conservation of trout fisheries, study the trout in the field. Although their investigations are directed to an applied end, their observations add to the store of knowledge about the life of the trout. Some of these results have never been published but others appear from time to time in books or periodicals, each author dealing with his special interest only. Recently, fishery biologists have studied the problem of conservation of trout waters for angling, especially in North America.

Angled trout is greatly appreciated as food by its captor and his friends. Stew-fed trout from Denmark, served in restaurants, may delight the diner and, bought deep-frozen, is a stand-by for the hostess. But until recently there has been little interest in the commercial culture of trout as food in the British Isles.

Zoologists' interest in comparative physiology is fairly young. Only about forty years ago did they seriously begin to compare fish with mammals and frogs. The trout was the most convenient live fish to use in the laboratory, because trout hatcheries were established and could supply fish at any time of year and these fish would be of specified size and known age and history. It is extraordinarily difficult to obtain most other species of freshwater or marine fish in good condition exactly when they are needed. They must be caught in the wild so their size and state are usually unpredictable. Tropical aquarium fishes are often too small but are useful for many investigations since they are easy to breed. But even though the trout has the disadvantage of breeding only once a year and starting to breed only when two years old or older, it is so convenient a subject for physiological work that there is now an extensive literature about it and its close relatives as studied in the laboratory.

Scientific investigation of the trout in the field has been carried out only during the last half-century and this pure research has yielded results of interest and of value both to the experimentalist in the laboratory and the angler and conservationist in the field.

The mass of literature, sporting, technical and scientific, about the trout is so extensive that it baffles the common reader. This book is an attempt to draw together information and ideas from multifarious sources and to present a unified account of the trout in the British Isles. The aspect which has most impressed us is the plasticity of the trout as shown by its variation in size and coloration in different waters.

The fisherman who visits the small streams of the uplands and mountains will catch many game little trout but they will all be small; if he wants to catch big trout, he will go instead to a chalk stream. Fishing a lakeland tarn, he will be pleased if his catch weighs four to the pound and delighted if he lands the odd half-pounder; but, casting the dry Mayfly over Lough Derg in the Shannon system, he will be disappointed if his catch does not average two pounds a fish. These trout will be silvery with black spots and so will be trout caught in Windermere, the latter ranging from a quarter-pound to two pounds or so. The trout in the tarns near Windermere are quite different to look at, with yellow bellies and red spots on their dark sides. The Windermere and Lough Derg fish usually have pink flesh like a salmon but the little fish from the tarns and becks in the Lake District have white flesh. In the chalk streams, some have pink and some have white flesh from the same water. All these are good to eat although pink flesh enjoys a slightly higher status among gastronomes. As trout swim and turn gracefully in their native waters—in rushing becks, placid lakes or yellow bog-pools—they are, simply, beautiful. It is because trout are so agile and so attractive that they are called "game fish"; and the angler increases his sport by laying down rules about gear and lures to make their capture difficult and exciting.

This problem of variability of growth has been recognised at least since the time of Izaak Walton but in this century three men have made specially important contributions to our ideas and knowledge about the trout. We shall refer to them often in the rest of this book, so let us introduce them now:

Professor Knut Dahl, of Norway, who died at the age of 80 in 1951, was a pioneer of scientific investigation of the brown trout. A born naturalist and a competent angler, he had a vivid interest in all aspects of the life of the trout and he studied its natural history, particularly growth and factors affecting it. *Salmon and Trout: a Handbook*, published in 1916 by the Salmon and Trout Association, records some of his findings but *Orret og Orretvann*, published in 1917 (translated in the Salmon and Trout Magazine (1918, 1919) as "Studies of Trout and Trout Waters in Norway"), is a more complete account. Some of his conclusions have not stood the test of time but he contributed to the study of almost every aspect of the trout's life and environment.

Rowland Southern was for many years Assistant Inspector of Fisheries in Dublin. While he was in charge of the Limnological Laboratory on Lough Derg, from 1920 to 1923, he formulated his hypothesis that the growth rate of brown trout was in some way connected with the presence or absence of limestone in the drainage area, and this was the basis of his very thoughtful and far-ranging paper in 1932. He realised the need for accurate comparative data about food supply and other environmental factors and he initiated the survey of the River Liffey to which many references will be made later. This Irish river is conveniently close to Dublin. It rises from acid moorland on granite but later flows over limestone so that at Ballysmuttan it is a typical upland river with soft, acid water whereas downstream, at Straffan, conditions are typical of hard-water rivers. The Liffey Survey was still in progress at the time of Southern's death in 1935 at the early age of 53. The results were published in a series of papers from 1929-1945. Southern intended to write a book on brown trout, indeed he was working on it the year before he died. He would doubtless have written a classic for he was a first class scientific naturalist and also a skilled fly-fisherman, with much delight in and wide knowledge of his subject.

Kenneth Radway Allen worked as Biologist with the Freshwater Biological Association at Wray Castle, beside Windermere, and studied the trout in that lake. He then became Freshwater Biologist at the Fisheries Laboratory of the Marine Department in New Zealand and undertook a survey of the Horokiwi River. This is a small stream on the west coast of North Island, near Wellington; it has probably held brown trout since their introduction in about 1883. Allen's study of "The Horokiwi Stream," published in 1951, is a classic; for it is the first thorough quantitative study of a population of brown trout and of their food supply. We shall refer frequently to his observations and conclusions. Perhaps mention should be made here of how we ourselves became interested in brown trout:

I (W.E.F.), a very junior colleague of Southern's, helped him in field and laboratory with his River Liffey Survey. The trout we needed for the work had to be caught by angling so Southern taught me how to fish with an artificial fly. This art has given me untold pleasure since and from its practice I have learned much about the trout in river and lake.

I (M.E.B.) sought a subject for research which might help the war effort and thus became interested in the growth of fish and their production for food. I worked with trout because of their convenience for experiments. My co-author gave me useful advice and told me much about the trout in natural conditions and thus stimulated me to be interested in it as a wild fish—but she has not as yet persuaded me to try to angle for it!

In spite of the interest in the trout of so many people over so many years, there remain considerable gaps in our knowledge, as will become apparent in this book: we hope that by drawing attention to these we will stimulate further observation and research. Many readers will find that we have not given exactly the information they want: this may well be because we do not have it but may sometimes be a consequence of the necessity to compress a great amount of information into a readable compass. We have not solved the problem of trout variability but we have clarified it in our own minds, at least, and offer here a progress report.

Chapter One

Anatomy and Physiology

Although the trout is a fairly primitive bony fish, it is well adapted to its habit of life. Here we consider the various functions performed by its body in turn and thus build up a picture of its anatomy and physiology.

Movement

The trout is an active animal and swims by using its tail which is moved from side to side by bending the body by shortening the muscles alternately on the two sides. As the tail moves, water is pushed backwards and the fish therefore moves forwards. The vertebral column provides a central support down the middle of the fish. There are usually fifty-eight or fifty-nine vertebræ, closely tied to each other with connective tissue so that the column can be bent easily from side to side but less easily in any other direction. The nerve cord is protected by a series of bony arches above the centra of the vertebræ and the principal artery and veins of the body are enclosed by the hæmal arches below. There are ribs protecting the organs in the body cavity and also ribs lying above these in the muscles; the unpaired fins, including the tail, are connected with the vertebral column through supporting bones. The first vertebra has a fairly rigid joint with the back of the skull, and the front paired fins (the pectorals) are also connected with the back of the skull through an elaborate bony girdle on each side. The hind paired fins (the pelvics) are supported only by small bony plates embedded in the belly muscles.

The body muscles make up about three-fifths of the volume of the whole fish and are the part we eat. They start at the back of the skull and along the back edge of the pectoral girdle, and extend down to the base of the tail—inserting on its supporting bones. They are divided on each side into a dorsal mass above and a ventral mass below the short ribs, and each of these masses is divided along its length into a series of blocks (the myotomes) corresponding in number to the number of vertebræ. These myotomes have a complicated shape which probably leads to more efficient bending of the body. Outside the muscles is the skin with scales embedded in it (see chapter 5, p. 88). The skin secretes a thin layer of slime (mucus); its surface is thus smooth and slippery. The shape is streamlined, offering least resistance to the water (see plate 4).

A trout has seven fins besides its tail. The small adipose fin seems to have no particular function, but the other six act as stabilisers, rudders and brakes. The front dorsal fin prevents the fish from rolling and yawing as it moves forwards; the paired pectoral fins prevent rolling and pitching, help the fish to turn, and can be used as brakes assisted by the pelvics. Anyone who watches trout swimming in a stream or in an aquarium must be impressed by the speed with which they can turn. This is a tribute to the mobiltiy of their bodies and the efficiency with which they can use their fins as rudders.

Most of the tissues of a fish are heavier than water, yet a trout can remain almost motionless suspended in water without sinking to the bottom. This is because it has an air-bladder. This is a sac lying beneath the vertebral column and kidney and above the body cavity. It is connected to the œsophagus by a narrow tube, the pneumatic duct, and thus via the œsophagus with the mouth. The bladder's silvery walls are of strong connective tissue and it contains air. It is used as a hydrostatic organ.

The specific gravity of a fish (i.e. its effective weight in water) depends on the amount of air in its air-bladder, and the fish can alter this by gulping air in through its mouth, œsophagus and pneumatic duct, or by forcing it out of its air-bladder by the same route. There may be a small amount of adjustment, too, by secretion of oxygen from the blood into the cavity of the air-bladder or absorption back into the blood. When the amount of air in the bladder is increased, the specific gravity of the fish is reduced and it floats nearer the surface of the water than when there is less air in the bladder.

How fast do trout swim? This question is not easy to answer. The fisherman who hears his reel screaming out as a large trout swims away from him may sometimes have the impression that the fish can do up to sixty knots, but it is much more probable that the average speed of a fast-moving trout is about eight to ten knots. The fish can be poised almost motionless in the water with slight movements of the fins and can suddenly dart away, accelerating very rapidly, perhaps up to twenty knots.

Dr. Bainbridge has deduced an equation from which the speed of a fish can be calculated if its total length and rate of tail beat are known. It is: $V = \frac{3}{4} [L(f-\frac{4}{3})]$ where V is the speed (in feet or cm. per second), L is the total length (in feet or cm.) and f, which must be greater than five, is the number of tail beats per second. It is interesting that this equation may apply to a great variety of fishes of all shapes and sizes and the difference between them must be related to the maximum frequency of tail beat which they can produce and maintain. This must depend on the form of the body muscles, their insertion into the tail and the efficiency with which they can contract and move the tail. Thus goldfish cannot move their tails as fast as dace and trout and whereas small dace can move as fast as small trout, large dace are less efficient and speedy than larger trout.

Breathing

The trout's energy for movement is produced within its body cells, during the process of respiration, by chemical reactions between substances derived from its food and oxygen absorbed from the water. One of the waste substances produced is carbon dioxide and this is released into the water. The oxygen is absorbed and the carbon dioxide passed out through the delicate gills. There are four pairs of these on each side lying in a cavity just in front of the fish's pectoral girdle; they are protected, on each side, by a flap of skin supported by bones, the operculum. The water is sucked in through the mouth and passes between the gill filaments and then out through a slit between the operculum and body on each side. There are valves inside the mouth and the opercula act as valves too; the floor of the mouth is a force pump which moves water past the gills as it is raised with the mouth valves closed. The outwards swing of the opercula suck water past the gills. The movements of the mouth are about one quarter of a cycle ahead of those of the opercula; thus when the mouth opens, the opercula are closed and as the mouth closes, the opercula are swung fully outwards; they swing inwards again as the mouth is about to open once more. These movements are continuous throughout the trout's life. During most of the respiratory cycle a stream of water is maintained past its gills. As the water passes between the gill filaments, oxygen is taken in and carbon dioxide passes out.

Trout can only obtain enough oxygen to supply their needs if the concentration of it in the water is fairly high. Fairly shallow or swiftly flowing rivers and streams and clear lakes contain plenty, while deep stagnant pools contain too little oxygen and too much carbon dioxide. Trout need more oxygen, and are more susceptible to carbon dioxide, than fishes found in stagnant water. Table 1 is a comparison of the survival of rainbow trout, perch, roach and tench in water with low carbon dioxide concentrations. These figures show that more oxygen is generally required at higher temperatures and how fish may survive adverse conditions for a short time but be killed over a longer period. Rainbow trout are slightly hardier than brown trout. There is evidence that trout are more active at 16°C (61°F) than at 20°C (68°F) and this may explain why the minimum requirement for three and a half days and seven days survival is higher at the lower temperature. Dissolved carbon dioxide may have a considerable effect. At $16.5°$c ($62°$F) rainbow trout survive at least twenty-four hours with only 2 ppm[1] of oxygen (20% saturation) if there is no carbon dioxide but most of them die in less than one hour when 15 ppm of carbon dioxide is present. Perch are also very susceptible but roach and tench can survive quite high carbon dioxide concentrations.

Table 1. The minimum concentrations of dissolved oxygen, expressed as percentages of the saturation values, at which all individuals survived at three different temperatures. (From Downing and Merkens, 1957)

Fish species	Duration of test	Temperature of water $10°$C ($50°$F)	$16°$C ($61°$F)	$20°$C ($68°$F)
Rainbow trout	3½ hours	15·3	19·1	23·4
	3½ days	16·7	30·2	28·8
	7 days	—	38·6	29·6
Perch	3½ hours	5·8	10·7	13·3
	7 days	9·3	13·6	13·9
Roach	3½ hours	3·2	6·5	12·0
	7 days	5·7	7·2	15·5
Tench	8 hours	1·9	4·7	
	7 days	3·1		

Another gas sometimes found dissolved in water is ammonia—one of the intermediate products in the normal processes of decay of organic matter, and an excretory product of most aquatic organisms including trout (see p. 31. If the ammonia concentration is only one part per million, the oxygen carried in the blood of speckled trout (*Salvelinus fontinalis*; see p. 47) is reduced to one seventh of the normal value—and brown trout are probably equally sensitive.

[1] parts per million.

The amount of oxygen which can be dissolved in water falls as the temperature rises; but fish need *more* oxygen for their normal activities when it is warmer. Thus their activity may be severely restricted if the oxygen saturation falls. Speckled trout, which resemble brown trout closely in their requirements, can take up only one quarter of the oxygen necessary for full activity at 68°F (20°c) if the water is only half saturated with oxygen.

Feeding and digestion

Trout are carnivorous animals and normally use their eyes for locating and identifying the animals on which they prey. The animals eaten by trout in different waters will be discussed in detail in chapter 8. The larger ones are caught in the trout's mouth, the fish using the teeth on its upper and lower jaws and on the vomer and palatine bones in the roof of its mouth. It does not masticate or chew its food and swallows by raising the floor of its mouth. Food passes through its œsophagus into the U-shaped stomach which lies in the body cavity. The stomach has muscular walls which can be distended by a good meal. There is a muscular sphincter between the stomach and the intestine, and just beyond this there are many hollow processes, like the fingers of gloves. These are the pyloric cæca, which serve to increase the area of this part of the intestine; their number varies greatly but is usually more than thirty. The rest of the intestine is a loosely coiled tube that opens to the outside by the anus, just behind the pelvic fins. At the front of the body cavity there is a bilobed brownish-red liver, with a spherical gall bladder from which the bile duct leads to the intestine a short distance beyond the pyloric sphincter. The pancreatic tissue is scattered in this region. A dark-red spleen is attached to the hind angle of the stomach (fig. 1).

Digestive juices are secreted in the stomach, the pyloric cæca, the anterior part of the intestine, and by the diffuse pancreas. The liver secretes emulsifying bile through the bile duct. The proteins, fats and carbohydrates in the food break down into amino-acids, fatty acids, glycerol and sugars, and by the time the food reaches the end of the intestine the animals of which it was composed have been so broken down as to be unrecognisable, except for indigestible hard parts.

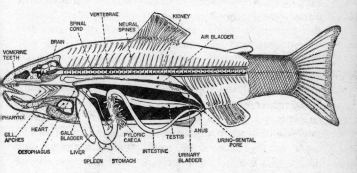

1. The internal structure of the brown trout, semi-diagrammatic. (Based on Parker and Haswell, 1928. Fig. 876)

In the intestine these breakdown products are absorbed by the cells of the wall. The amino-acids and sugars pass into capillaries and are carried in the blood through the hepatic portal vein to the liver. The undigested remains of the food pass out of the body, as the fæces, through the anus.

The liver cells remove sugars from the blood as it passes through and these are converted into glycogen, which is stored there until required by body cells. The glycogen can be converted back into sugars which are used as a source of energy in cell respiration. The amino-acids may be cir-culated through the body and used to build proteins by cells, in the processes of replacement and growth. Any excess is converted into sugar in the liver and stored as glycogen. The fatty acids are stored in fat deposits round the viscera and sometimes in the muscles. These reserve fats can be withdrawn and turned into sugars and used in respiration.

The major part of the diet of trout consists of proteins, fats and carbohydrates, but there are other important constituents such as mineral salts and vitamins. Most of these also are absorbed through the intestine. Calcium ions, too, may be absorbed directly from the water as well as in food. Some food organisms, such as shrimps and snails, contain the pigment carotene, and trout deposit this in the skin as red spots and sometimes in the muscles, giving pink flesh. Many different artificial diets have been used for rearing trout so that we have learned a certain amount about some of the constituents they particularly require. Raw liver appears to be a good food for trout fry; it seems to contain a vitamin affecting trout growth and survival and has been used to supplement artificial foods. Recent work on the survival of trout when under stress has shown that fish fed on modern artificial diets (pellets) are hardier than those fed on raw meat and liver, but wild trout on a natural diet are even hardier.

How much food does a trout need every day? This is not a simple question to answer, since there are a number of factors which must be considered. Every animal uses a certain amount of energy every day simply for the processes of living, and therefore requires a certain amount of food as a source of this energy. Living tissues are continually replacing part of themselves and this also uses up a part of the food intake. There is, therefore, a minimum daily requirement of food, called here the "maintenance requirement," which will prevent an animal from losing weight but is not sufficient to allow it to gain weight. This maintenance requirement is a measure of the amount of food being used to replace worn out tissues and to provide energy for the vital processes. The larger the animal, the larger will be its total maintenance requirement. We can compare animals of different sizes in terms of weight of food required per unit weight of fish. Smaller trout have relatively higher maintenance requirements, but for fishes weighing 90 g. (3 oz.) and more the requirement in units of meat per unit weight of fish is fairly constant under similar environmental conditions; it is 6½% per week at 53°F (11½°c). We shall be discussing later the effects of temperature and other environmental factors on food requirements of trout, but we must stress here that as the temperature rises, their maintenance requirement also rises since all vital activities are accelerated. It is therefore essential to know the water temperature when discussing how much food a fish needs.

An animal which is receiving more food than it requires for maintenance is able to use this extra food for growth. This growth may represent an increase in the living tissues of the fish or simply an accumulation of food reserves—both of these will be accompanied by increase in weight and the former, but not the latter, by increase in length. If the increase in weight over a period of time is divided by the total amount of food eaten during that time, we obtain a figure for the overall conversion of food into fish, expressed as increase in weight per unit (or %) weight of food eaten. Practical men may be more interested in the reciprocal value—that is, in the pounds of food which must be eaten for the fish to show one pound increase in weight.

The value for overall conversion includes the maintenance requirement of the trout and is therefore much affected by the rate at which the fish grow—since this determines the total time over which the increase in weight is added. A more accurate measure of the efficiency with which food is converted into flesh is obtained when the total maintenance requirement is subtracted from the amount of food eaten and this value is then divided by the increase in weight of the fish. This "net conversion" figure is meaningful in a variety of conditions which lead to very different rates of growth. Let us consider a trout weighing 100 g. (3½ oz.) at 11½°c (53°F). Its maintenance requirement is 6½ g. (⅕ oz) of meat per week. Let the net conversion value be 25%, which is an average value for laboratory conditions; then 1 g. increase in weight results from eating 4 g. of meat more than the maintenance requirement.

Suppose that the trout adds this 1 g. in	it must eat for its maintenance	plus for growth	Total food eaten	Overall Conversion
$\frac{1}{2}$ week	$3\frac{1}{4}$ g.	4 g.	$7\frac{1}{4}$ g.	14%
1	$6\frac{1}{2}$	4	$10\frac{1}{2}$	$9\frac{1}{2}$%
2	13	4	17	6%
4	26	4	30	$3\frac{1}{2}$%

This explains in part why figures for efficiency of conversion of food vary so much. It is not possible to compare different foods used under different conditions unless the net conversion is known; and this should really be based on the dry weight of the food used, since different foods contain very different amounts of water. Using dry pellets under optimal conditions in a hatchery, a yield of more than 1 pound of trout flesh for each 2 pounds of food used can be maintained through the year; the conversion of natural food organisms in wild conditions must be much less than this and will certainly show seasonal changes.

If trout are provided with an unlimited food supply, they eat certain definite amounts which vary from day to day but are relatively constant over longer periods such as weeks or months. These amounts of food eaten are a measure of the appetite of the fish and the appetite, like the maintenance requirement, varies with environmental factors, such as temperature. If the amount of food which the fish are allowed to eat is limited, so that their appetite is not fully satisfied, they use the food more efficiently. As the amount of food allowed is increased and decreased, the fish adapt themselves to the changed level of feeding by altering the efficiency with which they convert food into fish flesh. This leads to the somewhat surprising result that trout may show the same increase in weight when allowed to eat as much as they will and also when restricted to smaller quantities of food. So the trout in a river or lake may grow just as rapidly at a time when their food supply is sparse as when it is unlimited, provided that their food is of good quality and that it is more than is required for maintenance.

We have already mentioned some observations on artificial trout diets, but beyond these nothing is known of the effect of quality of the food on the efficiency of conversion. Natural trout diets vary considerably in quality from place to place and from time to time (see chapter 8), but it is not possible at present to assess the effects of these differences on the growth of fish.

Elimination of Waste and Regulation of Salts and Water in the Body

There is a constant wear and tear of the tissues in all animal bodies. The principal breakdown products are compounds derived from proteins, which contain nitrogen, and carbon dioxide produced during respiration. These must be eliminated, since they are poisonous if allowed to accumulate. Ammonia is the main nitrogenous waste product of trout and is eliminated from their gills in the same way as carbon dioxide. Small quantities of other nitrogenous substances and of other waste products are voided through the kidney. This is a long, dark-red organ, lying immediately below the backbone and above the airbladder and stretching from the head to the beginning of the tail (see fig. 1). It consists of many coiled tubes starting as small bulbs with a rich blood supply (the glomeruli) and all joining to form a pair of ducts, the ureters, which pass on either side of the rear end of the body cavity and then join to form a distensible bladder opening behind the anus. An ultra-filtrate of the blood passes through the glomeruli into the tubules, and farther along these there is some resorption of sugars and salts and there may be secretion of other substances into the tubules.

The kidney is most important to a freshwater fish as the organ through which excess water is eliminated. It is essential for the survival of animal body cells that the concentration of salts in blood should not deviate from a certain value and a certain proportion of different ions; for trout the concentration is approximately one third of that of seawater. The salt concentration of freshwaters is much lower than that of trout blood (approx. one thirtieth of seawater) and water therefore tends to diffuse into the blood through the gills. This water must be eliminated and this is done through the kidney where salts are resorbed through the tubule wall so that the urine, which is copious, is much more dilute than the blood.

In the sea the position is different because the salt concentration in the water is three times as high as that in the blood. A sea trout therefore tends to lose water by diffusion through its gills, and strict conservation of water is necessary. Bony fish in the sea absorb saltwater through the stomach wall and then excrete the excess of salts through special cells in the gills, while retaining the water; they produce sparse and concentrated urine. Fish such as the sea trout and the salmon, which spend part of their lives in the sea and part in freshwater, must be able to adjust the physiological processes which regulate the water and salt content of their blood according to the medium in which they are living.

The Blood and its Circulation

Growth, energy supply and the elimination of waste all depend on the transport of chemical substances between different parts of the body. This occurs in the blood. Blood is a fluid containing red and white corpuscles as well as colloids and substances dissolved in its plasma. The white corpuscles protect the body from infection. The red corpuscles contain the pigment hæmoglobin; and it is in combination with this, as oxyhæmoglobin, that much of the oxygen is transported from the gills to the tissues. Some oxygen is carried dissolved in plasma and this seems to be sufficient for the survival of goldfish under normal conditions, but trout have higher oxygen requirements and are poisoned by substances which prevent oxygen transport using hæmoglobin. Carbon dioxide, ammonia, sugars, amino-acids, fatty acids and hormones all circulate dissolved in the plasma.

The blood is circulated round the body through definite vessels by contractions of the heart which lies between the ventral ends of the two pectoral girdles. It consists of three chambers, the sinus venosus, auricle and ventricle; the last two, especially the ventricle, have muscular walls. The blood is forced from auricle to ventricle and thence round the body. From the ventricle, the ventral aorta takes the blood forwards into the afferent branchial arteries; each of these supplies gill filaments on either side of one gill bar, where there are spaces where the blood is separated from the water outside the gill by a single layer of cells only. Here carbon dioxide and ammonia diffuse out of the blood through the cells and oxygen diffuses in.

From the blood spaces in the gills, the blood passes through the efferent branchial arteries to the main dorsal aorta. This carries blood forwards to the head through the carotid arteries and backwards to the body. Arteries leave the dorsal aorta, which lies immediately below the vertebral column and above the kidney, and carry blood to the muscles and to all the internal organs. The arteries break up into capillaries among the cells of the body, and oxygen and sugar diffuses from these capillaries into the cells where they are used to produce energy by the chemical reactions of cellular respiration. Carbon dioxide, formed during these reactions, diffuses from the cells into the blood.

The capillaries join together to form veins through which the blood is returned to the heart. All the blood from the capillaries in the walls of the gut returns through the hepatic portal vein to the liver, and then through another set of capillaries to the hepatic veins. The main veins of the body and head join to form the sinus venosus, which opens into the auricle of the heart. Valves between the sinus and auricle, the auricle and ventricle and the ventricle and ventral aorta ensure that the blood flows always in the same direction.

The blood passing through the heart is poor in oxygen and rich in carbon dioxide, while that in the dorsal aorta is rich in oxygen and poor in carbon dioxide. The amino-acid and sugar level of the blood is regulated as it passes through the capillaries in the liver, and blood passing through the capillaries in the kidney is altered by the processes occurring there. Many organs in the body either add substances to the blood, remove substances or are affected by substances reaching them.

The Endocrine Organs and Chemical Co-ordination

Endocrine organs secrete chemical substances called hormones into the blood and thus affect parts of the body far away from them. Much of the co-ordination of the basic processes of the body is achieved by the secretion of hormones, most of which slowly produce relatively long-lasting effects. Rapid responses to external stimuli are mediated through the nervous system, as when a trout takes a fly, but the general level of metabolism and its relation to seasonal changes are controlled by hormones.

The pituitary, a small gland situated under the brain, is often termed "the master gland" because it produces several hormones which affect other endocrine organs. It secretes a hormone stimulating growth and hormones affecting the reproductive cycle and its activity is influenced, at least in part, by light. It also secretes a hormone causing dispersion of the black pigment, melanin, in cells in the skin and hence darkening of the body colour when the trout is on a dark background. The opposite response, aggregation of the melanin, in a fish on a light background, is caused by nervous impulses; so that paling of the body is quite a rapid process but darkening takes several hours. The eyes must be intact for both reactions to take place.

The thyroid consists of pockets of cells near the ventral

aorta and its hormone production varies seasonally and probably affects the fish's general metabolic level. "Silvering," like that of sea trout smolts, can be induced by injections of thyroxin.

The gonads contain endocrine tissue which probably controls the onset of spawning behaviour and the slight differences between ripe males and females. There are cells homologous with the types of cells found in the complex adrenal glands of mammals which probably have similar functions in trout but these have scarcely been investigated. There are also special pancreatic cells producing insulin and thus, as in mammals, regulating the sugar level in the blood.

Reproduction and the Gonads

The gonads lie in the body cavity above the gut. The male has a pair of testes which open to the outside through ducts leading to its urino-genital pore. The female has a pair of ovaries and the ripe eggs are shed into its body cavity and pass out through two pores at the base of its excretory duct and thence through its urino-genital pore. The gonads vary very greatly in size according to the maturity of the fish and the season. These changes and the microscopic structure of the gonads are discussed fully in chapter 4.

Nervous System and the Sense Organs

The brain and spinal cord are enclosed within the skull and vertebral column respectively. The most noticeable features of the brain (fig. 2) are the large optic lobes, connected with the sense of sight, and the cerebellum, connected with the control of movement. The brain receives sensory nerves from all the sense organs and distributes motor nerves to the head through the cranial nerves and to the body through the spinal cord and spinal nerves. A pair of spinal nerves emerges between each pair of vertebræ and carry motor nerves to the muscles and sensory nerves from the muscles and other organs back to the spinal cord. Rapid reactions always involve nervous impulses passing through the brain or spinal cord.

The most important sense organs of trout are probably the eyes which are large and placed on each side of the head, so that they look sideways with only a limited field

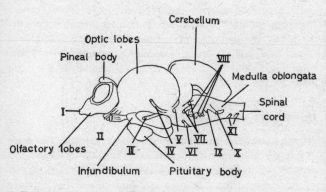

I-X Cranial nerves   XI Spinal nerves

2.   The brain of the brown trout. (Parker and Haswell, 1928. Fig. 877.) I-X, cranial nerves ; XI, spinal nerves

of view in front. Each consists of an eyeball lined with a sensitive retina and with a hole, the pupil, in the middle of the iris (fig. 3). Within the pupil is a large spherical lens which is moved backwards by a muscle and forwards by pressure within the eyeball so that an image of the outside world can be focused on the retina. The optic system resembles that in a camera fitted with a lens, iris, focusing device and sensitive film. Vision under water differs from that in air in several ways because the refractive index of water is greater than that of air. Light rays are absorbed and scattered more than in air so objects are clearly visible only over short distances, especially if the water is at all turbid. The colour of objects seen under water will vary with depth, turbidity and the actual colour of the water.

Ultra-violet and infra-red rays are completely absorbed near the water surface. Blue light rays penetrate to greater depths than red rays, but both penetrate deeper in clear water than in turbid water.

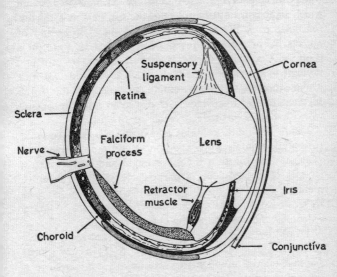

3. Diagrammatic vertical section of the eye of a typical teleost fish such as the brown trout. (After Walls, 1942)

Anglers are naturally interested in the extent to which objects in the air and on land are visible to fish in water. Fig. 4 illustrates conditions when the water surface is smooth and unrippled. Objects in the air directly above the fish are seen without any distortion. The fish's eye is, as it were, at the point of an inverted cone of light passing through the water surface and the fish can see everything from zenith to horizon in all directions. The amount of distortion increases as the horizon is approached and objects are seen more dimly. They appear very much smaller that similar objects overhead (see fig. 4). When the fish swims deeper in the water, it increases the actual size of the window so that objects near the horizon look relatively larger than when it swims near the surface. The absorption of light by water means, however, that the picture will not be so bright when the fish is deeper. The water surface which surrounds the "window" through which light from outside reaches the fish acts as a mirror, reflecting back to the fish images of the bottom and of objects in the water. Thus the fish lives, as it were, in a room with a ceiling made of mirrors except for a round skylight in the middle, through which the outside world is visible though distorted round the edge. If the water surface ripples, the window is disrupted and the outside world becomes virtually invisible to the fish.

The trout's retina contains cells of the two types found in vertebrate animals (rods and cones) and there is plenty of evidence that trout have good eyesight and can distinguish colours. The fish's eye is particularly sensitive to movements in the visual field. It has no eyelids, and so is unable to close its eyes; its eyeball can be moved to a limited extent by muscles within its eyesocket.

Trout use their eyes in feeding and normally are inactive in total darkness but may feed heavily during summer nights, although they are usually considered to be diurnal in habit. They also use their eyes when maintaining their position in streams. They do this by fixing the image of an object in the water or on the bank on a definite part of the retina and maintaining the image on the same spot by swimming against the current. Another response which is controlled through the eyes is the change in colour already described. Blind trout living in light are permanently dark in colour.

The ears of a trout are entirely inside the skull and are mainly concerned with balance although they are probably also able to detect some vibrations, i.e. sounds. Each ear (fig. 5) consists of three semicircular canals, the utriculus and the sacculus. The ampullæ (or sense organs of the semicircular canals) respond to acceleration of the body in various directions and enable the fish to swim straight even

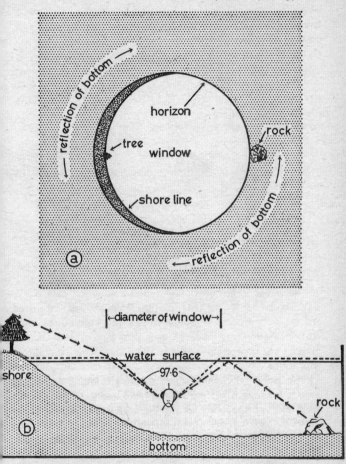

4. Visual field of a fish in the upward direction. (a) water surface and aerial window as seen from beneath. (b) explanation of the window; rays striking the surface at an angle within the window are refracted to the eyes of the fish but rays striking outside the window from beneath are totally reflected. Within an angle of 97.6° the fish sees out into an aerial hemisphere; but outside this angle it sees objects on the bottom, reflected in a silvery surface. The surface must be completely calm. (Walls, 1942. Fig. 129)

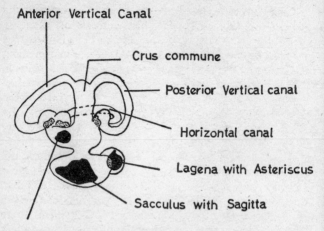

Anterior Vertical Canal

Crus commune

Posterior Vertical canal

Horizontal canal

Lagena with Asteriscus

Sacculus with Sagitta

Utriculus with Lapillus

5.   The ear of a trout. (Modified from von Frisch)

in darkness. The utriculus and sacculus contain large calcareous bodies, called "otoliths," which are supported on sensory processes. These enable the animal to know its orientation in space at any moment so that it can remain in an upright position; they may also respond to vibrations.

The principal organs which detect vibrations consist of canals forming a pattern on the head and extending along each side of the body as the "lateral lines." There are a series of small pores along each canal; these can be seen on the head, for instance, above and below the eyeball. The pores along the body open on a row of modified scales over the lateral line. Vibrations in the water cause the viscous fluid in the canals to move and to stimulate the ampullæ of the organs. This system is sensitive to vibrations of fairly low frequency (such as those caused by another fish moving) and it may be used to detect obstacles by the reflection of water waves back to the fish as in an "echo sounder."

The trout's pair of nostrils lead into nasal sacs lined with sensory epithelium, through which currents of water are moved by ciliary action. The epithelium is stimulated by chemical substances in the water. Very little is known about the sensitivity of trout to different chemical stimuli, though it has been suggested that they can recognise characteristic odours of streams. There is no connection between the nasal sacs and the mouth, and the part of the brain dealing with the sense of smell is relatively small and poorly developed.

Trout certainly have taste buds inside their mouths and perhaps also on the outside of their bodies; but very little is known of this sense of taste. There may be hot and cold receptors about their bodies, since trout show preferences for definite temperatures when placed in a gradient. There may also be receptors in their muscles indicating their degree of contraction, and there may be pressure receptors, but we still have very little information about the trout's sense organs and sensory discrimination apart from studies on the eyes and sense of sight.

Behaviour

Studies in tanks and in streams have shown that trout react to each other in definite and complicated ways depending on age, size and state of sexual development. Feeding on moving animals requires a high degree of muscular co-ordination, and observations reported in chapter 8 suggest considerable discrimination and learning from experience. The trout is perhaps less cunning and clever than some anglers' tales suggest, but its normal behaviour must be well adjusted to its normal environment since sufficient numbers of individuals grow and survive to spawn and continue the species.

Chapter Two

Taxonomy

SALMO. We know of no other group of fishes which offers so many difficulties to the ichthyologists with regard to the distinction of the species . . . as this genus.   *A. C. L. G. Günther, 1880*

Zoologists call the brown trout *Salmo trutta* Linn. because Linnæus first defined this species. The Atlantic salmon is *Salmo salar* Linn., a member of the same genus but a different species as also is *Salmo gairdneri* Richardson, the rainbow trout (which was first named by Richardson). The American brook trout or speckled trout, *Salvelinus fontinalis* Mitchill, is a species belonging to a different genus. All these fish belong to the order Salmoniformes which is believed to be the most primitive order of the main division of the Teleosts (bony fish). The air-bladder is connected with the œsophagus by an open duct and the pelvic fins are abdominal in position. The Cretaceous rocks, deposited one hundred million years ago, contain fossils of primitive teleosts such as the tarpons, the herrings, the osteoglossids (which include the modern arapaima) and the earliest salmonids. Of these four primitive groups, the Salmoniformes have been outstandingly successful since they were ancestral to a greater number of advanced orders of fish than were the other three groups added together.

The sub-order Salmonoidei, which includes the trouts, and is known since the beginning of the Eocene, seventy million years ago, has the following characters: (1) a pseudobranch, (2) two dorsal fins, the posterior one being the characteristic "adipose fin," (3) an upper jaw consisting of two bones (the premaxilla and maxilla) on each side, (4) a scale-bearing body but a scaleless head, (5) generally many pyloric cæca, (6) eggs which are shed into the body cavity, (7) no barbels (tactile sensory organs). Of all these characters, the most obvious and reliable in temperate waters is the presence of the adipose fin.

The sub-order Salmonoidei includes species which live in freshwater, species which are marine and others which are anadromous (breeding in freshwater and feeding in the sea). The freshwater species are indigenous to the arctic and temperate zones of the Northern Hemisphere. The variety of habit among the Salmonoidei is shown by the following British species: the argentines (*Argentina silus* and *A. sphyræna*) are entirely marine; they are caught in deep waters off the west and south-west of Ireland and are sometimes sold in English fish markets. The smelt (*Osmerus eperlanus*) is a valuable food fish which lives in the sea but comes into estuaries to spawn. The salmon (*Salmo salar*) spawns in freshwater and spends the first two, three, or four years of its life in freshwater but then migrates to the sea from which it returns to spawn in freshwater. The trout (*Salmo trutta*) generally lives in freshwater but may feed in the sea. The British chars (*Salvelinus alpinus*) are entirely freshwater but in Scandinavia fish of this species may be anadromous. The British whitefish, the gwyniad, the schelly, the powan, the pollans and the vendace (all species of the genus *Coregonus*) are entirely freshwater and each species inhabits only one or a few lakes.

This gradation in habit from entirely marine through estuarine and anadromous forms to entirely freshwater species raises the question of the ancestry of the whole group—are the freshwater forms more primitive and the marine forms more advanced or vice versa? There are two possible explanations for the present state of affairs. The ancestor could have been an entirely marine fish which developed the habit of laying its eggs in estuaries and then became more and more adapted to freshwater so that it bred farther and farther upstream until it lost the habit of returning to the sea even to feed. On the other hand, the ancestor could have been an entirely freshwater fish, living and breeding in freshwater, which began to forage in estuaries and then in the sea and at first returned to freshwater to breed but then bred in estuaries and finally bred in the sea, losing all connection with freshwater. The advantage of breeding in freshwater is the relatively smaller number of predators which may eat the eggs while the advantage of feeding in the sea is the relatively larger food supply. The physiological problems of life in the sea and in freshwater are so different that most Teleosts can only live in one or the other; thus, carp die if the salinity is increased while mackerel die if the salinity is decreased.

The family Salmonidæ is separated from the other six families of the sub-order Salmonoidei on several technical points. The end of their vertebral column turns up at the base of the tail and there are three vertebræ in the upturned part; this is the same as in tarpons and is probably a primitive character and the other Salmonoid families have only two or one upturned vertebræ. As well as trout, salmon and char (Salmoninæ) the family Salmonidæ includes the grayling *Thymallus* and the whitefishes (Coregoninæ).

Probably the most primitive living Salmonid is *Brachymystax* from Siberia. This fish is a generalised carnivore with a mouth of moderate size and teeth also of moderate size; it lays small eggs. It has a salmonine specialisation in that the supra-occipital bone separates the two parietal bones in the roof of its skull. The genus *Salmo* differs from *Brachymystax* in having jaws which are longer and stronger with larger teeth, and in laying large eggs. *Hucho*, with three species in Siberia and the River Danube, is intermediate between *Brachymystax* and *Salmo*. The grayling and whitefishes probably descended from a fish like *Brachymystax* but before the parietals became separated (fig. 6). The characteristic long dorsal fin of the grayling, with seventeen or more fin-rays, is a recent acquisition and the scales have indentations on the front, buried margins instead of being oval. The whitefishes diverged from the

ancestor by losing some and reducing other teeth, probably because they ceased to be predatory and fed instead
on plankton, like the ciscoes, or on detritus. One genus,
Stenodus, has returned to trout-like feeding habits but has
a quite different dentition. The arrangement of the teeth
on the vomer, a bone in the middle of the roof of the

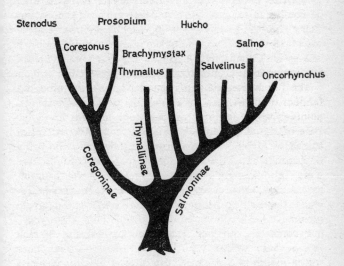

Salmonine-like Ancestor

6. The hypothetical phylogeny of the Salmonid fishes. (After
Norden, 1961)

mouth, may be used to separate the genera *Salmo* and
Oncorhynchus (salmon and trouts) from the genus *Salvelinus* (chars). In the two former genera the teeth form a
double or zigzag series over the whole of the vomer bone
while in the latter the teeth are restricted to the head of the
vomer (fig. 7). In *Salmo* there is only a small gap between
the vomerine and palatine teeth but this gap is wide in adult
Oncorhynchus (Pacific salmon). Probably the latter genus

has only recently diverged from the genus *Salmo* and the juvenile fish are very similar in structure. Other specialisations of adult *Oncorhynchus* are the closing of the dorsal fontanelles in the skull, the peculiar rostrum and the simultaneous ripening of all the germ cells (sperms and ova) so that these fish can spawn only once.

The Pacific salmon have the same habits as the Atlantic salmon but in exaggerated form; they are anadromous and migrate up the Pacific rivers in enormous numbers. This has led to the establishment of the salmon canning industry in Western Canada, U.S.A., Japan and U.S.S.R. There are five economically important species of Pacific salmon grading in habit and size from the large quinnat (king) salmon, *Oncorhynchus tschawytscha*, which migrate two thousand miles up rivers to spawn and average 25 lb., to the small pink (humpback) salmon, *O. gorbuscha*, which average 5 to 7 lb. and spawn only a few miles above the tidal reaches. It is the latter species that the Russians have recently been trying to introduce into the White Sea with the result that many have been caught in Norwegian waters and a few in British estuaries and rivers. In the unlikely event of their becoming established in Britain, they would not compete with our native salmon because of the difference in habits.

Chars (genus *Salvelinus*) can always be distinguished from trout by the fact that teeth are present only on the head of their vomer bone. They probably split fairly early from the Salmonine stem. Another useful difference is that chars have smaller scales than trout. Chars typically have a pattern of light markings against a darker background while trouts have dark markings against a paler background. Char vary greatly in colour which depends partly on sex, age and locality. Char are cold-water fish; they are generally found either in deep lakes or in mountain tarns. They feed to a large extent on zooplankton, i.e. small animals drifting in the water, and in lakes they generally spend the daytime in deep water. Many come to the shallower water to spawn or ascend rivers and streams.

Their systematics are still the subject of argument by experts and will not be discussed here.

Salvelinus fontinalis is an American relative of our char but the American angling fraternity call it the "brook" or "speckled trout." It has been introduced into Britain without much success but is acclimatised in certain waters on the European continent. It is indigenous in N. American rivers which flow into the Atlantic Ocean. It is easily recognised because its back and dorsal and caudal fins are

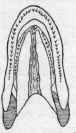 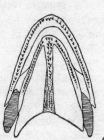 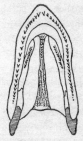

Salvelinus fontinalis   Salmo trutta   Oncorhynchus nerka

7. The palatine and vomerine teeth (from left to right) in the genera *Salvelinus* (chars), *Salmo* (Atlantic salmon and trout), and *Oncorhynchus* (Pacific salmon). (After Norden, 1961)

mottled and barred with black or olive, the actual pattern of mottling being very variable. The speckled trout seems essentially a river fish although often found in lakes; it has very similar habits to brown trout although in detail its spawning behaviour is more like that of Windermere char.

Salmo salar, the Atlantic salmon, is an anadromous fish, spawning in freshwaters connected with the Atlantic coasts of Europe and N. America. The young salmon "parr" live in freshwater for between one and five years but they usually become "smolts" at the end of their second or third year and migrate down the rivers into the sea. Here they feed and grow very rapidly and eventually they return to freshwaters to spawn. They may do this as "grilse" after only one winter in the sea or may not begin to spawn until five or six years old. After spawning, the "kelts" return to the sea but there is heavy mortality. Salmon rarely live to be more than eight or nine years old.

Dr. J. W. Jones (1959) has given a fascinating account of the salmon in this series. It is a close relative of the trout and the habits of parr are very similar to those of small brown trout but the older fish behave quite differently. There are no non-migrating races of salmon in Great Britain and with the spread of industrial pollution the number of salmon and salmon rivers has been sadly reduced.

Salmon parr can always be distinguished from trout parr by (1) the length of the maxilla, which reaches back only to the level of the middle of the eye in salmon but to below the posterior edge of the eyeball in trout, (2) the shape of the tail which is more deeply notched in salmon (middle caudal fin rays less than three-fifths as long as the longest rays compared with three-fifths or more in trout), (3) the shape of the pectoral fins, which are long in salmon and broad in trout, and (4) by certain colour features, e.g. in trout the adipose fin is usually orange and the anal fin usually has a white edge with a dark streak behind it and there are usually more spots on the operculum behind the eye and never three in a line as in salmon (fig. 8).

Salmo gairdneri, the rainbow trout, is indigenous to certain tributaries of the Sacramento River in N. America and was first introduced into Europe in 1882. In appearance very like the brown trout (pl. 4), it can be recognised by the spots on the caudal fin and the iridescent, magenta bands on the side of the body from which it takes its common name. It differs also from the brown trout in being able to withstand higher temperatures and less clear water and in being usually a spring spawner. It grows more rapidly than brown trout but lives only for four or five years. It is a migratory species, moving down rivers in spring and returning upstream to spawn in autumn, and it can survive estuarine conditions. In Britain it is known

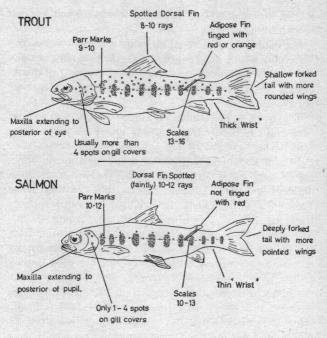

TROUT

Spotted Dorsal Fin
8-10 rays

Parr Marks
9-10

Adipose Fin
tinged with
red or orange

Shallow forked
tail with more
rounded wings

Maxilla extending to
posterior of eye

Usually more than
4 spots on gill covers

Scales
13-16

Thick "Wrist"

SALMON

Dorsal Fin Spotted
(faintly) 10-12 rays

Parr Marks
10-12

Adipose Fin
not tinged
with red

Deeply forked
tail with more
pointed wings

Maxilla extending to
posterior of pupil.

Only 1 – 4 spots
on gill covers

Scales
10-13

Thin "Wrist"

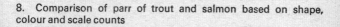

8. Comparison of parr of trout and salmon based on shape, colour and scale counts

to have become acclimatised and to breed successfully only in about a dozen waters, the northernmost being the River Wye, Derbyshire. In competition with native trout, rainbows have been more successful only in parts of the Derbyshire Wye, and in the Chess and Misbourne in the Chilterns. Elsewhere, the stocks are maintained by rearing in hatcheries and planting them out as required. This is only satisfactory in lakes and ponds since the fish will migrate downstream in rivers.

Another North American species, *Salmo clarkii*, the cut-throat trout, is characteristic of high altitude lakes in the

Rocky Mountains. This strikingly coloured trout has not been introduced here.

Having briefly considered the other species of *Salmo* and *Salvelinus* which may be met in the British Isles, we can now concentrate upon the brown trout, *Salmo trutta*, and discuss the many varieties which are included in this single polytypic species.

The trout is indigenous in Europe, N. Africa and W. Asia and has been introduced into nearly all parts of the world where conditions are suitable for its survival (see chapter 3 and map 1). There is great variation in form, colour and habit among individual brown trout from different localities. Linnæus named the "Swedish River Trout" *Salmo trutta* and distinguished two other species: the "Sea Trout," *Salmo eriox*, and the "Brook Trout," *Salmo fario*. Günther described ten different species from the British Isles: the sea or salmon-trout (*Salmo trutta*), the sewin or western sea trout (*S. cambricus*), the phinnock or eastern sea trout (*S. brachypoma*), the Galway sea trout, (*S. gallivensis*), the Orkney sea trout (*S. orcadensis*), the river trout (*S. fario*), the great lake trout (*S. ferox*), the gillaroo (*S. stomachicus*), the Welsh black-finned trout (*S. nigripinnis*) and the Loch Leven trout (*S. levenensis*). Tate Regan, however, grouped all these and the continental trout varieties together as *Salmo trutta*, one very variable species, and Dr. Trewavas, in her review of this problem in 1953, agreed with his conclusions.

If we take as our definition of a species a group of individuals which can produce fertile offspring from any mating, then it must be admitted that there is but one species of European trout. Eggs from sea trout can be fertilised with milt from river trout and vice versa and the offspring are fertile and grow like ordinary brown trout. Loch Leven trout can be cross-bred with any other variety and the offspring are fertile. (See chapter 6.)

"Sea trout" have the same type of life history as the salmon but differ from the latter in that they do not journey so far into the sea and they feed regularly while visiting

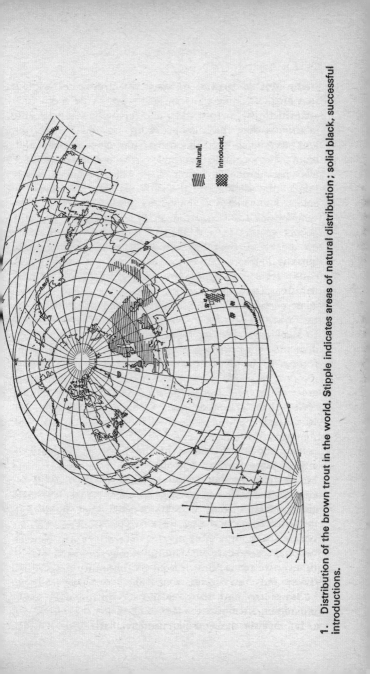

1. Distribution of the brown trout in the world. Stipple indicates areas of natural distribution; solid black, successful introductions.

freshwaters to spawn and may visit freshwater without spawning. We may thus consider them to be more fully adapted to life in freshwater and less well adapted to life in the sea than the salmon. Young sea and brown trout look very much like salmon parr (the differences have already been mentioned) and they grow at similar rates. Sea trout pass through a "smolt" stage which resembles closely that of the salmon and the adult sea trout are silvery in colour but have more numerous blackish spots than the salmon. Sea trout may remain in estuaries and generally do not venture far into the sea; they often return earlier up the rivers than the salmon. They do not grow so quickly in the sea.

Experts can recognise two local races of sea trout in British waters: the sewin of Wales, Ireland and the west coast of England and Scotland and the sea trout of the east coast. The former has a long head, larger mouth, stronger jaws and larger fins than the latter and the subopercular bone projects back beyond the opercular in the former. Even the experts, however, cannot always identify the race to which a given specimen belongs. There are a great many local names for sea trout, to mention only a few: sewin, phinnock, peal, whitling, herling, truff and scurf. Nall (1930) has given a full account in his book *The Life of the Sea Trout*.

In the brackish waters of the Loch of Stenness, in Orkney, there is a variety intermediate between sea and brown trout in habits and appearance; this constituted Günther's *Salmo orcadensis*. Certain Norwegian lakes communicate directly with fjords and some of the trout in them migrate to the sea when two years old and become typical sea trout; others may migrate at any age between two and seven years old. Until they migrate, they look and behave like typical brown trout but once they have visited the sea they become sea trout. Nine-inch brown trout can be transferred into seawater and survive for many weeks provided the temperature is kept at $50°$F ($10°$C) or less.

It has been shown experimentally that sea trout which

are prevented from migrating to the sea can grow and spawn in freshwater like typical brown trout, but as they grow older they become silvery in colour as do also the older brown trout in lakes such as Windermere. There are therefore no real grounds for considering "sea trout" as anything more than brown trout in which the migratory habit is very well developed. Indeed, typical brown trout transplanted to some parts of New Zealand and to the Falkland Islands found their way to the sea and became anadromous. There are no true freshwater fishes, such as roach and perch, in the rivers and lochs of the Hebrides, Orkney and Shetland, but there are many brown trout and it is very likely that these are the descendants of sea trout which have lost their migratory habit.

The brown or freshwater trout is thus a variety of *Salmo trutta* in which the migratory habit is not sufficiently strong for the fish to become anadromous. Many brown trout are migratory to some extent since they move upstream to spawn, or, if they live in lakes, move into inflowing streams to spawn. During most of the year, however, these trout frequent a definite locality and individuals probably have restricted areas within which they feed and rest. In this they differ from adult rainbow trout which may live in loose shoals and tend to move from place to place.

Trout from different rivers and lakes show a remarkable diversity in such features as size and colour but there is great constancy in basic structure and the variability is probably largely the result of environmental conditions. It is with this variability, particularly of size, and the conditions which may account for it that we shall be concerned in most of the rest of this book. Here we may mention some extreme types, usually differing in colour, which have been described as distinct species.

As a trout grows larger, there are slight changes in its general proportions; the snout becomes relatively longer and the eye relatively smaller while the tail loses its notch, becoming truncate instead of emarginate. Large male trout may develop a hook on the lower jaw during the breeding season and have relatively longer heads and sharper snouts than female fish. In some localities the trout never reach more than $\frac{1}{2}$ lb. in weight whereas in others trout of 5 lb. or even more are fairly common. In those places where fish are big, they will differ in bodily proportions from those in waters where no big fish are ever found. The Great Lake Trout (Günther's *Salmo ferox*) is thus simply a very large brown trout, *Salmo trutta*.

Coloration varies tremendously from place to place. Some trout are silvery-white, others quite blackish; the colour of the back varies from bluish-grey or olive through yellows and browns to nearly black while the belly may be white, silvery or golden-yellow and the sides may have silver or golden reflections; the spots may be red or brown, oval, stellate or haloed and they vary much in size, number and distribution. Trout from caves or holes may be very pale, almost white; those from muddy or peaty pools and streams are dark coloured, e.g. the black-finned trout of the Welsh mountains and some Irish bog pools (Günther's *Salmo nigripinnis*); those from large lakes are silvery, with black X-shaped spots; trout from clear waters generally have intense, haloed spots. The dark pigment cells in the trout skin are under control of the eye so that trout are able to change colour to some extent and to match their backgrounds. But in these colour variations different amounts of the black, white and red pigments (melanin, guanin and carotene) have been deposited in the skin during growth and arranged in different patterns. Blind fish from all localities are dark in colour and the examples already quoted show that colour varieties correspond to the general background colour except that fish in complete darkness are very pale.

When trout are kept in an aquarium and fed only on liver and meat they do not develop the bright red spots which are characteristic of most wild trout and it is probable that red spots are formed only if carotene is available in the diet. Fish reared in a hatchery and planted out in different waters soon assume the colour varieties typical of those waters. There is evidence that pink flesh and many red spots are characteristic of trout which eat a high proportion of crustaceans and snails.

The gillaroo of some Irish lakes (Günther's *S. stomachicus*) is a very handsome fish with a yellowish back with large brown spots and a golden belly with pink tints. There are large scarlet spots on and below the lateral line and numerous red spots over the fish. The name is said to be derived from the Irish "*giolla*" (fellow) and "*ruadh*" (red). The gillaroos are said to live only on molluscs and to have hard, thick-walled stomachs; fish from different lakes differ in size and form but have the same colours and thickness of stomach. Day records that brown trout from other localities, caught early in the season when they are feeding on snails, have thicker stomach walls than those caught later when feeding on mayflies. The gillaroo is therefore a variety whose characteristics are associated with specialised feeding habits.

The Loch Leven trout (Günther's *S. levenensis*) are silvery with black spots and very few or no red spots and they have always been esteemed as sporting fish of very fine flavour. They are said to have weak maxillæ and between forty-five and ninety pyloric cæca, while trout from other localities have only from twenty-seven to sixty-nine pyloric cæca. When Loch Leven trout are removed to other localities, they "deteriorate," that is, they become indistinguishable from the native fish. Their offspring then have fewer pyloric cæca. Day records that a rainbow trout (*Salmo gairdneri*) reared at the Howietoun hatchery, near Loch Leven, had seventy-one cæca instead of the usual forty; and it is reported that trout from large lakes on the Continent have larger numbers of cæca than those in rivers. There is no justification for considering Loch Leven trout to be more than a local race with characteristics depending on environmental factors. Day reports a fisherman's statement that they do not eat molluscs or crustaceans; this would explain the absence of red spots.

The "sonaghen" of L. Neagh and L. Melvin in Ireland

also have weak maxillæ and a single row only of vomerine teeth. They are dark-finned like the Welsh mountain trout.

This survey of the more striking sorts of trout supports Tate Regan's view that they are all varieties of one species, *Salmo trutta*, and that the differences between them are probably the result of environmental differences. There are also "freaks" some of which may be fairly common in certain localities, e.g. "bulldog nosed" and "humpbacked" trout and fish with notches in one or both opercula.

Chapter Three

Distribution

The trout *Salmo trutta* Linn. is indigenous to Europe, North Africa and North-western Asia. Sea trout are found from Iceland to Scandinavia, the White Sea and Cheshskaya Gulf in the north, in the Baltic, North Sea, English Channel and Atlantic Ocean as far south as the Bay of Biscay. Brown trout live in rivers emptying into all these seas and also in rivers entering the western Mediterranean and the northern part of the eastern Mediterranean but there are no sea trout in that sea. Brown trout also live in Corsica and Sardinia. There are trout in the Black and Caspian Seas and in their tributary rivers and in the Aral Sea and the River Oxus. The Russian expert L. S. Berg concluded that there are six subspecies, as follows:

Salmo trutta trutta in northern and western Europe,

S. t. labrax in the Black Sea and its tributaries,

S. t. caspius in the Caspian Sea and its tributaries,

S. t. aralensis in the Sea of Aral and the River Oxus,

S. t. macrostigma in the Mediterranean region and

S. t. carpione the large trout of Lake Garda in Italy.

There is some overlapping of the characters which separate these subspecies and also of their geographical ranges. It is interesting that the first four in the list each include varieties which range in habit from migratory "sea trout" through lacustrine forms breeding in streams but living most of their lives in large lakes, to almost sedentary "brook trout." The Mediterranean subspecies lacks "sea trout" but it is likely from the present distribution that such existed in the Ice Age and disappeared when the water warmed up. The subspecies in Lake Garda is probably descended from a lacustrine form of the Mediterranean subspecies. (See map 1, page 51).

The British brown and sea trout belong to the northern subspecies and their qualities as sporting fish and fine flavour have encouraged Britons working overseas to try to introduce trout into other parts of the world.

High temperatures and low oxygen concentrations are lethal to trout and suitable conditions of temperature and substratum for spawning are necessary if they are to establish themselves as a breeding stock. There are many parts of the world where suitable environmental conditions occur and brown trout may now be found in N. and S. America, many parts of Africa, India, Australia and New Zealand. Rainbow trout (*Salmo gairdneri*) are rather hardier than brown trout and have also been transplanted from their native waters in N. America to many parts of the world.

With modern methods of refrigeration and air transport it is relatively easy to move fish eggs all over the world but conditions were very different a hundred years ago. The first well authenticated attempt to transport salmonid fish to the Antipodes was made in 1852, when 50,000 eggs were shipped aboard the *Columbus* at London. The eggs were placed in a tub with gravel and water and began to hatch some six weeks before they had been expected to do so. In the tropics, the water became thick and putrid and by the time the ship reached Tasmania there were no traces either of eggs or young fish. It was concluded from this failure that the temperature of the water should be kept low during transit across the tropics.

In 1858, a committee of Fellows of the Royal Society of Tasmania reported to the Colonial Secretary on problems connected with the introduction of salmonids and in 1860 the Tasmanian Legislature appointed a body of Honorary Commissioners to manage the whole experiment. Much of the credit for their ultimate success must be given to James Arundel Youl who enthusiastically managed the British end of the attempts. In 1860 the *S. Curling* sailed from Liverpool with 50,000 salmon eggs and a supply of ice with which to keep down the temperature of the water in which they were contained, but the last of the ice melted on the fifty-ninth day and the last egg died on the same day.

The next attempt in 1862, in the *Beautiful Star*, was also disastrous because the ice melted before the end of the voyage but some eggs had survived for eighty-eight days after being stripped from the fish. Mr. Youl packed eggs in ice in England in the winter of 1862-63 and some of these hatched after having been buried in ice for 150 days. He therefore persevered and in 1864 the *Norfolk* set out with 90,000 salmon eggs and 1500 brown trout eggs and thirty tons of ice in a well built ice-house. The trout eggs were included at the special request of Frank Buckland who obtained most of them by stripping one pair of R. Itchen fish; the rest were sent by Francis Francis who collected them from Hungerford fish. They left Falmouth on 28 January and reached Melbourne on 15 April. One box was opened and a large number of eggs was found to be alive. Some were left in Melbourne and the rest were taken on to Hobart, in Tasmania, and were unpacked on 21 and 22 of April. It was calculated that 35,000 eggs had survived the journey, of which only 300 were trout and the rest were salmon. They were placed in hatching beds supplied with water from the Plenty River, a tributary of the Tasmanian River Derwent. The first trout egg hatched on 4 May, 1864, and the first salmon egg on the following day, and they continued to hatch until 15 June. In January 1866, 171 of these trout were still alive in the ponds and thirty-eight of them were released into the river.

A further consignment of 103,000 salmon eggs and 15,000 trout eggs were transported to Tasmania in the *Lincolnshire* in 1865; nearly half of them arrived alive and about 6000 salmon and 500 trout fry were hatched successfully.

In July and August 1866, some two-year-old trout began to spawn naturally in the Plenty River and others were caught in ponds and stripped. A large number of these eggs were infertile. The trout from the ponds were stripped again in 1867 and some of these eggs were sent to Victoria and to New Zealand. Many of these were also infertile and the ponds were remodelled so that the fish should breed naturally and these eggs, which were nearly all fertile, were then collected. An interesting point about the spawning of these trout is that it took place in the Antipodean winter which corresponds to the European summer; trout in Europe spawn during the European winter. Some of the three-year-old trout weighed more than three pounds; a four-year-old trout caught in 1868 weighed 9¼ lb.

From 1868 onwards, the Plenty River was established as a natural breeding ground for trout and a source of eggs and fry for Australia and New Zealand and for other Tasmanian rivers.

Meanwhile, it may be of interest to record that some of the salmon fry had become smolts and descended to the sea and some grilse were first observed in the River Derwent in February and March 1867. It was hoped at the time that they had become acclimatised, but thirty years later there was no evidence of the presence of *Salmo salar* in Tasmania, New Zealand or Southern Australia.

The first successful hatch of trout eggs in New Zealand was in 1868 at Otago, South Island, from Tasmanian stock. It is interesting that some of these descendants of British non-migratory trout became anadromous in the Waiou River, South Island, and others formed distinct colour varieties clearly related to their backgrounds. In 1882, a trout, captured at Canterbury, weighed 21 lb. and at Otago the average yearly increment in weight was from 1 to 2¾ lb.

In 1866, Francis Day attempted unsuccessfully to introduce brown trout eggs into streams in the Neilgherry Hills near Madras, but McIvor, in 1868, was successful with a batch of fry from Loch Leven. These bred in the hill streams near Ootacamund, and even developed red spots which are not found on the fish in Loch Leven.

Attempts to introduce trout into South Africa followed the pattern of the Tasmanian efforts. In 1875 and 1882 all the eggs being shipped were lost because of the heat in the tropics. In 1884, Mr. Maclean hatched 17,000 out of another batch of 20,000 eggs at Ceres, near Capetown, but lost most of these from zinc poisoning and other disasters. Three survivors died in 1890 when they weighed 3 lb. each at six years old. The first completely successful venture in Cape Province was in 1892 when Ernest Latour took charge of imported brown trout eggs and started the successful hatchery at Jonkershoek.

Trout were first introduced into Natal in 1890 for the Natal Government by John Clarke Power, when 600 brown trout fry were released into the Mooi, Bushmans and Umgeni Rivers, and later in the same year 800 Loch Leven fry were also placed in the Mooi. In 1893 there was no evidence that the trout had become acclimatised and Government interest waned but six years later trout were found to be well established in the three rivers and a hatchery was then built at Tetwork, from which fry were distributed to other waters.

These Natal rivers start as torrents in the Drakensberg Mountains, form larger streams in the foothills and flow thence across the coastal plain with the water temperature rising as the altitude decreases. Spawning is very successful at 5000 to 5500 feet above sea level. The average size of the trout is greatest in the middle reaches, e.g. about thirty miles below the source of the Bushmans River, which is still populated by progeny of the fry originally introduced more than seventy years ago. Downstream from this, trout survival and growth decrease as water temperature rises while upstream of this optimum region there are very large numbers of small trout, especially in the upland valleys. Some of the indigenous fish still live alongside the introduced trout, for instance, the small catfish *Amphilius* and the large barbel *Barbus natalensis*, but it is possible that a small "minnow" *Labeo quathlambæ* has been eaten out by the trout.

Major Ewart Grogan introduced brown trout into Kenya in 1905 when eggs were hatched at 9500 ft. on the Gura

River; the Game Department took control of the trout waters in 1926; by 1939 there were 373 miles of river containing brown trout in Kenya. There are no other fish in these trout streams, except perhaps the catfish *Amphilius* and eels. They are all over 5800 ft. above sea level, and rise on Mount Kenya and the Aberdare Mountains. There are waterfalls between the trout zone and the warm plains. The trout may reach 5 lb. in weight; the majority breed in the long rains from October to December. Rainbow trout have also been introduced into Kenya and may reach 10 lb. in weight at four years.

The first attempt to introduce trout into Tanganyika Territory was organised by Major Sandwith in 1926 and only fifty-seven fry survived from 3000 eggs. Another batch of 3000 eggs arrived from Kenya in April 1927 and was followed unexpectedly by a batch of rainbow trout eggs in May. In spite of waiting for hours on a station platform in a shade temperature of 90°F, many of the latter survived and 1700 brown and 1457 rainbow trout fry were released or escaped into the river in the western Usambara Mountains that year. The rainbow trout flourished and weighed 2 to 3 lb. at two years old but the brown trout seemed usually in poor condition and failed to spawn. Subsequently streams in other mountainous areas were stocked with varying success.

Brown trout eggs were sent from Germany to New York in 1883 and eggs from England followed in 1884. Eggs from Loch Leven trout were introduced into Newfoundland in the same year; from four centres in the Avalon peninsula, these brown trout spread through salt water to many other streams up to sixty miles away and populations of these "sea trout" are now well established. Trout from the Caledonia Hatchery, New York, were released into Lac Brûlé, Quebec, in 1890. The first introductions into Ontario were in 1913 and into the Maritime Provinces in 1921. In the Guysborough River, in the Maritimes, some of the brown trout migrated into the sea and have colonised the adjacent Salmon River. Anadromous "sea trout" are now found also on Vancouver Island where they are the descendants of introduced brown trout. Brown trout are stocked in many waters in Canada and U.S.A. but, on the whole, they do not spawn successfully and are less esteemed by anglers than the excellent native "trouts," *Salmo gairdneri, S. clarkii* and *Salvelinus fontinalis*.

Brown trout from England were introduced into Argentina between 1904 and 1910 and into Chile in 1905. The species is now well established in many southern waters of these countries, including streams in Tierra del Fuego; these are at present the southernmost limit of its distribution. Farther north, brown trout come into competition with imported rainbow trout and the latter is more successful.[1]

The early transplantations were followed by a spectacularly high growth rate in many of the waters colonised and there have been speculations about the reasons for this rapid growth especially as it has been stated that the rates declined later to more usual values. For New Zealand, Percival in 1932 concluded that the fish grew as well as ever but the angling pressure was such that they did not survive long enough to reach spectacular weights. This seems to be true also of some Kenya rivers where a rest from fishing for three years led to "recovery" of the water because of the survival of older larger fish. In other waters it is possible that over-stocking has brought about a decline, the early rapid growth being the result of an unlimited food supply. This is illustrated by data from Natal, where weather conditions drastically reduced the trout populations between 1944 and 1946 and later allowed them to build up again. Trout in the Mooi River averaged $8\frac{1}{4}$ inches when one year old throughout the trout zone in 1947, but they averaged $7\frac{1}{2}$ inches in the lower reaches and only $5\frac{1}{2}$ inches in the upper reaches of the trout zone in 1952. The corresponding lengths of two-year-old fish were $13\frac{1}{2}$ inches in 1948 and $11\frac{1}{4}$ and 8 inches

[1] We are grateful to Senor D. A. Conroy, of the Instituto de Biologia Marina in Argentina, for this information.

Chapter Four

Life History

Adult trout change in "fatness" during the year and this can be measured by changes in the condition factor, K (see p. 86). These changes are mainly the result of alteration in size of the gonads—the testes of the male and the ovaries of the female fish. The gonads are small in spring but fill the body cavity in autumn; besides changing in size, they change in histology (cell structure) resulting in the production of sperms and eggs in autumn.

In late winter and spring, the ovaries of an adult trout (a fish which has already spawned at least once) are long bodies lying below its air-bladder, close-knit structures with small bead-like swellings among which are a few larger pellucid swellings (fig. 9). The latter are remnants of spawning from which the fish is just recovering. Often there are one or two collapsed full-sized eggs loose in the body cavity, these were not shed when the fish spawned in the previous autumn. The ovary is composed of a large number of "follicles"; seen under the microscope these consist each of a layer of follicle cells surrounding a single cell which will become an egg. The nucleus of such a cell undergoes special division (meiosis) so that the number of chromosomes in the egg is half that in a normal body cell. The eggs are budded off from the layer of germinal epithelium which forms the outside of the ovary. The number of eggs and their surrounding follicles is determined each year in March in Great Britain.

During the summer the eggs grow in size. A few of them break down and their follicles probably produce a hormone which is necessary for the successful maturation of the remaining eggs and for the onset of spawning activity. The other eggs grow by incorporation of yolk which they obtain from the follicle cells; these extract food substances from the blood circulation and pass them into the eggs. The yolk is derived partly from the fat stored in the gut wall; for trout in Wraymires hatchery, Swift found that this was 23% of body weight in July but had been reduced to only 5% when the fish were ripe. The protein content of the ovary rose by 16% between June and October and its fat content by 3% while its water content fell from 84% to 64%.

In autumn, the ripe ovaries fill the body cavity and may comprise up to 20% of the total weight of the fish. Each egg is full of yolk and about ½ cm. in diameter, the follicles are stretched, become very thin and disappear. The whole ovary is surrounded by a transparent limiting membrane which becomes ruptured so that the eggs lie loose in the body cavity when the fish are ready to spawn. The eggs are shed through the urino-genital pore behind the anus and can easily be squeezed out of a ripe fish by pressing along its body. Each egg is surrounded by a tough "shell" within which is a thin vitelline membrane. There is a hole (the micropyle) in the shell through which a sperm can enter to fertilise the egg. Some nearly mature eggs may be resorbed, and their follicles are the larger pellucid bead-like structures which can be seen during the next winter.

After the eggs have been shed, the spent fish (slat or kelt) has a long flaccid ovary, usually bloodshot, with a few large pellucid swellings. As the next season's follicles develop, the picture becomes transformed once more into the ripening ovary of late winter and spring and the cycle of changes is repeated again.

In immature female trout, that is, fish which have not yet spawned, the ovary is one quarter the length of the body cavity or less and is hidden by the liver and stomach when viewed from below. The ovary is widest at its anterior end and tapers like a carrot; it is always orange or yellow in colour. The eggs are small (about 1 mm.) and the follicles are tightly packed together and of uniform size. Some sexually mature trout do not spawn every year; during the resting year their ovaries look very like those

9. The ovary of a trout in different stages of development. 1, "immature," eggs just visible, has never spawned and will not ripen to spawn at next breeding season; 2-5, "maturing," i.e. ripening to spawn: (2-4, ripening, eggs begin to fill body cavity and grow larger; 5, ripe, eggs ready for shedding, large, free in body cavity); 6, spent, eggs shed, ovary narrow, often a few unshed eggs in body cavity. When recovered from spent state a fish is "mature." (Diagram from Sømme, 1948)

of immature fish but are longer (about half the length of the body cavity) and wider. Microscopical examination reveals that small old follicles are present and these are never found in immature ovaries.

The cycle of events in male trout is somewhat similar. In winter and early spring the testes (soft roe) of an adult trout, one which has already spawned, are the long, narrow, crimson-pink "tough" structures of a spent fish. By about mid-May they are growing in width and becoming creamy in colour. Progressive increase in volume and creaminess occurs during late summer, and they reach their maximum size in October and November. Testes never completely fill the body cavity, as do the ovaries.

The histological structure of the testes is quite different from that of the ovaries. Testes consist of seminiferous tubules with a limiting layer of basement cells and these contain the developmental stages of the sperm together with supporting and nourishing cells (Sertoli cells). Inconspicuous interstitial cells between the tubules produce the male hormone. The tubules are held together by the testicular membrane, and all of them open into a common space which leads to the genital opening behind the anus. The developmental stages of the sperm include meiotic division so that mature sperm contain only half the number of chromosomes of body cells. A mature sperm consists of a body containing the nucleus, and a tail; it is very much smaller than a mature egg and contains no food reserves. Male trout produce infinitely greater numbers of sperm than the numbers of eggs produced by female trout of the same size and age, but the weight of the mature ovary is greater than that of the mature testis.

When the fish is ripe, gentle pressure on the sides of its body cavity will express drops of white "milt" through its urino-genital pore. After spawning, the testes of a spent fish look shrunken, pellucid and bloodshot and gradually widen and become creamy, as the next season's sperm are produced and develop.

In an immature trout, the testes lie below the swim

bladder against the wall of the body cavity and extend along its whole length. Each testis is a white narrow string of almost the same width for the greater part of its length but becoming very thin at its posterior end. It becomes tinged with pink and then (as the young fish matures) swollen, particularly in the anterior and middle portion, and creamy coloured.

In the British Isles, brown trout may become ripe and spawn between October and February; they are never found in breeding condition outside this period. The cyclical changes of the gonads depend on the physiological state of the body and are probably controlled by activity of the pituitary gland. External factors may affect the reproductive cycle; for instance, artificial shortening of the hours of daylight can lead to spawning six weeks earlier than normally. There may be an intrinsic annual rhythm which is independent of environmental changes, because fish in tanks under constant environmental conditions become sexually mature at the right time of year. A male trout captured in an underground stream in Durham was ripe in early December, although it had almost certainly been in total darkness for a period of at least two months and perhaps for much longer.

The normal time for spawning is November and December, but there are local variations. In the upper Avon, Wiltshire, and in Driffield Beck, Yorkshire, February is the chief spawning month but in the River Derwent, only twenty miles away from Driffield Beck, spawning takes place in November and December.

Spawning usually takes place in running water and trout living in lakes migrate into feeder streams. In some instances trout living in rivers move up the main river and into the tributaries to spawn, even, as in the Thurso River and the Tweed, ascending fish passes and weirs in this migration. Allen, however, found no movement of spawning trout in the Horokiwi stream in New Zealand and none was observed by my colleague Mr. Le Cren, in some small lakeland becks. On the other hand Mr. C. Myers and the late John Bevins noticed that some of the mature trout in the River Wyre which lived in the river below Abbeystead Lake, where spawning grounds were presumably adequate, move upstream, ascend a long fish ladder into the lake, and then migrate out of the lake into the two inflowing streams where they spawn.

As the trout living in lakes and tarns normally migrate into inflowing streams to spawn, they provide us with the best material for a study of spawning migrations. The time of this migration is determined by external and internal factors. The internal factors include the state of ripening of the gonads and the gonadial hormones.

Working from the Freshwater Fisheries Laboratory at Pitlochry, Scotland, Stuart found that when their gonads were ripe, there was an abrupt and marked change in the behaviour pattern of the trout in Dunalastair Reservoir, for then these fish, normally solitary, congregate and form shoals near the entrance of the spawning stream. His colleagues Munro and Balmain saw, during 1953, large numbers of trout shoaling near the mouth of the main spawning stream of Loch Leven on 2 October. They noted that at the end of August and through September fishing tends to become concentrated in the areas around the mouths of the spawning streams, which suggests that the trout are tending to congregate there.

The fish which are to spawn may start their upstream migration several weeks or only a few days before they spawn. From Windermere there is often a considerable migration of brown trout into Troutbeck in August, although they also enter this (and other streams) in October and November and spawning usually occurs in November. Trout of Poulaphouca Reservoir may run up the inflowing River Liffey as early as mid-June. In two small mountain lochs, Lochan an Daim (1080 feet) and Loch Moraig (1105 feet) spawners entered the inflowing streams from early to mid-October respectively, on the other hand in Dunalastair Reservoir, a larger water at 600 feet, the spawning migration began at the end of October. In a four-acre tarn above Windermere the trout enter the tiny inflowing stream in November. Thus on the whole breeding trout leave a large lake with long tributary streams and distant spawning grounds earlier than those living in a small body of water with short tributaries.

Although trout may enter their spawning streams over a period of four months, this migration, whenever it occurs, is usually (perhaps always) associated with a rise in water level, a coincidence of events which has long been recognised by anglers and fishery workers. The heavy rains which usually fall in August in the Lake District bring the first run of maturing trout out of Windermere into the flooded Troutbeck, but in 1955 there was a long drought and the first run of trout did not occur until mid-September when the beck was in spate for the first time in several weeks. In 1952 the mature trout of a five-acre moorland tarn began to run up the inflowing beck early in November. There was then a drought until mid-December and no more trout ran upstream, although the fish assembled at the beck mouth were so gravid they gave eggs when handled. Migration from Loch Leven always began after an increase in water level although there was sufficient water to enable the fish to enter the stream at other times.

It is not known how the rise in water level stimulates the trout to migrate, but there are several changes in physical and chemical conditions that coincide with the rise. There seems to be no consistent relation between the temperatures of stream and lake at the onset of migration, but too great a temperature difference may be inhibitory. Van Someren believed that dilution of the stream water by floods was the main stimulus to upstream migration of rainbow trout in Kenya. Increased acidity of streams derived from peaty ground may inhibit migration. Extreme turbidity may be the factor which inhibits the run at the peak of a spate in Loch Leven where a "run began as the water level rose, slackened as the spate reached its peak and then reached its maximum as the water level began to fall."

Thus there is an association between a rise in water level and the upstream movement of trout, and this occurs whether the rise results in a small spate or a flood, suggesting that the trout respond to a relative and not to an absolute increase in the height of the water. A similar response is shown by silver eels in their *downstream* migration.

The final upstream run which immediately precedes spawning may well depend on water temperature. Stuart found that it always occurred when the temperature of the stream into which the trout migrate had dropped to 6°-7°c (44°F) and in every case he observed this was the first time it had fallen to this level.

The site on which the trout in due time will spawn has certain physical characteristics which apparently provide the stimulus for the construction of redds and the laying of eggs. A "redd" is the area of gravel in which the trout deposits her eggs in one or more pockets (or nests). The spawning places are usually in fairly quickly flowing water of moderate depth but not in turbulent riffles; such conditions are found at the tail of a pool or at the edge of the river. The width of the stream appears to be immaterial, for trout (both large and small) will ascend both the wide rivers and those (even in the same region) which are only a foot or two in width. Stones of a certain size and a substratum permeable to water currents seem essential. Stuart found that trout utilise gravels composed of stones up to three inches in diameter with a large proportion of smaller materials, the effect of which is to consolidate the mass while leaving it permeable to water. There are characteristic water currents through such a substratum when it is situated at the tail of a pool (fig. 10). He showed also that these currents have a path at right angles to the surface of the gravel and that they pass through the egg pockets deep in the bed of the stream and emerge beyond, thus producing a continuous current through the redd. Moreover their force is such that all traces of sand and silt placed on the surface of the gravel are removed. When these conditions for a stable silt-free well-aerated redd are present trout will spawn even though the site be unsuitable in other respects, as when fluctuations in water level may leave the redd high and dry.

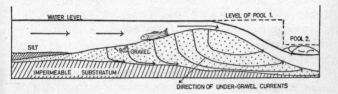

WATER LEVEL   LEVEL OF POOL 1.

POOL 2.

SILT   GRAVEL

IMPERMEABLE   SUBSTRATUM

DIRECTION OF UNDER-GRAVEL CURRENTS

10. Diagrammatic section through the substratum of a typical stream pool showing the principal water currents and the position of the female on the gravel bank before excavation of the redd. (T. A. Stuart)

Where stony wave-washed shores of lakes present gravel banks resembling those of running waters, trout may spawn in such "still waters." I have seen redds on the shores of a small peaty tarn and a large calcareous Irish lough. In the first of these cases the obvious reasons for the lake spawning habit were the useless peaty bottom of the one inflowing stream; in the second there were only three small streams which provided inadequate spawning ground for the large population of trout in the lough. Stuart, who found that trout spawned on a gravel patch in Lough Moraig, suggested that they did not enter an easily accessible stream because of a high temperature barrier.

At the breeding season, trout change their shape and colour to some extent; this may start early in the spawning migration and become more obvious at the actual spawning time. The male develops a hook (neb or kype) on its lower jaw and is therefore at this time reliably distinguishable by external characters from the female. Colour varies greatly, but the spawning male generally has dun-coloured flanks with copper coloured spots and a dingy cream-bronze belly, although I have seen an almost ripe male with the golden yellow belly and red spots of the non-breeding fish. The throat may become grey-black in colour and the anal fin edged with an intense white. The ripe female may have an overall coppery look, or have steely mauve flanks; its belly colour grades from white to a dingy greeny white. Some large (4 to 6 lb.) ripe female trout in Windermere have no hint of copper colour but only a rather drab cast over their usual colouring of silver with black spots.

There are but few records of the sex ratio of breeding trout based on a census of the total spawning population— and these are inconsistent. There are records from different waters of males being more numerous, less numerous and equal in number to the females. Males tend to remain longer in the streams than the females, which, having spawned, retreat rapidly, and it is likely that some mate with more than one female. Stuart found that larger trout ran up earlier and spawned farther upstream than others, but this was not the case in Loch Leven.

The spawning activities themselves are concentrated into two or three weeks. They have long attracted attention, but much recorded information is fragmentary and some erroneous. Recent investigations in the field, particularly by Stuart, together with observations and films made in laboratory tanks by Jones and Ball of Liverpool and by Stuart, have now provided an accurate picture of the activities of the breeding brown trout (see plates 1 and 2).

Spawning may occur at any time of day. Greeley found the trout more active during the midday period when the light was bright than in the early morning and late evening. The female arrives at the spawning place before the male and explores the territory, selects a suitable site and then begins to excavate the egg pocket or nest by "cutting" the gravel. She may begin this operation in the absence of the male but usually cuts when males are in the vicinity. To cut, the female "turns over on her side and by alternately bending and straightening her body produces a vigorous vertical flapping of her tail as a result of which

gravel immediately beneath the spread caudal fin is dislodged as the fin moves upwards and forwards quickly"
(Jones and Ball). The suction produced by the upward
movement of the caudal fin causes the gravel to move
downstream. The nearby males take no part in selecting
the site nor in excavating the bed but spend their time
chasing and fighting each other until one attends the
cutting female and defends his position against other
intruding males. This male darts alongside the female and
quivers against her. This quivering is a short sequence
of rapid shudders involving the whole body. After some
exploratory cuts the female concentrates her cutting to a
limited area and the male becomes more attentive and
quivers against her frequently. In between cuts, the female
every now and again sinks into the depression she has made
and "feels" it with her anal fin. Cutting and quivering
activities go on for some time and then when the depression
is about two to three inches deep the female descends into
it with a curious "slow bounce," inserts her anal fin between two of the larger stones and assumes the "crouch"
position when "the head is elevated and the pelvic region
fits snugly into the gravel." The crouch is retained for a
second or two and may be repeated a few times. Then
when the female finds the nest is suitable she remains on
it, opens her mouth and the male darts alongside her
quivering violently. Eggs and sperm are then extruded,
almost simultaneously, as the fish lie in the nest with their
mouths wide open; most of the eggs pass down between
the two loose stones where the anal fin lies. During the
spawning act, which is over in a second, the female is in a
state of extreme muscular tension with her head slightly
raised and her body arched.

The nest made by an eleven-inch trout is "a saucer shaped
depression ten to twelve inches in length and three inches
in depth to the top of the gravel," and the time taken
from the first cutting to extrusion of the eggs is about one
and a half hours. There is only one oviposition in the nest
and Jones and Ball found 233, 220 and 141 eggs in three

successive nests made by a three-year-old female. Immediately after shedding her eggs the female moves upstream of the nest and with vigorous cutting activity covers the eggs taking only one or two minutes to do so. By this cutting to cover she also begins the depression for her next nest, which will thus be just upstream of her first one. Each redd may consist of several nests. The number of nests and redds made no doubt depend on the size of the female but there is no evidence from the field about this nor about the time taken for a female to spawn herself out.

The eggs are fertilised while being shed into the nest by the female. The sperms shed by the male become active when ejected into the water; they swim by lashing their tails and they are probably attracted to the eggs by chemical stimuli and can enter through the micropyles. When a sperm has entered an egg it loses its tail and its nucleus fuses with the egg nucleus. Since sperm and eggs each have only half the number of chromosomes of body cells, the result of this fusion is that the fertilised eggs has the full number of chromosomes. After fertilisation, the egg membrane becomes impermeable so that the developing embryo is insulated from the surrounding water.

Only one sperm can fertilise each egg and the number of sperm present during the spawning act is many times the number of eggs. It is possible to preserve trout sperm in concentrated frozen condition for many months but once diluted with fresh water an individual sperm can survive for less than one minute. However, sperm can live in seawater for about fifteen minutes. In trout hatcheries, ripe female trout are stripped of their eggs into bowls and milt from ripe males is squeezed into the same container. After thorough mixing of eggs and milt, water is added and later, after washing, the eggs are set out in trays. Under these conditions a hundred per cent fertilisation may be obtained: under natural conditions people used to consider that reproduction must be an inefficient process with many of the eggs remaining unfertilised. Hobbs, however, dug up all the eggs in redds in a New Zealand river soon after they had been spawned and reared them in a hatchery and found that ninety-seven per cent had been fertilised.

The eggs are laid, as described above, among gravel, and being heavier than water sink into interstices. Although chemically insulated from the surrounding water by the egg shell, the developing embryo is very susceptible to mechanical shock during early development until the stage when the eyes of the young fish can be seen through the shell. Until it starts feeding, the embryo lives entirely on the yolk present in the egg; after hatching it also absorbs water. The rate of development depends on the temperature, being faster at higher temperatures. A good proportion of the eggs can hatch successfully at temperatures between 5 and 13°c (41 and 55°F); above and below these temperatures the mortality increases markedly. Table 2 gives the number of days taken to complete development to the hatching stage at different temperatures. Eggs of equal size will produce equal-sized fry ready to begin feeding at all temperatures between 7 and 12°c but at higher or lower temperatures the alevins will be smaller since at these less favourable temperatures they use more yolk to provide energy and less for growth.

Hatching occurs soon after the eggs become "eyed." The egg membrane is dissolved away from the inside by a "hatching enzyme" and becomes transparent. The young fish wriggles actively inside, the thin membrane splits and the alevin wriggles out by lashing movements of head and tail. A newly emerged alevin is shown in plate 3. The yolk sac is attached below and usually contains a large oil globule. The heart can be seen beating and the principal blood vessels show clearly through the transparent body. The eyes are relatively large with plenty of black pigment, the fins are present but not well differentiated. At first the young alevin remains quiet but after two or three days (depending on temperature) it responds to light by wriggling; if placed on the surface of gravel it therefore tends to burrow down away from the light.

Table 2. The average time between fertilisation and hatching for brown trout eggs at different temperatures. (Modified from Davis 1956 after Embody, 1934)

| Water temperature | | Incubation time |
°C	°F	days
2	35½	148
3·6	38½	118
4·7	40½	97
6	43	77
7·8	46	60
10	50	41
11	52	35
12	53½	27

As they grow older and use up their yolk, the alevins grow more like the familiar trout with streamlined body, well-developed fins and pigmented skin. When the yolk supply is nearly exhausted the alevins change their behaviour and move towards the light and orientate themselves to face a water current. Stuart followed the dispersal of alevins from egg pockets in streams and in tanks and found that, after spending three or four days at rest, they move away from the pocket and towards the surface so that a plot of their position forms an inverted cone with the egg pocket at the apex and the most advanced alevins farthest away and nearest the surface. If they become exposed to light during this period they turn and burrow in another direction. Trout alevins feed on their yolk sacs for two or three weeks, depending on temperature, but when they are about one inch long the yolk sac has usually been absorbed and the fry begin to feed. They rest on the bottom but will swim upwards to any small moving object which under natural conditions is generally a small organism suitable as food, e.g. a midge larva. This first feeding stage may occur as early as mid-March if there has been a mild winter. Soon the fry, up to 1¼ inches long, become poised in mid-water and take their position in the stream, where they are found in shallow water two to three inches deep. Some are in mid-stream, others in pools behind big stones, all maintaining their positions by swimming against the current, while yet others may occupy almost static backwaters. These fry are spaced about three inches apart and each one has its territory, an area in which it feeds and lives and from which it will chase other fry. In aquaria there are usually individuals in each group of trout fry which never begin to feed; these die of starvation in a few weeks depending on temperature. The fry which start feeding earlier acquire an initial advantage in size over others which start later and they typically maintain this greater size if all the fry are left together in one group. In a stream the larger fry probably hold the more "desirable" territories with better feeding facilities, and so grow faster. As the season progresses the disparity in length between smallest and largest fry increases so that in the Liffey, for instance, fry at the end of their first year may measure from 2 to 5½ inches (5 to 14 cm.).

In form and colour, the fry are recognisable as little salmonids from the beginning. The "parr marks," visible even in the young fry, become more obvious as the fish grows older and may remain throughout life (plate 4). The red edge of the adipose fin, so characteristic of *Salmo trutta*, appears early in fry life. Dark spots and red spots appear on the back and flanks as the fish grows older, and later also on the belly; some develop a red border to the tail.

The mortality during early life is enormous. Allen calculated for the Horokiwi River in New Zealand that in a good year the total egg production would be about 900,000, and about 500,000 fry would begin feeding three months later. After feeding for three months, only 12,000 of these would be alive; after a further three months, about 7500; and at the end of the first year of life only 4500. The most

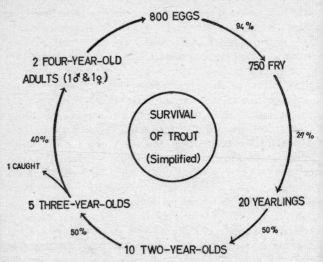

11. Diagram of the survival of a typical trout brood. The small figures indicate percentage survival from one stage to the next. (Le Cren, 1961)

hazardous time for survival of trout in the Horokiwi is during the first six months after fertilisation, for 44% die before beginning to feed and only 2% of the young fry are alive three months after they begin to feed. After that time, natural losses appear to be such that about 20% of the trout alive at the beginning of each year will survive for twelve months or longer.

Allen's figures for mortality of eggs and alevins are higher than those recorded here and in the U.S.A. Le Cren has estimated average survival figures for a good trout stream and these are shown in fig. 11. Here, 94% of the eggs may develop into fry ready to begin to feed, and of these 2.7% are still alive at the end of the year. Thus the survival from eggs to yearling fish is 2½%. Le Cren assumes an annual survival of 50% after the yearling stage and this is higher than Allen's figure of 20%. Figures for Three Dubs Tarn are given in fig. 12 and show the expected low

We must digress to mention briefly the terminology used for trout of different ages. The newly-hatched fish, living on its yolk, is called an alevin here (sac-fry in U.S.A.). In its first year of life, the trout is a fry or fingerling (0+ fish); in its second year, it is a yearling (1+ fish); in its third year, a two-year-old (2+fish); and so on. A fry in the autumn (0+fish) is sometimes called a "yearling" commercially, but the trout's year should really begin between January and March when the eggs hatch into alevins.

The yearling trout in a river have the same kind of habits as older fish, each keeping station within its territory from which it seeks food. This territorial habit, expressed in the "lie" of an older trout, characterises trout living in running water (it has much bearing on trout stream management, chapter 10).

Movement of trout during the fry stage is that of individuals that cannot find a territory, these migrate downstream. In some rivers older trout may move from place to place. A study of the movements of trout in the River Wyre by Mr. C. Myers and Mr. R. S. Fort showed that the fish of varied sizes and ages moved upstream and to some extent downstream at all times of the year. Allen however found that trout in the Horokiwi River moved very little during their lives. When the mature fish live in lakes but spawn in streams, the young fry live and feed in the streams. Those that grow fastest may move down into the lake when about one year old, the rest at two, three or even four years old, the larger ones migrating earlier than smaller ones. Growth is usually faster in the lake, so the larger fish, which move down into it earliest, tend to remain larger for the rest of their lives. If the inflowing stream is very small, all the young fish may move down in their first year, as in Three Dubs Tarn. Stuart has found that young trout drop from small streams into lochs during autumn but return to the streams in spring, repeating these annual movements until they become mature. The trout may show periodic movements in lakes; in Windermere none are caught in shallow water between June and

September. In this and other deep lakes, large trout, more than 5 lb. in weight, seem to spend all their time in deep water where they may be caught when trolling for char or by setting gill nets.

Pacific salmon spawn only once and then die, but it is characteristic of trout that they spawn several times before death. After each spawning, the trout which have migrated out of lakes return to them and those which have moved upstream in rivers probably move downstream; they then feed and recover condition; their gonads begin to mature again and in late summer they migrate upstream once more. In many trout populations each surviving fish spawns every year after it has first spawned, but this is not always so. Certain trout living in large lakes, such as Windermere, may "rest" for a year and spawn only once every second year. In a Swedish lake, Runnström found that out of thirty-four trout which had spawned twice, thirty-one had rested for a year between. Stuart found that fifty per cent of the mature females from Dunalastair Reservoir and Lough Moraig were not ripening in any year while the others were clearly maturing again after having spawned the year before.

The study of marked fish is producing evidence that trout which live in a lake return to spawn a second and further times in the same stream. Runnström has recorded this in Sweden and Stuart in Scotland. The latter has recaptured many trout marked in seven spawning streams the previous year; all were caught in the stream in which they had been marked and some were caught in the same stream in three or four successive years. When gravid trout from each of two streams from opposite sides of Dunalastair Reservoir were exchanged, one third of these returned to their original streams, some within twenty-four hours; none were found in other streams. Trout marked in nursery streams as small fry have moved into the loch in winter and back to these streams in summer, repeating these annual migrations until they become mature. Thus there is sound evidence for a "homing instinct" in trout, expressed by their return to spawn again in a particular stream which is very probably that in which the fish was hatched and lived as a fry. The means whereby the trout find their way back to their own stream is not yet established.

Figures showing the survival and frequency of spawning of adult trout are difficult to come by but Stuart has recorded the same fish spawning for three years in succession. Runnström found one quarter of his Swedish trout had spawned at least twice, some a third time and one a fourth time, but most of these had rested for a year after first spawning. Southern caught one trout in Lough Derg, in December 1918, and calculated that it was at least twelve years old and had spawned eight times, in its fifth to twelfth years. He could find no trace of gonad so concluded that it had become sterile through old age. One ten-year-old and two eight-year-old trout, caught in the 20's in Lough Derg, had each spawned four times in consecutive years.

The question of length of life and "natural death" will be discussed more fully later. It is probably the fate of most trout which live more than six months to be eaten by some predator. As a fish grows older and larger, it is less likely to encounter a predator large enough to kill and eat it. But the older, larger trout needs more food than the others and so is more liable to become weak or die of starvation: it is also more likely to have become heavily infected by parasitic organisms. Losses through parasites and disease are very difficult to assess. For each trout water there seems to be a natural term of life, and individual fish which exceed this term are very rare. But the effective causes of death have not been investigated.

Chapter Five

Age and Growth

Freshwater biologists all over the world investigate many different sorts of fishes, and there is now an established routine (see appendix 1, p. 272) for examining and recording a mass of information which may later prove useful in understanding how they live and grow. Anglers, though, often record only the weight of the trout they catch.

An ideal fish does not change shape as it grows, so its weight is proportional to the cube of its length; this is so nearly true for a trout that it is accepted as true. It means that, if a fish weigsh 4 oz. when it measures 8 inches, it must weigh 32 oz. when it measures 16 inches. From measurements of a large number of trout, the following length-weight relationship has been established:

$$\frac{Weight\ in\ pounds}{Length\ in\ inches^3} = 0.000427$$

or

$$\frac{Weight\ in\ grams}{Length\ in\ centimetres^3} = 0.01$$

Thus, to convert weight into length or vice versa, we can use the following formulæ:

1000 $\times$ weight in pounds = 0.427 $\times$ length in inches^3
or,   100 $\times$ weight in grams = length in centimetres^3.

The values obtained from these formulæ are approximations because they are based on averages obtained from a large number of trout and individuals that depart from the ideal may be very different from this average.

Anglers are often anxious to know whether their fish are in "good" or "poor condition"—that is, whether the fish is heavier or lighter than the average fish of that length. The condition factor, κ, is calculated from a formula derived from the length-weight relationship, thus:

$$\kappa = \text{approx. } 1.0 = \frac{1000 \times \textit{weight in pounds}}{0.427 \times \textit{length in inches}^3} = \frac{100 \times \textit{weight in grams}}{\textit{length in centimetres}^3}$$

The average trout has κ equal to 1; if κ is less than 1, the fish is in poor condition since it weighs less than expected and is long and thin; if the fish is fat, its weight will be more than expected and κ will be more than 1. Thus κ, the condition factor, is a measurement of the individual fish's well-being, its fatness and the state of its gonads; κ is high in mature fish with ripe gonads and low in spent fish.

The weight of an animal can also vary greatly according to the fullness of its gut and type of food as well as with the state of its gonads, the amount of fat reserve and the degree of muscular development. Length is a much less variable quantity and fish do not decrease in length as they may in weight; we shall therefore consider mainly changes in length in the rest of this chapter but increase in length is, of course, usually accompanied by proportional increase in weight.

Routine examination can tell us not only the present state of a trout but something of its past history, particularly its age and growth. These may be deduced by three methods.

(1) A large and unselected sample of fish is netted or trapped. The fish are measured and the lengths obtained are plotted on graph paper to give a length frequency distribution. If the lengths fall into a series of well defined

groups, these are regarded as representing age groups (fig. 13). This is generally known as the Petersen method.

(2) Fish of known length and age are tagged and released. Later when they are recovered the increase in length gives the growth made during the period between release and recapture.

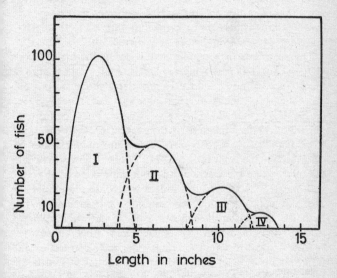

13. Petersen method of ageing fish. Each well defined length group, indicated by the broken line is regarded as representing an age group, shown in Roman numerals. Based on data from brown trout taken from Troutbeck

(3) Certain bony parts of the fish, such as opercular bones, otoliths, vertebræ and scales, record the growth of the fish by well defined periodic differences in their structure. If these can be shown to follow an annual or other cycle of known duration the age and growth of the fish may be deduced. These deductions may be checked by means of tagging fish and also by the occurrence of a "good," i.e. a particularly numerous, "year class" which

can be followed throughout many years' samplings of fish.

In trout studies, the scale method is usually favoured for determining the age of a given fish. The structure and development of fish scales have been studied by biologists since the seventeenth century, and the idea that a record of the age of a fish might be found on its scales has interested scientists since Leeuenhoek first suggested that this was the case in the eel (1686). Here we refer only to a few investigations which are of immediate interest to the determination of age from scales in brown trout.

The scale lies in a pocket in the dermis or inner layer of the skin. That part lying towards the tail projects above the surface of the fish but does not pierce the epidermis or outer layer of the skin. The anterior and much larger part is deeply embedded in the fish's body. These points are illustrated in the diagram of the section of the skin of a trout (fig. 14). How to remove, clean and mount scales is described in the appendix (p. 274). Under a low power of the microscope the cleaned out trout scale is an oval plate with more or less concentric ridges which are more numerous and continuous on the anterior (and greater) part, than on the posterior exposed part of the scale. These ridges, some of which are widely, and others narrowly spaced, are called circuli or rings. The scale consists of an upper or outer layer and a lower or inner layer, and both layers are formed by special cells in the dermis. The upper layer is "a form of bone and as such consists of an organic framework *plus* certain inorganic salts, principally calcium phosphate and calcium carbonate" (Neave). This bony substance is raised into the characteristic ridges of the scale (the circuli) and new material is mostly laid down only round the margin. The lower layer of the scale consists of a fibrous, non-calcareous material which is laid down in thin plates superimposed below each other; this layer grows over the whole of its area.

The trout is naked when hatched. Scale papillæ appear when the fry is about 2.6 to 3.0 cm. (1 to 1¼ inches) long, and the scales themselves appear when the fish is about 3.5

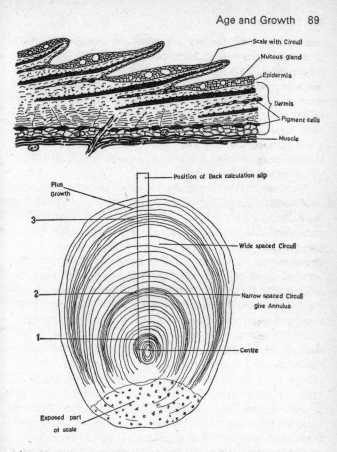

Scale with Circuli
Mucous gland
Epidermis
Dermis
Pigment cells
Muscle

Position of Back calculation slip
Plus Growth
3
Wide spaced Circuli
2
Narrow spaced Circuli give Annulus
1
Centre
Exposed part of scale

14. *Above,* section through the skin of a trout showing scales in pockets of the dermis. *Below,* diagram of a trout scale. The circuli are widely spaced in summer, narrowly spaced in winter, the latter giving the winter band, usually called the annulus

cm. so that by 4.1–4.5 cm. (1¾ inches) there may be one to three circuli on each of them. The scales show first along the lateral line of the fish, then spread dorsally and ventrally above and below it, the region posterior to the dorsal fin being the first to be so "colonised." In spite of this, scales used for age determination are usually taken from the area just in front of the dorsal fin. The circuli stand up as dark hills alternating with light valleys when seen by transmitted light. They may extend wholly round the scale, but the majority end at the junction of the anterior and posterior parts of the scale. Some circuli do not extend so far but are "cut off" at the "shoulder" (see plates 6 and 8). The circuli are widely or narrowly spaced and normally a group of the one type is succeeded by a group of the other.

Hoffbauer (1898) experimented with carp and found that the widely spaced circuli were laid down in the summer and the narrowly spaced ones in the winter, from which structural difference it was therefore possible to tell the age of the fish. Dahl in 1910 examined the scales of brown trout caught in Norway at different seasons of the year and studied those of artificially reared trout of known age. He found that in the summer the circuli were widely spaced and gave what is known as the summer zone or band, and that in the winter the circuli were narrowly spaced and gave the winter zone or band (sometimes called the "annulus"). He summed up: "It is therefore quite clear that the summer-zones and winter-bands on the scales of trout are respectively formed in the corresponding seasons, which affect their growth, and that these zones indicate annual epochs in the life of the fish. If, therefore, we count the number of these zones we can ascertain the age of the fish."

It is possible, however, to use the scale to determine not only the age (in years) but also the growth made by the fish during each year of its life. This determination, often referred to as "back-calculation," means that the growth of the scale is correlated with the growth in length of the body and thus the amount of scale growth made by the end of the first, second, etc. winter band is interpreted in terms of length attained by the fish at the end of its first, second, etc. winter. This use of the scale for calculating the amount of growth in length made each year by the fish is based on the assumption that the scales, once acquired, are present throughout life and that their numbers remain constant, and that the increase in size of the scale is proportional to the increase in size of the fish. Calculation from the scale of the annual length attained by the fish means that more information about age and growth of the fish can be obtained than is found by using the scale for age determination only. It is therefore a most useful tool.

The principle of back-calculation, established for sprats and herrings by Norwegian workers, was first used by Knut Dahl for brown trout. He assumed proportional growth throughout life but with some misgivings. Recently the problem has been investigated by several workers including Miss Kipling of the Freshwater Biological Association (1962). The scales appear when the fry is 1½ inches (3.8 cm.) long and grow relatively faster in length than the little fish itself until the fish is about 4 inches (10 cm.). If thereafter the trout is a fast grower then the scales grow almost exactly in proportion to the fish's growth in length so there is a change from the allometric (disproportionately rapid) scale growth when the fish was small to isometric (proportional) scale growth when it is bigger. It has been shown that trout which grow slowly never achieve isometry, so the growth rate of the fish is important, too.

In fast-growing fish, isometry probably starts by the time the fish has reached 4 inches (10 cm.) in length and there is no error in back-calculation using simple proportion for fish which reach or exceed this length by the end of their first year of life. For fish which grow fairly fast, but do not attain 4 inches in their first year, back-calculation will mean that their length at one year old is underestimated. For slowly growing fish, when allometry persists through life, back-calculation means that lengths at all ages are underestimated. It is very important to know how great this error is likely to be so some estimates are quoted in table 3. Miss Kipling concludes that an error greater than 1 inch (2.5 cm.) is very unlikely at any time for any fish, so any differences greater than this 1 inch can be taken as

each summer plus winter band (the annual growth) and using the measurements for calculating the length of the fish at the end of each winter. (See appendix, p. 274, for method.)

The circuli are therefore the fundamental units on which the scale method of determining age and growth is based. In Windermere, K. R. Allen found that the percentage of fish with wide circuli at the edge of the scale rose in February, was greatest in May and June (in one year July-August), began to fall in July to August and was lowest in January. On the River Liffey at Straffan the percentage of fish with wide circuli at the edge increased in March, rose rapidly to a peak in May and June, began to fall in July and thereafter declined constantly until by October no wide circuli were present; at Ballysmuttan on the same river, the periodicity of fish with wide circuli at the edge was much the same except that here they first appeared in April and were absent in September.

In Llyn Tegid (Lake Bala), N. Wales, the majority of trout formed the winter band of narrow circuli between August and November and then stopped growing completely in the winter and started forming wide circuli in February or March; all the fish had wide circuli at the scale margin in June. Nearly one third of the fish, however, had a few wide circuli at the scale margin in mid-winter and Ball and Jones suggested that these started to grow fast again in autumn after completing the winter band and had very suddenly stopped growing for the winter. Five trout had extremely wide bands of widely spaced circuli and it seems that these may have failed to produce a winter band by continuing rapid growth through the autumn, stopping abruptly and starting equally abruptly the following spring. Thus in the British Isles the time of year when the wide and narrow circuli are laid down (and probably when growth of the fish is rapid or slow) corresponds roughly with spring–summer and autumn–winter respectively; the factors which underlie the periodicity in circulus formation are still not fully known.

The first and obvious suggestion is that food is the responsible factor. Bhatia found that starved rainbow trout (*Salmo gairdneri*) had narrow circuli on the edge of the scales and well-fed fish had wide circuli, irrespective of whether the temperature was high or low; he concluded that the food supply and not the temperature was responsible for the width of the circulus. It may thus be argued that in nature the scarcity of food in winter is the reason for the narrow circuli (winter band) on the scales. We shall show later (chapter 8) that the quantity of potential food is not markedly diminished during the winter months.

Van Someren discussed annulus formation in scales of rainbow trout from Kenya streams. These fish lived at altitudes of 6000 feet and more on the Equator where the annual variations in temperature and daylight are very slight. He was able to correlate the percentage of fish with narrow circuli at the edge of the scales with the percentage of fish which were ripe, spawning or spent at different times of the year. He could find no association between the occurrence of narrow circuli at the edge of the scale and variations in food supply, feeding intensity or mean water temperature. Van Someren therefore concludes that the "winter check" is a "maturity check" and that an innate physiological rhythm without actual ripening of the gonads accounts for the presence of annuli in maiden fish.

The scales can thus give us information about the age and the growth in length made each year by the trout; it is possible however to deduce even more of the trout's history. The scales of spawning trout look as though they have been worn down at the margin. This is usually termed "erosion," a term which suggests that the wearing away is the result of some mechanical agency. As this is not the case, Crichton's term "absorption" is preferable. This absorption of the scale is definitely associated with spawning of the fish, and varies considerably in its extent. It begins at the posterior end and often only affects this part, but may extend any distance from here to the apex of the scale. Sometimes the surface of the scale is also ab-

sorbed. After spawning, renewed growth forms the "spawning mark" which looks like a scar or a blur on the scale
surface (see plates 7 and 8).

Scales of salmon and sea trout typically show spawning
marks but those of brown trout do so very unusually.
Scales from the large quick-growing trout of Lough Derg
may show considerable absorption but those from the small
slow-growing fish of nearby Lough Atorick show none; in
the River Liffey the scales of all the trout, whether quickly
or slowly growing, show no absorption at all. Thus although
the presence of a spawning mark is positive evidence of
sexual maturity, the absence of the mark is no proof that
the trout is a maiden fish.

There are certain difficulties in using scales for age and
growth determinations. If a trout loses some scales for any
reason, they are replaced, but the "replacement scale" has
a centre of scar tissue and the normal circuli appear round
this. The extent of the central scar depends on the size
of the fish when the new scale grew. Only perfect scales
give a full record of the trout's growth so replacement
scales must be discarded. (See plate 6).

Some scales show "summer checks" of a few narrow
circuli set between bands of a wide circuli, each of these
being narrower than a typical summer band at the same
age. Checks differ from true winter bands (annuli) because
the circuli are regular and extend round the scale and
are not cut off at the shoulders as are the outer circuli of
an annulus.

Occasionally, the summer band is very wide and probably denotes a fish that has failed for some reason to form
a winter band (see p. 93), and whose apparent age is one
year less than its true age.

If eggs hatch late and fry grow very slowly, as they may
in some Highland lochs and burns, scales may not develop
at all until autumn or later so the normal first annulus
will be missing. These fish will also appear to be one year
younger than their true age.

Records of the length and weight of trout at different

ages can thus be obtained either by direct observation of individual fish or from a study of the annual rings on the scales and "back-calculation" of the length at the end of each year. These records can be used to compare the growth made by individual fish within a population or the average growth of different populations of fish. There are several ways in which the size data can be used for making these comparisons.

The back-calculated lengths of fish of different ages from various British waters are given in appendices III and IV (pp. 280-3). The figures for each water show that the length increases as the fish grows older. When these figures are plotted as a graph against the age of the fish they form a curve which is less steep in the first year and may become so again in later life. This is shown in fig. 15 which is a graph showing the lengths of fish of different ages from Straffan and Ballysmuttan (River Liffey) and from the Clare-Galway River (part of the Lough Corrib system). The lengths are calculated for the ends of successive years, so that any seasonal variation in growth rate during the year is concealed.

Another way of treating the size data is to calculate the annual increments, that is, the amounts by which the average lengths of the fish increase during each year. These increments for the same three waters are shown in fig. 16A. The figures for each water show that the increments rise to a maximum in the middle years of life (here the second year) and fall off as the fish grow older.

An animal's body may contain non-living material, such as mineral deposits, but the greater part of it consists of living cells. These are continuously growing and multiplying so that the amount of growing tissue increases as the animal's body grows larger. If the living tissues of the body grew at the same rate throughout the life of the fish a graph showing total size against age should look like the right half of a U, but in fact the curve for the trout is more like an S (fig. 15). The annual increments can be expressed as a percentage of the size at the beginning of

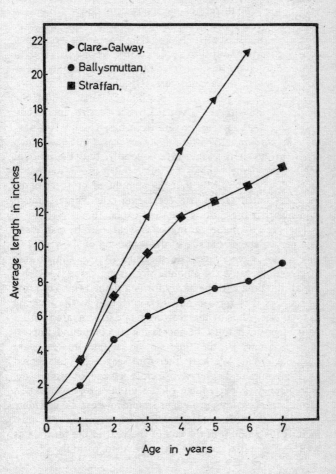

15. Annual growth in length of trout from the River Liffey at Ballysmuttan and Straffan (Went and Frost, 1942) and from the Clare-Galway River, Lough Corrib system (Went, 1942). This familiar type of growth curve is based on lengths back-calculated for the ends of successive years

each year, and these values should be the same every year if the growth rate of the living cells does not change. This value has been calculated for the data for the three localities and is shown in fig. 16B. Far from remaining constant throughout life it decreases, having its highest values during the first year at Straffan and in the Clare-Galway and in the second year at Ballysmuttan.

There are at least three possible explanations of the shapes of these three curves (i.e. those of size, increment, and percentage increase as shown in figs. 15 and 16); first, that the amount of growing tissue decreases but that which is left grows at the same rate; secondly, that the amount of growing tissue remains the same but it grows more and more slowly; or thirdly that the amount of growing tissue increases but it grows at a decreasing rate. There is much evidence that the third is the right explanation.

The growth made during each year can be expressed as a percentage of the size at the beginning of the year. But this is not a very accurate measure of the annual rate of growth, because the amount of growing tissue is increasing all the time and the newly formed tissue begins to grow as soon as it is formed and so contributes to the increase in total size. Thus, if the growing tissue is compared with a bank deposit, it must be increasing at compound interest rates accruing all the time not at simple interest paid once each year. We must therefore seek a formula based on the compound interest principle instead of using "the increment as a percentage of the initial size," which is a formula representing growth as simple interest. To calculate the rate at which compound interest was paid we must include the amount at the end of the year in the formula as well as the initial amount. A convenient formula is:

$$Y_T = Y_t . e^{g(T-t)}$$

The symbols have the following meanings:

Y_T is the final size (the size at time T),

Y_t is the initial size (the size at time t),

T and t are expressed in units of time and T is later than t.

e is the base of "natural logarithms,"

g is a growth rate; it has been given many names, for instance: geometric, incremental, instantaneous, logarithmic, multiplicative, and specific growth rate.

Of these synonyms, we shall use the term *specific growth rate* in this book. The formula is more convenient to use when transformed thus:

$$G = \frac{\log_e Y_T - \log_e Y_t}{T - t} \times 100$$

$\log_e Y_T$ and $\log_e Y_t$ are the natural logarithms of the values of Y_T and Y_t; they can be looked up in tables of natural logarithms. (Natural logarithms are $2.3026 \times \log_{10}$). G is $100 \times g$, and it is the percentage specific rate of growth in size per unit time. The formula may perhaps look formidable to those with little mathematical training, but in practice it is very easy to use if a table of logarithms is available. (See appendix, p. 285, for an example.)

The "simple interest" method of assessing growth, i.e. by using the increment expressed as a percentage of the initial size, will give almost the same value as the specific growth rate when the time interval is very short or when the increase in size has been very small. Over long periods and when the size increases markedly the specific growth rate gives a much clearer measure of the actual rate at which the fish was growing than does the other. When calculating G for long periods of time it is important to realise that the figure obtained from the formula above will be the *average* specific growth rate over that period. If the rate of growth is changing, the figures will be most accurate if the time interval (T—t in the formula) is very short. There is an annual cycle of rapid growth in summer and slow growth in winter in the British Isles. Growth rates calculated from annual measurements are the averages of these high and low growth rates and also depend on the relative lengths of the periods of rapid and slow growth.

One advantage of using the specific growth rate instead of the other methods of assessing growth is that the formula takes account of both the initial and final sizes of the fish, and therefore gives a much more accurate comparison of the growth rates of fish of different sizes than does any other method. The average annual specific growth rates of fish from selected British waters are given in appendix VI, p. 287. These rates for fish at Straffan and Bally-smuttan and in the Clare-Galway are shown in fig. 16c. The rates generally decrease as the fish grow older so the fish grow at the highest rate during the first or second (Ballysmuttan) year of life and after that they grow less rapidly each year but this decrease in the growth rate becomes less marked as the fish grow older.

The fall in specific growth rate as an individual grows older is characteristic of all animals. This was first pointed out by Minot (1890) who equated the decreasing growth rate with increasing senility. Mammals and birds have first a period of "embryonic" growth and then a "juvenile" stage during which they grow rapidly until they reach an "adult" size. After this the specific growth rate becomes zero, since the adult animals stop growing, but they breed and show the greatest development of their faculties. They may reach a "senile" stage. Many fish, such as the trout, have quite a different growth history because they continue to grow throughout their lives, though at decreasing rates. The time at which they begin to breed may depend on their age or on their reaching a certain minimum size, but they normally continue to grow in size after they have started to breed and may breed several times.

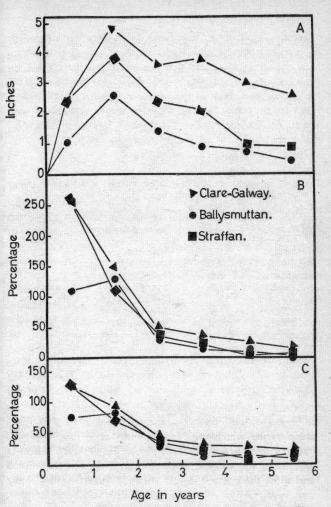

16. Expression of the length/age data for trout from the River Liffey at Ballysmuttan and Straffan and from Clare-Galway River (fig. 15) as:

A, annual increments, i.e. amount of increase in length during each year of life

B, the annual increments expressed as a percentage of the size at the beginning of each year

C, the average annual specific growth rate. (See p. 99)

We shall now consider in more detail the growth records of brown trout from different parts of the British Isles. It is important to realise that almost all the figures which are given in the appendices, pp. 280-3, for the lengths at the end of each year of life in the different waters are derived from "back-calculation" from measurements of the annuli on the scales. For all these it has been assumed that the scales grow accurately in proportion to the growth in length of the fish. (But see p. 91.)

Table 4. Average lengths of trout (in inches) at the end of their third year in various British waters.

Still waters		Running waters	
Wastwater	6·1	River Rhydwen	5·1
Lough Atorick	7·0	Raise Beck	5·7
Windermere	8·5	River Dart	7·0
Loch Leven	11·1	River Forss	7·9
Malham Tarn	11·3	River Bela	8·2
Lough Derg	11·6	River Fergus	12·1
Lough Rea	13·8	River Kennet	13·3

Study of any trout population reveals that fish of the same age may be of very different sizes. The "back-calculated" lengths of one-year-old trout from Straffan in the River Liffey showed a range of 4 inches (10.4 cm.) between the minimum of $1\frac{1}{2}$ inches (3.8 cm.) and the maximum of $5\frac{1}{2}$ inches (14 cm.), the average being $3\frac{1}{2}$ inches (8.9 cm.). Fish that were smaller than the average when one year old remained smaller than the average as they grew older with a few exceptions. Records made from scale readings of other wild populations show similar ranges in size between fish of the same age.

The figures in appendices III and IV and those used for the map on p. 158 show that the average sizes of fish of the same age from different waters vary greatly.

The average lengths of three-year-old fish from various waters are shown in table 4. Some have grown to twice the length of others so there must be differences in the average specific growth rates of trout in these waters.

Specific growth rates for waters selected to give a wide range are given in appendix VI. For each water there is a progressive decrease in growth rate which we have already seen to be characteristic of all living organisms. There is also a fair amount of variation in rate between fish of the same age in different waters, but the most striking differences are in the specific growth rates during the first year of life: these we shall discuss first.

Let us at once consider certain sources of error which can account for part of the differences between growth rates in different waters—especially for those during the first year of life. The first source of error derives from the difficulty of locating the first annulus and measuring it accurately, when reading a trout scale. The second derives from the difficulty of allowing for the allometry of scale growth relative to that of the body either in the first year only or throughout life (see pp. 91-2). Where the back-calculated length is less than 4 inches (10 cm.) it has certainly been underestimated. A third source of error derives from the absence of figures from different waters for the length of trout fry when they begin to feed. In calculating the figures in the appendix, it has been assumed that the initial size of the fry is 0.95 inch (2.4 cm.) for all waters. The actual range of size between the smallest and largest fry at this stage is probably less than $\frac{1}{8}$ inch ($\frac{3}{4}$ cm). A fourth source of error derives from the fact that the actual growing period may be longer in some waters than in others. Since the rate of development of trout eggs depends on the temperature of the water, eggs laid in warmer water will hatch earlier in the year than those in colder water so that the fry in the warmer water will have a longer growing period. The same actual specific growth rate maintained over a longer proportion of the year will give a higher average rate.

We need more information about conditions in the field before we can evaluate with certainty the significance of these four sources of error. We can, however, say that the error due to allometry will not exceed one inch (2.54 cm.) and is probably less.

Table 5 shows the figures for Straffan and Ballysmuttan adjusted in various ways to illustrate the effects of correcting the underestimate of the length at the end of the first year, applying various corrections and assuming different alevin lengths at the beginning of the growing period. The

Table 5. Annual specific growth rates for length for the first year of life (0–1) for trout at Ballysmuttan and at Straffan calculated to show the possible effects of two sources of error. (Rates expressed as % per annum)

Assuming that the fry length at first feeding was:	Assuming that the length at the end of the year was underestimated by:					
	0	$\frac{1}{4}$ inch	$\frac{1}{2}$ inch	$\frac{3}{4}$ inch	0	$\frac{1}{2}$ inch
	Ballysmuttan				Straffan	
0·90 *inch*	80	85	102	120	—	—
0·95	75	79	97	106	128	140
1·00	—	—	—	—	122	136

average specific rate at the two localities becomes the same if the Ballysmuttan length is increased by 1 inch (the maximum possible adjustment) and the Straffan length not at all (which is unlikely) and furthermore if the alevins are one tenth inch longer at Straffan when they begin to feed (again, unlikely). The most probable adjustment to the calculated lengths is less than 1 inch at Ballysmuttan and $\frac{1}{2}$ inch at Straffan; these figures are used in table 6 to show how the average monthly specific growth rate varies if it is assumed that all the growth is concentrated into a few months. Rates become equal at the two localities if all growth occurs in only six months at Ballysmuttan but in eight months at Straffan. These are part of the same river system and Ballysmuttan is only 700 ft. above sea level so it is unlikely that the periods of rapid growth, if determined by climate (see p. 150), are so very different.

We may conclude from the analysis that the sources of error involved in estimating G in the first year of life are not so great as to make insignificant the very striking differences between the calculated figures. In other words, there seems to be a very real difference in the specific rates of growth of fish in their first year of life in different British waters.

Table 6. Average monthly specific growth rates for length (as % per month) for trout in their first year of life at Ballysmuttan and at Straffan assuming that both start feeding when 0·95 inches long, calculated to show possible effects of two sources of error.

Assuming that the length at the end of the year was:	Assuming that all growth was concentrated into:			
	4 months	6 months	8 months	12 months
at *Ballysmuttan*—				
2 inches	19	12½	9½	6¼
3 inches	26½	17½	13	9
at *Straffan*—				
3·4 inches	32	21½	16	10¾
3·9 inches	35	23½	17½	11¾

The specific growth rates for the second year of life are fairly similar in all waters although the fish are of varied sizes as a result of the differences in growth in the first year (see table 7). The rates fall markedly in the third year and there are greater differences between different waters. These seem to be associated with the effects of the onset of maturity. In the year when most of the trout first spawn, the average specific growth rates often decrease markedly when compared with those in the preceding year and continue to be very low thereafter. Where the fish become mature over a period of years, this effect is not apparent.

A decrease in the average annual rate of growth of fish which are spawning is easily explained since increase in size of the gonads uses up food material which might otherwise have been incorporated into more permanent parts of the body. Behaviour associated with spawning such as migration upstream and construction of redds uses up much energy and this must be derived from the food eaten or from food reserves in the body. Thus ripening of the gonads and spawning must reduce the amount of food which is available for growth.

Table 7. Specific growth rates for length (as % per annum) for each year of life for various waters in the British Isles

Water	Specific growth rates (% per annum)					Age at which majority spawn
	0–1	1–2	2–3	3–4	4–5	
R. Test						
fast-growing	170	70·3	25·8	7·1		3
slow-growing	133	85·9	42·5	25·1	14·5	5
R. Avon						
fast-growing	168	69·3	21·9			3
slow-growing	139	73·1	34·0	14·3	7·5	4
R. Forss	93	72·2	41·8	15·2	2·1	4
R. Rhydwen	97	49·5	21·8	16·3	9·5	
R. Teifi	112	80·7	25·7	19·4	4·8	
R. Fergus	151	70·5	33	20·8	16·1	
Blagdon Reservoir	141	84·7	36·9	26·0	16·6	
Windermere	88·4	85·4	45·4	27·6	23·0	
Malham Tarn	101	96·1	50·8	23·5	11·9	4
Fincastle Loch	97	89·2	35·5	9·9		
Llyn Tegid	133	51·1	34·8	21·1	13·4	
Lough Derg	108	85·7	56·4	30·9	16·3	
Lough Corrib	121	78·3	47	23	10·8	4
Lough Inchiquin	151	74·9	28·5	17·4	10·5	
Lough Bofin	88	85·4	30·6	13·0	10·4	3
Yew Tree Tarn	74	78·9	35·9	21·4	7·4	4

The tables in appendices III and IV include (where it is known) the age at which the majority of trout in each water have started to spawn and it is obvious that there is variation although most British trout mature at four years old. In those waters where many fish do not begin to spawn until they are older than this, there is a fair amount of variation among individuals as to the age at which they become mature and in some of these waters the fish may spawn every second year instead of annually, as appears to be the general rule. We shall discuss possible reasons for this in the next chapter.

Trout appear to live to different ages in different waters. This is deduced from the fact that the maximum number of annuli which can be seen on the scales is thirteen or more in (for instance) Lough Derg and Windermere, but it is only seven in Three Dubs Tarn. One possible explanation is that the scales with only seven rings were considerably "eroded," a number of outer rings having thus been lost, but there is no evidence that this has actually happened. Another possibility is that the fish with few annuli have grown so slowly in their later years that it is impossible to distinguish between "summer" and "winter" growth, and thus to age the fish. If this were so, there should be an unusually wide zone of "winter" growth at the outer edge of the scales of some (the older) fish, but scales of this type are not found. It is therefore probable that there is a real difference in the longevity of trout in the different waters.

This study of the specific growth rates of trout from different British waters has thus revealed three factors which appear to determine the size of fish in those waters. These are:

(1) The specific growth rate in the first year of life, which varies considerably,

(2) the age at which the fish begins to spawn, which varies slightly and may mark a transition from more rapid juvenile to less rapid adult growth,

(3) the length of life.

These three factors show a certain amount of correlation since a low growth rate in the first year of life is generally associated with early spawning and a short life, e.g. in Three Dubs Tarn and Ballysmuttan. This is not always so, however, for some fish with a high growth rate in their first year begin to spawn when three years old and die young—e.g. the fast growing trout from the chalk streams described by Gerrish. The largest trout of all, however, are those that grow well in their first year, do not begin to spawn until fairly old and live for a long time.

We now want to know why trout in different waters

Chapter Six

Heredity

We have already stressed the fact that the brown trout is a very variable fish in appearance and in size. Those who have kept a few trout in an aquarium over a length of time will have observed individual differences in temperament as well as in appearance—even if all the fish are of the same age and came from eggs from the same female fertilised with milt from the same male. We shall discuss in this chapter how far individual differences can be ascribed to heredity and how far they are probably the result of environment.

Trout are not convenient animals for genetical experiments because they breed only once a year and take at least two years and usually longer before they attain sexual maturity. They require water of sufficient purity and at temperatures near 50°F (10°c); and the space required for rearing large numbers of families of trout is likely to be prohibitive. It is therefore not surprising that relatively little is known about the genetics of trout; where genetical work has been done in hatcheries, one of the objects has usually been the "improvement of stock," i.e. the selection of strains of trout which will grow fast and survive well under the hatchery conditions.

The genetical mechanism of fishes, as of mammals and birds and the fruit-fly *Drosophila*, is based on the chromosomes contained in the nucleus of every living cell of the body. Each egg receives a half-set of chromosomes from the female and the number is made up to the "diploid" value by a half-set of chromosomes contributed from the male when the egg is fertilised by a sperm. The diploid number for the brown trout is eighty and the same number of chromosomes are, of course, found in sea trout; salmon (*Salmo salar*) have only sixty chromosomes, char (*Salvelinus alpinus*) have eighty and speckled trout (*Salvelinus fontinalis*) have eighty-four. The mechanism of sex determination through the chromosomes has not been investigated.

The most fully documented series of experiments to investigate the inheritance of differences between naturally occurring varieties of brown trout are those by Gunnar Alm at Kälärne Hatchery in Sweden. He called his two varieties "*fario*" and "*lacustris*"; the former spend all their lives in streams and seldom grow to more than 12 inches (30 cm.) long while the latter are spawned in rivers and remain there for two or three years (until they are 8 to 12 inches—20 to 30 cm.—long) when they migrate into lakes and may eventually reach weights of between 6 and 30 lb. (usually up to 10 lb.). Besides these differences in habit and growth, the two varieties differ in colour and in age of sexual maturity. Males always become mature when younger than females and the *fario* (river) males mature when two or three years old whereas the *lacustris* (lake) males mature at five to seven years old; the female *fario* spawn annually after becoming mature but the female *lacustris* probably spawn every second or third year only. The *fario* trout are brownish green with black and red spots and in all of them the anal fin is edged in black and white and in eighty per cent of them the ventral fins are similarly coloured; *lacustris* fish, however, are silvery with black spots only and the anal fin is edged with black in eighty per cent, the ventral fins also in twenty per cent while twenty per cent have no black edging to the fins.

Alm collected eggs from the two varieties of trout and grew the alevins and fry under identical conditions in adjacent ponds in the hatchery; when they matured he took eggs from them and reared these and eventually was able to report on two generations of *lacustris* and three of *fario* —by the autumn of 1951, there were sixteen fish of the second generation of *fario* (six were then fourteen years

Table 8. Sexual maturation in two races of brown trout reared at Kälärne Hatchery in Sweden. (From Alm, 1949)

Age	fario (river trout)	lacustris (lake trout)
First generation— end of 4th summer 5th	58% ripe (2 ♂♂:1 ♀) 93·7% ripe (1 ♂:1 ♀)	12·3% ripe (all ♂♂) 51·3% ripe (9 ♂♂:1 ♀)
Second generation— end of 3rd summer 4th 5th 6th	nearly half ♂♂, no ♀♀ ripe nearly all ♂♂, ⅔ ♀♀ ripe all ♂♂, about ¾ ♀♀ ripe all ripe	none ripe none ripe ⅔ ♂♂ ripe, no ♀♀ ripe (the ♀♀ began to mature at 8 or 9 years old)
Third generation— end of 3rd summer 4th 5th	a few mature ♂♂ a few mature ♂♂ all ♂♂ and ♀♀ mature	no data

old and ten were twelve years old) and seven fish (twelve years old) of the second generation of *lacustris*. Alm reported his observations in detail in 1949. There was no significant difference between the early growth rates of the two stocks—so differences in wild conditions must be the result of environmental effects. The two stocks continued, however, to show consistent differences in age of maturity and in colour of the fins and these are summarised in tables 8 and 9.

Alm noted that when the fish grew faster, they became mature earlier and he attributed the later maturing of the third generation of *fario* fish (table 8) to the fact that they did not grow so well as the earlier generations. Under his conditions, the fish which had grown well and matured early continued to grow well after spawning. He found, however,

Table 9.   Percentage of individuals with black and white edges to the fins belonging to two races of brown trout reared at Kälärne Hatchery, Sweden. (After Alm, 1949.) F1, F2, F3—first, second and third generation reared at the hatchery.

| | *fario* (river trout) | | | | *lacustris* (lake trout) | | |
	wild	F1	F2	F3	wild	F1	F2
ventral and anal fins	80	58	69	80	20	20	30
anal fins only	20	39	29	19	60	60	55
neither fin	0	3	2	1	20	20	15

that female fish of the *fario* stock spawned every year whereas the *lacustris* stock did not spawn regularly every year. Thus the differences in age of first spawning and in regularity of spawning were apparently inherited features of the two races of trout and continued to be displayed when the two races were grown under identical artificial conditions.

The general coloration was also, apparently, inherited. It became more intense with age in the *fario* stock but less so in *lacustris* fish (which presumably grow more silver with age); the characteristic edging of the anal and ventral fins continued to appear in approximately the same proportions of individuals of later generations of the two stocks.

In 1934, Davis described breeding experiments with speckled trout (*Salvelinus fontinalis*). By selecting and breeding from those fish which grew most rapidly in each generation, he obtained rapidly growing fish which, with "improved diets," would reach in one year the size normally attained after three or four years' growth. He stated that experiments with brown and rainbow trout showed that more rapidly growing strains could be obtained by selective breeding of these, too.

Donaldson and Olson summarised in 1955 the results of twenty-three years of selective breeding of rainbow trout (*Salmo gairdneri*) at Seattle (Washington). They started with local races; the fish matured when four years old when they weighed about $1\frac{1}{2}$ lb. and each female produced 800 to 1200 eggs. The largest and strongest batches of fingerlings of each year were reared to provide the brood stock. After ten years, the workers began to select individual fish instead of groups of fingerlings with the object of producing a "strong" stock with rapid growth, early spawning at an early age and high egg production. They therefore chose individuals on the basis of their growth rates, "strength," date of spawning, age of first spawning and number of eggs laid. The fish they selected represented about one per cent of the total number of eggs laid by the stock fish. At that time, most of their fish first spawned at two years old.

In 1955, the 1953 year class were twenty-two months old, they measured an average of $19\frac{1}{2}$ inches and weighed 4 lb. and they were ready to spawn. The 1952 year class, then thirty-four months old, had spawned once, measured $23\frac{1}{2}$ inches and weighed $6\frac{1}{2}$ lb. while the 1951 year class, then forty-six months old, measured only $21\frac{1}{4}$ inches and weighed $4\frac{1}{2}$ lb. Thus the youngest year class had reached in two years almost the same size as fish two years older while the three-year-old fish were markedly longer than the fish of the year before them. As all these trout were reared in the hatchery, these considerable differences should not be due to environmental factors. The fish spawned first at two years old and the average number of eggs laid was 2032 by the 1951 year class and 3894 by the 1952 class; when three years old, the 1951 class produced on average 4985 eggs per fish. It appears that the number of eggs laid varies with the length of the female—the logarithm of this number is directly proportional to the length —but there is a great deal of variation between individuals. However, the longer the fish are when they begin to spawn, the more eggs they will lay, and on average each increase of one inch in length of the female parent meant a yield of 230 eggs more.

The results of these twenty-three years of selective breeding are certainly striking. Compare the 1952 year class with their ancestors of 1932. The 1932 class spawned first when four years old; their descendants at two years. The 1952 year class fish weighed more than twice as much at two years old as the 1932 year class fish had done when four years old, and produced an average of more than twice as many eggs. Thus the potential yield to the fisherman of selected stock can be much greater than that of wild fish—unless there are other factors which make the selected fish less fit when released into lakes and streams.

There are some apparent discrepancies between Alm's results with wild stocks of brown trout and Donaldson and Olson's results with wild stocks of rainbow trout. Alm found no differences, under hatchery conditions, in the early growth of those trout which eventually reached very different sizes in the wild and he found that the age of first spawning appeared to be genetically controlled so that the two stocks continued to become mature at different ages. However, Alm was not consciously selecting his fish and there was variation between individuals of the same stock in their rates of growth and age of maturity; further, as he noticed, both his stocks showed a correlation between good initial growth and earlier sexual maturity, which he believed to be a general feature of freshwater fishes. Thus it seems probable that selection within brown trout stocks in Sweden for rapid growth and early sexual maturity could be as effective as it was for rainbow trout in Washington.

Although detailed figures are not available, many hatcheries have their own brood stock. These have been selected for rapid growth, early maturity and number of eggs and show marked "improvement" in these features compared with most wild stocks. We discuss the management of fishing waters in chapter 10 and consider the conditions under which stocking with fish from hatcheries is necessary and beneficial. These conditions are fairly widespread in Britain, particularly among the chalk rivers of southern

England, and the practice of stocking some of these waters is long-established.

In the mid-thirties Gerrish examined a number of trout scales from these rivers and concluded that there had been a change in the pattern of trout growth. He attributed this to the planting of fry from hatchery stocks instead of from wild stocks. He argued that the wild trout characteristically grow steadily, mature late, produce small eggs and live for many years, whereas the hatchery stocks are selected to grow fast and mature early. Their growth falls off when they mature and they die after two spawnings or so, having laid large eggs. He suggested that these fish feed well but when mature use the food to lay down large eggs instead of to increase true body weight and thus they lose "condition" when three or four years old. According to him, the really large trout are usually old wild type fish which have matured late and he argued that this type of fish must disappear since their initial growth rate is lower than that of fish of hatchery stock so that they will not compete successfully with the latter. Gerrish did, in fact, find scales recording the two types of growth history. Those fish which had lived longer and reached the greatest lengths had grown more slowly in their early years but thereafter had maintained a reasonable growth rate. The other fish grew faster when young but their increments in length fell off markedly after their second year (see tables 7 and 10). His observations are of interest because they are consistent with the existence of heritable growth patterns and ages of maturity in the same natural environment.

Gunnar Alm's conclusions about age, size and maturity are important and interesting. He has shown that maturity is a function of growth rate and size so that in any population of trout, those which grow fastest mature earliest. Whether any individual fish becomes mature will depend on whether it has reached a certain minimum size by a certain time of year. If not, it will continue to grow and will mature the following year provided that it then exceeds the minimum size. As the trout grow older, however, the required size probably decreases so that old, slow-growing individuals become mature when smaller than their faster-growing contemporaries. If the average growth rate of a trout population is accelerated by improving the diet or the environment, then the average age for maturity will be lowered. This is well illustrated by the results of the experiments at Seattle.

Table 10. Annual increments in length (inches) back-calculated from scales for first three years of life to show contrast between fast-growing and slow-growing trout in three chalk streams. (After Gerrish, 1935)

Year of life early growth	First fast	slow	Second fast	slow	Third fast	slow
River Nadder	4·7	3·6	5·8	3·9	2·9	3·8
River Avon (Bulford)	5·1	3·8	5·1	4·1	2·6	3·2
River Test (Romsey)	5·2	3·6	5·3	4·9	3·1	4·5

The Swedish experiments showed that different "races" of trout may have genetical differences in their pattern of growth and maturity. Thus, the male *fario* trout usually matured when two or three years old and the male *lacustris* fish not until they were five to seven years old even though all these fish were growing at identical rates under the artificial conditions of the hatchery. The *fario* males were much smaller at maturity than the *lacustris* males but within each group, the biggest males matured earlier than the smallest. Alm described several possible patterns of life history, each genetically determined. First, trout may be long-lived with good initial growth and late maturity at large size. Secondly, trout may mature early which may be associated either with good initial growth falling off after maturity, or with slow growth from the beginning: thus the fish may be potentially short- or long-lived (see fig 17). *Lacustris* trout belong to the first category, Gerrish's "hatchery stock" and *fario* trout to the second category.

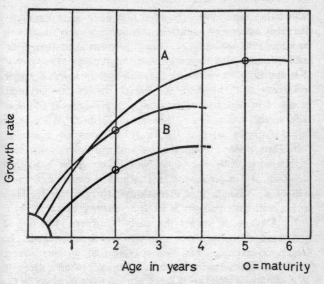

17. Diagrammatic growth curves for forms of trout with genetically conditioned age of maturity (after Alm, 1959). A, large-sized, mostly long-lived forms with good initial growth and late maturity. B, small-sized forms with early maturity and short or long lives: the upper curve indicates good initial growth soon slowing down, the lower curve shows slow growth throughout life.

The latter usually show poor initial growth and are thus small when they spawn, while "hatchery stock" usually show good initial growth falling off at maturity and thus spawn when quite large. Within all these stocks, good environmental conditions leading to rapid growth result in earlier maturity while poor conditions and consequent slow growth would delay maturity.

The genetical differences between existing races of trout must be the result of natural selection in the past. In a population with slow initial growth, the fish which spawn when small will be able to reproduce themselves earlier than those whose heredity requires them to become larger before they can mature; the latter may never spawn at all. If mortality becomes high after three or four years, there will be a natural selection of young breeders and hence the establishment of a race with early maturity.

If the initial growth is good, this will establish a larger average size than where the initial growth rate is poor. Larger females produce more and larger eggs; it is therefore likely that more of the many offspring of a large female survive than of the fewer offspring of a smaller fish. Thus where growth is rapid and mortality is not very high among older fish, there will probably be a natural selection of the progeny of the largest spawners and there will be no advantage in precociously early maturity. Thus a race with late maturity is likely to survive best.

In Alm's experiments the early spawners, which had grown fastest, continued throughout their lives to be larger, on average, than late spawners of the same race; there was thus no evidence that spawning caused a decrease in growth rate. However, these fish were all stripped in the hatchery of their eggs and milt and they were fed daily with adequate quantities of food of good quality; they did not have to carry out the arduous activities involved in natural spawning (see pp. 70-6), nor did they have to seek for food. The *fario* and *lacustris* fish lived for ten to twelve years in the hatchery so the fact that the former had matured earlier and spawned more frequently than the latter did not seem to have decreased their life span.

Length records for British waters often show a decline in growth rate at the age when the majority of trout in that water are mature (see pp. 105-6). Where the fish mature early, very few old fish are ever caught so the average life span seems to be about four or five years only. This early death may result from predators attacking the spawning trout: fish exhausted after spawning may well be more susceptible to adverse conditions, to diseases and to starvation where food is difficult to find. This exhaustion may also lead to slower growth in subsequent years so that under natural conditions maturity may mark the end of faster "juvenile" growth and the beginning of slower "adult" growth. The effects of maturity are least where the fish mature late at large size. Many such trout, like Alm's *lacustris* fish, spawn only in alternate years.

The number of eggs produced by a female fish varies, as does their size. In general, the number depends on the length of the fish. The size probably depends on the level of feeding of the fish during the period between the beginning and end of maturation of each crop of eggs, i.e. March to October. Both number and size are very variable, though Southern pointed out in 1932 that in any given water the larger females produce more and larger eggs than the smaller ones. Females of very different sizes from different waters may, however, lay eggs of the same size. Southern found a 1½ lb. trout from the Owenea River (a very large fish for that water) with eggs larger than those of the average Lough Neagh trout of 4½ lb.

The size of the eggs is of interest because of a possible correlation between egg size and growth; if fry from large eggs always grew faster it would be an advantage to select large eggs and discard smaller ones. It is certainly true that smaller eggs hatch into smaller alevins if all other conditions are identical, so the problem is whether these small alevins grow more slowly than larger ones.

If the alevins all grew at the same specific growth rates, the proportional size difference would be maintained and the larger ones would become larger fry; if the larger alevins grew at higher rates, the size difference would become much greater, and if all the fish became the same size after a time, the smaller alevins must have grown faster. Knut Dahl first investigated this problem. His larger alevins *did* grow faster, but all his growth rates were rather low. In experiments in Germany the larger alevins, again, grew slightly faster. But Higgs in Canada found that rainbow trout alevins of different sizes had very similar rates.

In the experiments summarised in table 11, some of the largest alevins grew very well, as illustrated by family x and family A, but others grew more slowly as shown by family B. The smallest alevins, those of family Y and family A, grew better than the large alevins of family B. There was a lot of difference between groups starting with the same size range, as shown by families X and Y, and this was as great as the differences between the graded groups of family A and of family B. These experiments do not show any consistent correlation between alevin size (or egg size) and early growth. *Mortality* was much higher, however, among small eggs and small alevins; so there is an advantage in using large eggs in hatcheries.

Table 11. Comparison of the early growth of three individuals from groups of alevins grown under similar conditions at 53°F (11·5°C) to show the effects of starting weight (depending on egg size) and of heredity. (Brown, unpublished.)
SGR—specific growth rate as % per week.
W—weight of fry at end of 8th week (families A and B) or 9th week (families X and Y) in milligrams

Female parent	Time weeks	Groups of alevins	Starting weight (mg.)	Fish 5 SGR W		Fish 10 SGR W		Fish 15 SGR W		Comments
X	9	two of similar range	104–130	21	820	19	665	17	555	one group
			104–130	18	580	16½	505	16	485	grew much better
A	8	three of graded sizes	101–110	19	489	18	455	16½	395	largest grew
			95	17½	379	15½	331	13½	271	best; others
			80–89	17	339	16	310	14	267	much alike
Y	9	two of similar range	64–94	16½	406	15	356	12½	264	one group
			64–94	14½	324	10½	212	10	193	grew much better
B	8	two of graded sizes	120–130	12	319	11	301	10	274	smaller grew
			90–100	15½	332	14	293	13	272	better

At Kälärne Hatchery Alm's two races had eggs of very different sizes but grew at similar rates. The Freshwater Biological Association hatched large eggs from large trout from a reservoir and small eggs from small trout of Scandale Beck, Westmorland, at their hatchery and found no differences in the size range of the fish at the end of one year.

Larger eggs, those giving alevins of 90 mg. weight and upwards, are hardier and easier to rear in a laboratory and would probably show less mortality in nature. The fact that small, early-maturing trout produce eggs which are larger, in relation to their body size, than those of large late-maturing trout is probably the result of natural selection. Of the small eggs of small trout, the slightly larger will have the greater probability of survival whereas all the eggs produced by late-maturing trout will probably exceed the minimum size above which there is virtually equal probability of survival.

There is such an enormous loss during the early months of each year class of trout (see pp. 79-82) that it may seem that only through the production of very large numbers of eggs can the species survive and maintain relatively constant populations. However (as we shall show later) there is an upper limit to the number of fry which are likely to survive in any stream, so production of more eggs than are necessary to give this maximum number of small fry is really wasted effort. There are high numbers of trout in moorland streams where they mature early and at small size. Natural selection will favour relatively large eggs, and when the number of spawning females is high it will be of no disadvantage to the species that those producing larger eggs also produce fewer at each spawning.

So far there has been no demonstration that brown trout inherit obvious characters in simple Mendelian ratios—as, for instance, eye colour in man. Most of the colour varieties appear to be the result of environmental influences such as the food supply and the colour of the background. Those characters which have been shown to be inherited— such as age at maturity and potential growth rate—are the sort of characters which are controlled by many sets of genes, probably on many chromosomes, and therefore it is possible to "improve" the stock progressively by selection. However, as with height in man, the type of environment determines the extent to which the potentialities of the individual can be expressed and most of the striking differences observed between wild populations are probably the result of environmental differences.

Hybrids

"Pure" sea trout can be grown from eggs and milt stripped from adult fish migrating up rivers. "Pure" brown trout can be bred from known non-migrating parents. It is interesting to compare them.

The relation between the development of the eggs and water temperature is very similar for these two pure lines. But if a cross is made between a sea trout female and a brown trout male or vice versa, the "hybrids" show a different relationship especially at higher water temperatures. This suggests that there is a genetic difference between the sea trout and brown trout, for the "hybrids" show a typical "heterosis." Salmon eggs have temperature relations during development slightly different from those of trout; and salmon×trout hybrids show a heterotic effect which is more marked than that in the sea and brown trout "hybrids."

Sea trout can be reared to maturity in ponds, and Skrochowska has shown in Poland that the migratory "instinct" persists in the first generation but is lost in the second generation of pond-reared fish. The generation produced by breeding "hybrid" sea×brown trout among themselves showed a segregation into some migratory and some non-migratory forms. The pond-reared pure sea trout grew at similar rates to brown trout, but their colour was variable and usually changed to the silver characteristic of migrating sea trout, the larger fish changing earlier than those growing more slowly. The larger fish also became sexually mature earlier and very well-fed specimens matured at two (males) and three (females) years old which is earlier than is usual for wild sea trout.

Salmon belong to the same genus as brown trout but have only sixty chromosomes: trout have eighty. Hybrids have seventy chromosomes. It has been reported that milt

from a salmon male×trout female hybrid successfully
fertilised salmon eggs leading to a second generation
back-cross hybrid. The salmon-trout hybrids are more successful if the female and male are of similar size: sea
trout eggs are easier to fertilise with salmon milt than are
brown trout eggs. Breeding is also more successful if the
female parent is the species with larger eggs; so brown
trout milt will fertilise salmon eggs more easily than in
the reverse cross. Mortality is high in eyed egg and alevin
stages and specially marked during hatching. The hybrid
fish look more like trout than salmon, and their growth
patterns are intermediate between those of the two parents
when all three types of young fish are grown under identical conditions. This again supports the view that potentialities for growth are genetically determined but depend
on polygenes. When brown trout are crossed with rainbows (*Salmo gairdneri*), the hybrids are spotted and brownish in colour and they are all sterile.

A hybrid which has sometimes been recommended as a
sporting fish is the "tiger trout" or "zebra trout" which is
the hybrid between female brown trout and male speckled
trout. This is an intergeneric cross, since the speckled
trout (*Salvelinus fontinalis*) is really a char. One fully
fertile male hybrid has been reared but usually the fish
are sterile or nearly so. It is because they cannot breed
that they have been recommended for planting under conditions where it is desirable to have complete control
over the number of fish in the water. They grow at comparable rates to brown trout and are said to be hardy and
to be good sporting fish. However, under most conditions
it is probable that ordinary brown trout or speckled trout
will be as satisfactory: the mortality in rearing the hybrids
is greater than for the pure species. It is interesting that
these particular hybrids should have a very distinctive
pattern which is unlike that of either parent. The cross
has occurred naturally at least once in Britain for two
small zebra trout have been caught in Wise Een Tarn
where both parent species are present.

Chapter Seven

The Physical Environment

And, certainly, as some pastures breed larger sheep; so do some rivers, by reason of the ground over which they run, breed larger Trouts.   *Izaak Walton* (1653)

Topography

The brown trout is able to live and do well in running water (rivers, streams) and still waters (lakes, tarns, etc.). The two kinds of water differ widely in their physical characteristics of temperature and dissolved oxygen, and also in gradient, width, depth and substratum. We will now consider the direct effect of these topographical characteristics on the presence and numbers of trout in any water. Trout must have running water for spawning although they clearly do not *need* rapid water for living in. Let us deal first with the relationship between topography and the trout in rivers and streams.

Kathleen Carpenter in 1928 found the trout to be characteristic of rivers where the gradient is steep, the current strong and the river bottom of solid rock, stones and boulders—also where the gradient is easier but the flow of water is still quite swift and the bottom is stony. M. Huet (in his classification of rivers based on gradient) finds the trout to be the chief fish where the gradient is steepest with rapidly flowing water, to be present where the gradient is easier and flow less rapid, to be less abundant where the gradient becomes less steep and the river widens and to be rare where the gradient is negligible, be the river narrow or wide. Huet finds that certain species of fish characterise each of these zones in Western Europe, and his conclusions apply in general to the running waters of the British Isles.

In the rapidly flowing narrow streams of hills and moorland the trout is often the only fish, with the bullhead (*Cottus gobio* L.), minnow (*Phoxinus phoxinus* L.) and young salmon sometimes present. Such waters are typical of the mountains and moorlands of northern and western England, Scotland, Wales and Ireland (map II). Many typical trout streams are found where the landscape is hilly rather than mountainous with cultivated valleys; these occur particularly in northern and western England, the lowlands of Scotland and parts of the central plain of Ireland. Here the grayling (*Thymallus thymallus* L.) may be present and also salmon parr; perch (*Perca fluviatilis* L.), chub (*Squalius cephalus* (L)), eels (*Anguilla anguilla* (L.)) occur and sometimes pike (*Esox lucius* (L.)). The trout is not so common in slower, wider rivers flowing through fields and a level countryside and there are more cyprinid fish such as roach (*Rutilus rutilus* L.), rudd (*Scardinius erythrophthalmus* (L.)), and sometimes dace (*Leuciscus leuciscus* L.) together with the pike (map vii). This type of river is found in the Midlands and in the south of England, rarely in Scotland and Wales. Where the river is wide and deep and flows strongly through a flat and somewhat uniform landscape, as in south-east England, then trout are indeed rare and cyprinids, including the bream (*Abramis brama* L.) and perch and pike are the main fish.

Why is the trout so rare in those parts of a river where pike, perch and cyprinids (e.g. rudd, roach, dace, chub, etc.), which are collectively often termed "coarse fish," predominate? These water courses are usually found in lowlands and are characterised by their slow flow; they are less well aerated, have higher summer temperatures and more silt than waters where trout are the principal fish. Trout in these rivers may not obtain enough oxygen, may encounter lethal temperatures, and cannot spawn efficiently. That trout do occur in water where such conditions prevail indicates that they can tolerate them but their rarity suggests that they are near the margin of their tolerance. On the other hand the physical environment is favourable to coarse fish and they are numerous. The physical characteristics of the environment—oxygen supply, temperature régime and type of substratum—may solely account for the relative scarcity of trout in the lower reaches of rivers where coarse fish predominate: but biological factors of competition and predation may also be contributary causes, and these are discussed in chapter 9.

This distribution of trout in a river's course is primarily related to the obvious topographical factors of gradient and width, and particularly to the nature of the river bed. Hynes has classified substratum as either "eroding," i.e. of rock, stones or gravel, or "depositing," i.e. of silt or mud. The trout is generally (though not invariably) associated with an eroding substratum, which is called stable or unstable according to whether the stones are still or shifting.

Eroding and depositing substrata are distributed through a trout river in different "types" of water, such as cascades, riffles, runs, flats and pools; in the first three the bottom is primarily eroding, and in the last two mainly depositing. Allen has defined such water types very precisely. Each has its peculiar speed of current and character of substratum. The proportion of a trout stream which is taken up by each water type will differ but there will always be less variety in the lower reaches where the stream is deeper and wider.

The different water types tend to have certain trout populations although the trout, being a mobile animal, may move from one type to the other according to the season or time of day. In general, however, trout are few in the cascade reach which, with its turbulent water and steep gradient, offers few lies for fish. Riffles, with their rapid flow of broken shallow water and fairly stable stony bottom, often have fair numbers of smaller trout, with bigger fish coming in at dusk. As there can be little shelter from the current it is probable that riffles attract fish because the stony substratum produces a fair food supply. Runs have greater depth and a smooth gliding flow, there is less current to contend with, and the eroding substratum presents suitable spawning ground and also good feeding; thus there are good lies (a favourite being at the tail of the pool) and trout are numerous. Flats have deeper water with slight to moderate current giving a smooth flow so that silt settles, to varying extent, and any stony substratum is usually stable. With few loose gravelly areas spawning facilities are limited and a silted bottom produces poorer feeding than a stony one. Silt does however encourage weeds which hold trout food organisms and provide shelter for the trout: so that flats can offer suitable lies and fair numbers of trout may occur there. Pools because they are deep and sometimes weedy give shelter to trout, but the substratum being silty there is no spawning ground and the supply of available food animals is poor. Moreover, pools provide suitable conditions for coarse fish, e.g. pike and perch, so that the trout shares this "water type" with predators and competitors. The trout population in pools is therefore small and probably confined to bigger fish.

Species of fish have different preferences among these water types. Thus riffles and runs may hold grayling, minnows and bullheads, on flats some cyprinids such as chub are found, and in pools some cyprinids and pike and perch. Sawyer found that as a result of mud deposition in a trout stream dace, roach and even lampreys increased at an alarming rate and loach and bullhead practically disappeared. Altered proportions of eroding and depositing substrata can thus alter the number and kind of coarse fish present and hence affect the number of trout in a trout stream.

Thus within a trout stream trout are more numerous where the bottom is eroding than where it is depositing. As trout only spawn successfully on eroding substrata (see chapter 4), this is a primary requirement for natural maintenance of the stock. When the stony shallows of the upper Avon became coated with silt and mud, few trout spawned and their total numbers were much reduced, but when the shallows were cleared of mud the trout spawned thereon and maintained a good stock. Eroding substrata are common in those rivers which flow over hard rocks and many in the north and west of England and in western Scotland and Ireland have excellent and extensive spawning grounds.

The speed of the current may have a direct effect on the growth of trout. We can assume that trout which live in turbulent and swift water may grow more slowly than those in quieter waters, since much of their energy must be spent in maintaining position. We know that the metabolic rate of trout fry grown in tanks with a swift flow is significantly greater than in those with still water. Sømme studied the growth of trout in rivers of Gudbrandsdal (Norway) and concluded that "in parts of the river with pools and slowly running water the trout grew more rapidly than in swift parts of the river." The present day slower growth of the trout in a river in Westmorland may be, in part, the result of a swifter flow since it was dredged out some years ago. The trout are now subject to a swift current over most of the river's length whereas before there were many places of quiet flow where presumably the fish could put into growth the energy they now use to combat the current. It is generally true that larger trout in any river are found in the less turbulent reaches, but they may not have lived there all their lives, nor need they be individuals showing good growth.

Many trout rivers are liable to spates and floods. The severe floods in the Horokiwi stream in 1941, examined by Allen, greatly disturbed the shingle both during and after the spawning season and caused abnormally high loss of trout eggs and young fry, amounting to about eighty to ninety per cent of the eggs laid. In the previous year, when water levels were normal, the loss was negligible. After the floods there were also substantial losses of older trout; their number was reduced from a quarter to a half of

1   Female trout excavating her nest by violent lateral flexions of her body.
The pectoral fins act as brakes and the water round the hind half of the fish is
moved very forcefully, shifting the gravel and, in this shallow tank,
dimpling the surface. The stones are moved because of the water movements
and not by physical contact with the fish

2 Brown trout spawning

Above, courtship, the female is testing the site for a redd while the male performs a 'figure of eight' courtship 'dance' over the female. *Centre,* courtship, the male, nearest the camera, 'quivers' against the female who is settling into the excavation. *Below,* the spawning act, the female, furthest from the camera, is crouching in the nest with her mouth wide open and is extruding eggs. The male is releasing sperm (milt), visible as a faint white cloud

3 Early stages of brown trout, usually passed buried in gravel in the redd. **a,** egg (×16) at 'eyed ova' stage with the large eyes of the young fish visible through the eggshell. **b, c,** the eggshell splits and the young fish wriggles free (both × 14). **d, e, f,** the newly hatched fish ($\frac{3}{4}''$ long) are called 'alevins'. The yolk sac contains a large oil globule and has a rich blood supply. Alevins can move by lashing the body violently (**e,** ×13) and thus penetrate more deeply into the gravel. In **f** (×5) there is an empty eggshell near the two alevins

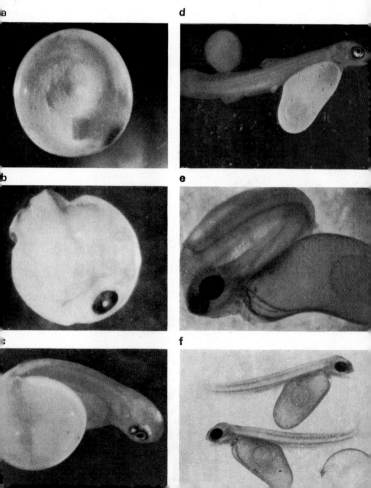

a

d

b

e

c

f

4 *Above,* alevin older than those in plate 3. The large oil globule has been reduced to small droplets; the body is beginning to have a colour pattern; the heart and vitelline veins are clearly visible. Alevins live on their yolk sac alone for about three weeks, but emerge from the gravel and start to feed on small animals before the yolk has been used up completely. *Centre,* trout fry, $2\frac{3}{4}''$ long, about five months old (0+), showing clearly the 'parr marks' —the dark, thumbprint-like bars on the side of the body. This attitude, resting on the pectoral fins, is very typical of trout fry at this stage. *Below,* adult brown trout (*Salmo trutta*) and rainbow trout (*S. gairdneri*). The rainbow trout has spots on the tail (a diagnostic feature), more spots on the top of the head and a characteristic magenta flush along the sides

Typical trout lakes

Above, Wastwater, English Lake District. This deep, steep-sided lake with rocky shores lies among mountains and moorlands; its water is poor in nutrient salts. Trout and char are the principal fish species; eels and minnows are also present; salmon pass through on their way to their spawning streams. *Below,* Smallwater, English Lake District. This typical mountain tarn, near Mardale, Westmorland, lies at an altitude of 1485 ft and contains only trout

Scales from trout in rivers

6   a: Fast-growing fish from River Itchen. 13″. 3+. May. Note contrast between the widely-spaced circuli of the summer growth and narrower spacing of winter growth (annulus). On this and on Plates 7 and 8 the annuli on each scale are indicated by guide-lines and numbers

b: Slow-growing fish from Scandale Beck, Windermere. 5″. 4. December. This small scale shows the same alternation of summer and winter growth, but with far fewer circuli

c: A young fish from Cunsey Beck, Windermere. 3¼″. 1+. June

d: A regenerated scale (see p. 89), useless for age determination since the centre circuli, clear in **c**, have gone. In fact 3 years old

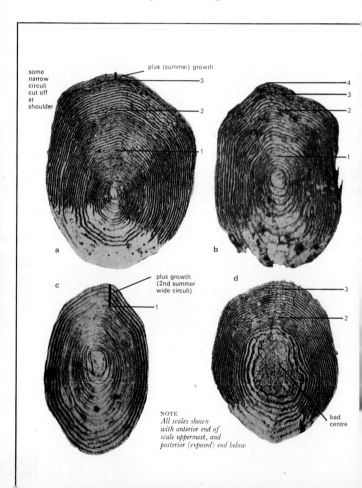

some narrow circuli cut off at shoulder

plus (summer) growth

3
2
1

4
3
2
1

a

b

plus growth (2nd summer wide circuli)
1

c

d

3
2

bad centre

NOTE
*All scales shown
with anterior end of
scale uppermost, and
posterior (exposed) end below*

Scales from trout in lakes

7   **a:** Windermere. $8\frac{1}{2}''$. 3+. May. Note accelerated growth in second year after leaving beck for lake. Contrast **6a** opposite

b: Also from Windermere. 21''. 7. December. The jump in growth is here in the third summer, so fish probably spent two years in the beck

c: Wastwater. $6\frac{3}{4}''$. 4. August. Much slower growth in this lake: no apparent change after leaving beck

d: Malham Tarn. 19''. 6+. August. Fast growth, with no contrast between beck and lake. Note the erosion and spawning marks, which very rarely occur in brown trout

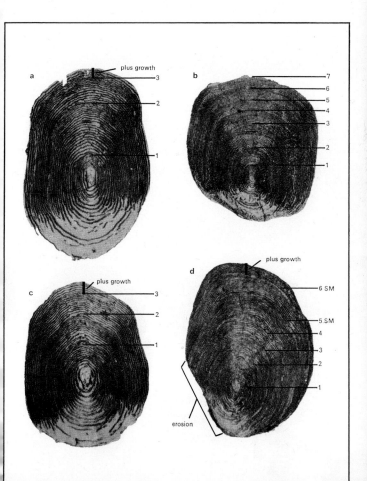

8 **a**: The brown trout scale shown in Plate **7b.** Silvery with black spots, large Windermere fish resemble sea trout

b: Sea trout, from R. Duddon. **c.** 30″. 3+ 5+. The contrast between river and sea growth (the diagnostic feature) is unusually clear in this picture. Note also the spawning marks (S.M.) and erosion

c: Salmon. Cairnton Water. 31¾″. 3+2. 11½ lb. May. Three years in river, then descent to sea, where it spent two years before returning to river to spawn. The river/sea contrast is much more striking than in sea trout and salmon rarely live more than three years in the sea

d: Rainbow trout. Lough Shure, Arranmore Island, Co. Donegal. 10″. 2+ May. Circuli (both wide and narrowly spaced ones) are more numerous than in brown trout

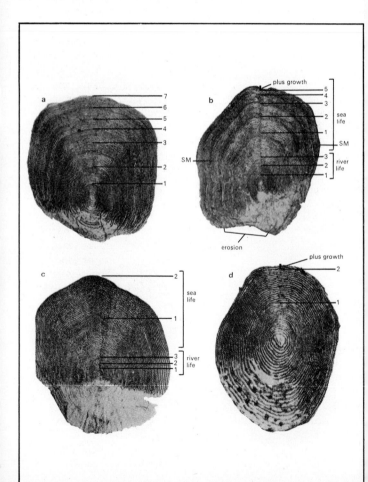

that found previously and their growth was also definitely reduced.

The quantity of bottom fauna in the Horokiwi in the flood year was reduced to less than half of what it had been in the previous year. An even greater potential loss of trout food due to floods was noted in the River Towy where invertebrates were reduced from 300-1000 to 40-48 per square metre (Jones, 1951). Even in those rivers where the violence of floods is tempered by gentle gradient and much weed growth, a sudden rise in water level has been known to sweep the bottom fauna on to the surrounding fields, as in the upper Avon. Aquatic animals may also be destroyed by the silt brought down by a flood, as in the Test. Thus floods reduce the food supply for trout, and where they are frequent and the bottom is unstable, as in the River Duddon, Cumberland, they may prevent the establishment of an abundant bottom fauna, since rolling stones gather little or no moss (or algæ) to give the necessary food and shelter.

Dearth of water can also be harmful, although not perhaps to the same extent. A drought in a river with a steep gradient and rapid run off can kill hundreds of trout. In a Lake District beck during the prolonged dry summer of 1955 dead trout were found stranded on the dry river bed or dying in the few remaining lukewarm pools, each heavily congested with fish. Small fry appear to be more resistant to drought than larger fish for they can survive if able to find damp gravel; but we have seen a beck in which even this remnant of water had gone and the fry lay dead on the dry bed. In most chalk streams the likelihood of drought is reduced because the stream is fed by springs; therefore the water level is not so directly dependent on the immediate and local rainfall. But in long spells of dry weather the springs may be reduced and the amount of water in the stream falls below normal; in such circumstances, in the Test, mud settled on the weeds and the great scarcity of "fly life" noted subsequently was attributed to this blanketing of the vegetation.

T.—E

Topographical factors directly determine the aquatic vegetation. The plants associated with different current speeds and types of substrata (eroding and depositing) are given in table 12. The invertebrates associated with the vegetation are listed, as are the commoner animals found on different types of substrata; here we shall discuss only the plants and leave the discussion of the animal associations until chapter 8.

Water mosses are the only plants found where the flow is swift and the substratum is rocky and stable. The plants provide no shelter for the trout but hold a varied and often abundant invertebrate fauna. In slower flows a stony stable bottom supports a variety of water plants; of these water crowfoot, water starwort and water milfoil, almost totally submerged, give better shelter to the trout than the semi-emergent water celery and water parsnip. Where the stony bottom is unstable, rooted vegetation is absent, the only plant life being the algal felt. With a still slower rate of flow and partially silted substratum, the pondweeds (*Potamogeton*) appear, and provide sheltering weed beds for the trout. The water cress, mare's tail and bur-reed are less valuable as shelter because they are partly emergent plants. This also applies to emergent plants, such as bulrush and sedges, which live where the flow is slow and substratum silted, but here there also grow submerged plants like Canadian pondweed (*Elodea*) which give the trout some cover.

Weed beds can damp down the disturbing effect of floods on trout redds. By collecting silt, weeds may lessen its deposition on spawning beds. Weeds are not themselves food for trout, but inasmuch as they provide living places, food and shelter for many animals upon which trout feed they play an important part in their lives (see also chapter 8). It is difficult as yet to relate any particular plant with a certain fauna.

The value of aquatic vegetation to the trout is that it can provide "good lies," that is places where, undisturbed by the current, hidden from enemies and on a good feeding ground, they find a satisfactory living place.

Trees and bushes on the river bank give shade, shelter, and hiding places and thus also provide "good lies" for trout. Moreover the decayed leaves of deciduous trees are food for aquatic invertebrates so bank vegetation can tend to increase the bottom fauna and hence the trout's food supply. But things can go too far. Really dense overhanging vegetation excludes the light necessary to the growth of algal felt, which is also a food of the invertebrates. But on the other hand terrestrial insects fall from the trees and bushes bordering the stream and so augment the food supply of the trout, often greatly. Aquatic insects, such as the caddis and alderflies and duns of mayflies, find shelter in bank vegetation and so are not blown away from the river to be themselves lost as immediate trout food, and ·to leave no progeny to be future food.

The kind and amount of bank vegetation varies with the local topography. A river in a rocky moorland terrain, such as the Troutbeck in Westmorland, is practically treeless and has few bushes in its highland reaches; but its banks lower down have the occasional rowan tree and some alder bushes and, when it reaches the valley, more and varied trees and bushes. At best, however, this bank vegetation of such a river is sparse compared with that which borders rivers flowing through lowland cultivated lands and meadows.

In running water topographical features largely determine the number of trout "lies" and as good "lies" usually mean good trout (i.e. those which grow well and are of an acceptable size to the angler) the importance of the relation between topography and such "lies" cannot be overemphasised.

There are many different types of still waters in the British Isles, each with characteristic fish faunas (see maps II and VII). Steep-sided lakes with rocky shores, among mountains and moorlands, are typical trout waters, usually holding minnows also, sometimes, char. Stony streams (with plenty of suitable spawning grounds for trout) enter these lakes, which vary in size from a few acres—like some tarns of the Lake District and lochans of the Scottish highlands—to several hundred acres as Wastwater and Loch Rannoch. Typical trout lakes are found in northern England, the highlands of Scotland and Wales, and in the mountainous districts of Ireland.

When the landscape is hilly rather than mountainous, and the lake is less steep-sided and has silted bays along its stony shore, then the fish community is one of trout, pike, perch and probably char or whitefish (*Coregonus* spp.). The eel, bullhead and stickleback probably occur but there are seldom any cyprinids except minnows. Examples of this kind of lake where trout and char are associated with perch and pike are Windermere, Buttermere and Lough Mask: examples where whitefish are present and char are absent are Loch Lomond and Llyn Tegid. When there are few stony and many silted areas and a less rugged countryside, there is a tendency for trout to be less important than pike and perch, and the cyprinids such as bream and rudd may be present. Some of the large loughs of the Shannon system, such as L. Derg and L. Ree, are of this kind. In these catchment areas there may be fewer suitable spawning streams.

Finally, lakes surrounded by low-lying, cultivated land, flat or undulating, will have silted or muddy bottoms, with few, if any, stony patches. They are usually shallow. Trout are seldom found in these waters, unless planted there by man, nor are there any other salmonids. Pike, perch, and cyprinids are important, and in some lakes the last predominate; the eel, stickleback and minnow are present. In England, the Norfolk Broads are such typical coarse fish waters; in Wales and Scotland such waters are rare. In Ireland there are many in certain localities such as Co. Cavan, and they usually hold pike, perch, bream and rudd. Most of the lakes described in this last paragraph have poor spawning streams because the siltiness which characterises them, is also characteristic of the waters running into them.

This account of the distribution of the trout and of other fish in still waters once more raises a question. Why is the trout less common, or even rare, in those waters where coarse fish are common or predominate? The oxygen supply and temperature conditions in summer are more favourable to cyprinids than to trout in typical coarse fish lakes, but the trout can usually find parts of the lake where conditions are more suitable for them. The nature of the substratum also favours the coarse fish; the silted substrata of inflowing streams limit trout breeding grounds. In lakes such substrata increase the spawning capacity of coarse fish, since siltiness encourages weed, and many coarse fish spawn on weeds. On the other hand, where the lake substratum is stony, the streams are too, and ensure spawning grounds for trout, whilst within the lake the breeding grounds for coarse fish are relatively few. Thus because of differences in breeding habits differences in substratum result in either the coarse fish being numerous and the trout few, or the trout are numerous and the coarse fish are few. Trout are therefore faced with more predators and probably more competitors in silted weedy lakes whereas they are numerous and dominate the fish fauna in stony lakes. Instances of trout living successfully in waters essentially suited to coarse fish, such as lowland reservoirs and gravel pits, serve to stress the importance of the biotic factors of predation and competition, since usually man has reduced or eliminated pike, perch and cyprinids from these waters before attempting to make them into trout fisheries (see chapter 9). Should the control of the non-salmonid fish be stopped in such reservoirs the trout quickly become reduced in number and may even disappear.

In still waters, depth and substratum determine, directly, the nature of aquatic vegetation. This in turn affects the number and kind of invertebrate animals present and hence the trout's food supply.

Table 13 summarises the plants and the invertebrates

associated with different substrata; a further discussion of the fauna will be found in chapter 8.

The plants in shallow water with eroding substrata are clinging mosses or low growing lake- and quillworts. Neither provides shelter for the trout itself, but their invertebrate fauna, especially that of the swards of lakewort, is a valuable source of food. The emergent plants hold a varied invertebrate fauna which includes many organisms which trout eat and the same is true for submerged plants. Indeed, in still waters aquatic vegetation is chiefly important to the trout because it harbours food animals. When trout are seen in weed beds they are primarily seeking food and not shelter. Weeds do certainly protect them to some extent from the angler but on the other hand the pike also tends to frequent weed beds which somewhat reduces their protective value to the trout. In still waters the trout does not need to seek shelter from the current as it does in rivers.

Dr. Macan compared the total number and in general terms the total weight of invertebrates found among and on the lakewort (*Littorella*), the semi-emergent sedge (*Carex*), the pondweed (*Potamogeton*) and the water milfoil (*Myriophyllum*) in a small tarn near Windermere. He concluded that the amounts of food held by these four plants were roughly in the proportion of $4:3:2:1$. Further information of this kind is obviously desirable in view of the major role of plants as trout-larders in still waters and their no less important part as such in running waters.

The bank vegetation of a lake or tarn plays much the same part in the life of the trout as it does in running water. Trees and bushes along the shore provide shade and shelter, although shade is not so valuable as in running water since the trout can move offshore into deeper and cooler water. Overhanging trees shelter aquatic insects and provide a supply of food in the form of terrestrial insects. In Windermere a trout was an almost permanent resident under a certain oak tree infested with caterpillars of the winter moth. The value of bank vegetation to trout in a lake depends on the size of the body of water. If there are but few trees along the shores of a big lake it is of little consequence, but even poor bank vegetation on the shores of a small tarn may make all the difference to the trout's food supply.

Lakes fluctuate in level but seldom as violently as rivers. Only very rarely do they dry out in Britain. Nevertheless, a fall in level may have a harmful effect on trout food supply. In Tunhov Fjord, when the water level was lowered by 18 m. in winter, snails and caddis larvæ were much reduced in number and shrimp disappeared, and in Paalsbu Fjord, although alterations in the height of water favoured the increase of the shrimp *Lepidurus* and the weed-living water flea *Eurycercus*, the fluctuations were fatal to *Gammarus*.

There is some evidence that trout grow faster in larger lakes and rivers than in smaller ones when other characteristics of the waters, including density of food supply and of fish fauna, are similar. Thus Allen found that trout grew faster in the Main Water of the Horokiwi River than in Zone 5 of that water, and the only apparent difference between these two parts of the river was that the former was larger than the latter. Alm wrote, "trout are usually bigger in large than in smaller lakes." The poor growth of three year and older trout in Three Dubs Tarn (area 4 acres) compared with that in the adjacent lake, Windermere (area 5½ square miles), seems to constitute another example of a direct relationship between water volume and fish growth. The degree of crowding, its measurement and its effect on trout population, structure and growth, is further discussed in chapter 9.

Climate

Everyone who lives in the temperate zones of the world is aware of the annual variation in daylight and temperature. In the British Isles, we have a climate without extremes, because of our position beside the Atlantic Ocean. We may also have rain in every month of the year, but usually it is highest in spring and autumn when floods are most likely to occur. Freshwater organisms are thus subjected to annual cycles in the amount of daylight, the water temperature and the water level and flow. Some effects of floods and droughts have already been discussed. The longest day-length and highest light intensity occur at mid-summer (June) and the least at Christmas (December), and there is a regular change in day-length and light intensity between these two extremes. In a "typical" year, the highest water temperatures occur in July or August and the lowest in February. The maximum and minimum temperatures thus follow the maximum and minimum amounts of light.

The annual cycle of events in the life of brown trout is naturally linked with this environmental cycle. Trout spawn in November and December when the light and temperature are both decreasing; the fry begin to feed in March or later, when daylight and temperature are both increasing. If the presence of wide circuli at the scale margin indicates rapid growth (see pp. 90-4) then in many British waters some fish begin to grow rapidly in February or March and all are growing rapidly in May and June. Slow growth, accompanied by narrow circuli at the scale margin, may begin in August and is general in September and October. In winter, from November to February, growth is either very slow or ceases completely.

Swift measured yearling trout at intervals in the Freshwater Biological Association's hatchery stewponds and noted a similar cycle. There was a peak of rapid growth in early summer, especially in May, and sometimes another (less marked) peak in late summer or early autumn. Growth was slow in July, when water temperature was high, and growth rates decreased rapidly in November and were very low in winter. Yearling hatchery fish released into Scale Tarn in March 1957 had a marked growth rate peak in May and June and a much smaller peak in October and November, and similar fish released into a netted-off part of Windermere showed similar changes in growth rate.

After examining scales of wild trout from Windermere and measuring recaptured marked trout, Allen found much variation in detail between individuals but showed that in general growth was twice as rapid between February and July as during the rest of the year, and that three-quarters of the fish grew rapidly between May and August.

Trout kept in an aquarium at a constant temperature and in artificial light of constant intensity for a constant number of hours each day may still show an annual cycle in rate of growth. Two-year-old trout living at $53°F$ ($11.5°C$) with twelve hours of artificial light per day showed an autumn check in growth, a spring maximum, rapid summer growth and another autumn check which coincided with maturation of their gonads as they became three years old. This suggests that there may be a "physiological rhythm" in the fish which can be independent of the stimuli of the solar cycle; but we do not know at all how it occurs, and Swift has not been able to confirm that it exists in yearling trout. Some such rhythm was postulated by van Someren to account for the formation of narrow circuli on the scales of maiden rainbow trout in Kenya. It could be a cycle in hormonal secretions and would explain why individual trout breed only once a year even on the Equator, where conditions are suitable throughout the year, as in Kenya where some breeding trout are caught in each month.

When trout are transplanted to the Antipodes, they show an annual growth and maturity cycle just like that of British fish but with fastest growth in December and spawning between June and August. Their annual cycle of growth bears the same relationship to the annual climatic changes in their new environment as did the annual growth cycles of their ancestors to the British climatic cycles. Trout are generally transplanted as eggs: it would be very interesting to see how a mature trout would react to such a transplantation. All this suggests that the "physiological rhythm" is normally synchronised with or governed by the annual climatic cycle and can be altered (at least in very young fish) if the climatic cycle is altered. We will now consider separately the information we have about the effects of light and of temperature on trout.

Since brown trout normally hunt their food by sight, the longer the hours of daylight (including twilight, when trout can still see well enough to take a fly) the more time is available for them to catch their food. Trout seem to have definite appetites, and may not feed through all the daylight hours in waters rich in food. But if the food supply is short, they may feed whenever there is enough light. A slack feeding time is generally around noon. In the Liffey, trout at Ballysmuttan appeared to feed over longer periods of the day than those at Straffan.

Four trout in special cages in Windermere showed patterns of activity with bursts of swimming at dawn and dusk, intermittent activity during the day and very little at night. Swift found that they were most active in May and June and three of them showed increased activity again in August. The following year, three trout in these cages were fed once a day with liver, and these fish were ten times as active as the unfed fish and showed the same diurnal pattern with a very sharp rise in activity at dawn, great activity during the day and very little at night. Two other fish were fed continuously with liver and these were altogether less active and showed no consistent rhythm. It thus appears that the diurnal activity rhythm is related to the need to search for food.

The amount of light can have a direct effect on the growth of the trout. When three groups of trout of the same age were kept under similar conditions but with artificial light for six, twelve, and eighteen hours per day, there was no difference between the trout with twelve and eighteen hours of light per day but those with only six hours daily grew more than four times as rapidly as the rest. Thus while longer daylight allows more time for food consumption, shorter day-length may result in more rapid growth in trout if there is plenty of food available.

The amount of daylight can also affect the maturation of

the gonads in many animals. This has been shown to apply to salmon and speckled trout and is almost certainly true also for brown trout. If the numbers of hours of daylight to which the fish are exposed are reduced in summer, they mature several weeks earlier than control fish with the normal amount of daylight; when given extra light they mature several weeks later. The effect of the alteration of day-length is thus to alter, by a few weeks only, the date of maturation of the gonad. These experiments were performed on fish which were about to breed and had lived for at least three years in natural daylight. Much greater effects might be expected on younger fish, and it is probable that the reversal of the normal spawning cycle shown by trout in the Antipodes is really the result of their having been exposed all their lives to the reversed day-length cycle characteristic of the southern hemisphere.

Table 14. Lengths (in inches, back-calculated from scales) of brown trout at the end of the first four years of life from five similar small mountain rivers—

| Age | Southern England | | Ireland Liffey (Ballysmuttan) | Northern Scotland | |
	Tamar	Dart		Forss	Gisla
end of year 1	2·3	2·4	2·0	2·4	2·3
2	4·5	5·4	4·6	5·2	5·0
3	6·9	7·6	6·0	7·9	7·0
4	8·3	9·6	6·9	9·2	8·6
number of fish	20	62	366	64	20

The amount of light available of course varies directly with latitude, except at equinoxes. The greatest contrast between long summer days and short winter days is found in the far north and far south and the days are approximately twelve hours long throughout the year on the Equator. In the British Isles, any considerable effect of daylight on growth should be detectable as a latitudinal effect—that is, there should be a contrast in growth history between fish living in comparable waters in southern England and northern Scotland. Data for growth of trout in four such waters are given in table 14. These are all rapidly flowing streams rising on igneous rocks. The Liffey at Ballysmuttan is of similar size and figures for it are given too: in latitude it lies between the other two pairs of rivers.

The lengths attained at the end of each year of life in these five waters are surprisingly similar and there is certainly no clear latitudinal effect, no contrast between the English and Scottish rivers. Thus differences in daylength seem not to be important enough to account for the marked growth differences among British trout.

Very much more is known about the effects of temperature upon fish than of the effects of light. But there are still considerable gaps in our knowledge. Trout are cold-blooded animals (poikilotherms), which means that their body temperature is the same as that of the water in which they are living and must change as that of the water changes. Most of the vital activities of the body are affected by temperature, and the ability of a trout to live and grow at various temperatures must depend on the balance between its various vital processes. As the temperature rises, a trout's respiratory rate increases so that more water is passed over its gills; its heart beat is increased so that more blood circulates round its body; its tissue respiration is increased, so that more oxygen is extracted from its blood; its digestive enzymes work more rapidly and their breakdown products are more quickly absorbed. All this means that the energy turnover of its body is greatly increased as the temperature rises. This increase in energy turnover happens even in a resting fish: if the trout become more active at higher temperatures, there will be an even greater increase in their expenditure of energy.

Brown trout are essentially cold water fishes and it is therefore of interest to know what extremes of temperature they can endure. At the lower limit for survival is the freezing point of water ($0°C$ or $32°F$). Trout cannot survive being frozen in ice, but they can live in water under ice because the temperature there is above freezing (though below 4°c). Their survival depends on the amount of oxygen in the water; if this is used up they die of asphyxia. Plants produce oxygen if they have enough daylight but use it up in the dark, and trout have died in frozen ponds when heavy snowfalls have prevented the light penetrating the ice. This "winter kill" occurred in a tarn in the Lake District in the very cold winter of 1941, when there was heavy snow, but in 1963 this same tarn was frozen for six weeks but *not* covered in snow, and all the trout survived.

The upper limit of temperature tolerance for brown trout (in tank experiments) seems to lie between $72\frac{1}{2}$°F (22.5°c) and $77\frac{1}{2}$°F (25.3°c) for periods of exposure up to seven days. The temperature they can withstand depends on their previous history as is shown by table 15. The "acclimatisation temperature" is that at which the fish have been living for at least the previous forty-eight hours and the lower this temperature, the lower the maximum temperature at which half the trout are able to survive.

Trout can survive for short periods at temperatures of more than 80°F but cannot survive for long above $77\frac{1}{2}$°F. They can live at temperatures above 68°F (20°c) only if the water is fully saturated with oxygen; their temperature

Table 15. The maximum temperatures at which half the brown trout survived for different periods. (After Gibson, 1951)

| Acclimatisation temperature | | Duration of test | | | | | | | |
| | | 12 hours | | 24 hours | | 48 hours | | 7 days | |
°C	°F	°C	°F	°C	°F	°C	°F	°C	°F
5	41	22·5	$72\frac{1}{2}$	22·5	$72\frac{1}{2}$	22·5	$72\frac{1}{2}$	22·5	$72\frac{1}{2}$
10	50	24·5	76	24·2	$75\frac{1}{2}$	24·2	$75\frac{1}{2}$	24·2	$75\frac{1}{2}$
15	59	26·2	79	25·6	78	25·1	77	24·4	76
20	68	26·5	80	26·3	$79\frac{1}{2}$	25·8	$78\frac{1}{2}$	24·8	$76\frac{1}{2}$
23	$73\frac{1}{2}$	27·8	82	26·6	80	26·4	$79\frac{1}{2}$	25·3	$77\frac{1}{2}$

tolerance is markedly decreased if the oxygen in the water falls. As already explained (p. 24) the amount of oxygen which can be dissolved in water falls as the temperature increases.

We cannot yet say exactly why trout die in hot water, whether it is the result of respiratory failure or of some more subtle change in their tissues. They become very excitable at temperatures above 20°c (68°F); any fall in oxygen concentration or rise in ammonia concentration will then lead rapidly to their death. Exposure to high temperatures has a cumulative effect unless the fish can spend periods of several hours at temperatures below about 21°c (70°F).

Although brown trout can survive for brief periods at temperatures exceeding 80°F (27°c), they do not grow successfully at temperatures much exceeding 68 F (20°c). The same thing happens at low temperatures within their tolerance range; trout can survive at temperatures near the freezing point of water but they do not grow at these temperatures. To understand this, we must consider the effects of temperature on their feeding and activity.

The total energy turnover of a fish can be measured as its *maintenance requirement*, expressed as weight of food absorbed per unit weight of fish when the fish's weight is constant (see pp. 25-6). The maintenance requirements of brown trout of 50 gm. weight in (otherwise) identical aquaria at different temperatures are shown in fig. 18. The values increase with temperature but the points lie along an S-shaped curve with the greatest increase in maintenance requirement per unit temperature between 8 and 15°c (46 and 59°F). The maintenance requirement as estimated here includes energy expended in movement as well as energy required for vital processes. Theoretically, the latter should increase exponentially with increase of temperature giving a curve like the right-hand half of the letter U. The S-shape can be explained if the activity 59°F), and decreased markedly above 15°c (59°F). An 59°F), and decreased markedly above 15°c (59°F). An

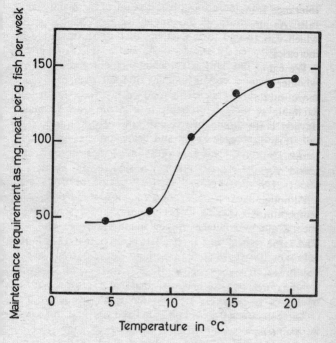

18.   The maintenance requirements of trout of 50 grams weight at different temperatures. (Brown, 1946c)

activity curve for the speckled trout (*Salvelinus fontinalis*) is of this type, with an activity peak at 13°c (56°F). Its curve rises again above 20°c (68°F) to another maximum at 24°c (75°F) from which it rapidly falls towards the lethal temperature at 27°c (80.6°F). No values for maintenance requirement for brown trout have been measured above 20°c (68°F) but there is probably a very marked rise in the maintenance requirement.

The effect of increase in temperature, then, is to increase the amount of food required by the trout to maintain its body weight. Growth in weight can only be achieved if the fish can eat more food than it requires for maintenance at any temperature. If the amount of food which can be collected is related to the activity of the fish, it should be greatest between 10 and 15°c (50 and 59°F). Trout living in tanks and fed daily have definite appetites and will not eat more than a certain amount of food each day. Since trout living in rivers rich in food do not feed throughout the day, the same is probably true in the wild. In tanks, appetite is maximum between 10 and 19°c (50 and 66°F) and falls off sharply above and below these temperatures.

The relation between growth and temperature is still controversial. Certainly, growth is slow below about 7°c (44½°F) and also above 19°c (66°F). One of us (M.E.B.) found that two-year-old trout grew most rapidly between 7 and 9°c, less quickly at 11½°c and above this there was much more individual variation but the average rate was higher between 16 and 19°c. Swift believes that 12°c is the optimum for yearling (and perhaps for all) trout and I found that fry grew better at 12°c than at 10°c. Swift follows Wingfield in believing that trout grow faster at temperatures below 12°c when the water temperature is rising than when it is falling, but I did not find this effect in an experiment which was designed to show it if it existed. I found an annual physiological rhythm in my two-year-old fish which Swift did not find with yearlings; this may be one reason for the existing confusion. If this rhythm exists, then growth will be more rapid when water temperatures are rising (in spring) than when they are falling (in autumn) and the same result would be observed if increasing photoperiod (more hours of daylight) promoted growth and decreasing photoperiod depressed growth. No one has yet experimented with regularly varying amounts or intensities of light in a constant temperature. All our interpretations are based on small numbers of fish of varied ages and origins so there is plenty of room for argument. There are genetical factors concerned with growth rate and different stocks may perhaps behave differently at different temperatures. Some of the published observations are listed in table 16.

All these figures, however, bear out the general conclusion that trout growth is maximum at temperatures between 7 and 19°C (45 and 66°F) so that within their limits of temperature tolerance (0-25.3°C, 32-77½°F) good growth is to be expected only in this more·limited range. Trout generally live in lakes or fast-flowing rivers. In the latter, there is little temperature gradient at any one place,

Table 16. Optimum temperature ranges for growth and feeding of brown trout quoted by different workers—

Author	Age of trout years	Growth optima °C	Feeding optima °C
Brown 1951	0 to ½	12 better than 10	
Brown 1946	2 to 3	7 to 9 and 16 to 19	10 to 19
Gerrish 1935	all ages?		5 to 13 and 16 to 19
Hewitt 1943	all ages?	15 to 19	
Myers 1946	0 to 1		7 to 15
Pentelow 1939	½ to 1½	10 to 15	10
Swift 1955	3 to 4	8 to 12 and 15 to 16	
Swift 1961	1 to 2	12	
Wingfield 1940	½ to 1½	10 to 15	

but the lower reaches are usually warmer than the upper ones. Small streams rising from springs probably show little annual or diurnal variation in temperature but these may be large in other small streams especially where the water runs off hard rocks with little percolation.

Dr. Macan (1958) used a temperature recorder continuously for more than three years in a small lakeland beck; the daily cycle showed a minimum at about 6 a.m. and a maximum about twelve hours later. As expected, the lowest temperatures were recorded in January and February when daily fluctuations were as large as 5°C; these fluctuations were even larger, up to 7°c, between March and June when the average temperature rose progressively; in July and August, the average was high and fluctuations were very slight and in the autumn, the temperature fell and showed small fluctuations of less than 5°C. The highest temperatures were recorded when the sun shone strongly after rain and the maximum was 19°c. On a sunny day, temperature in a wooded stretch of another small beck was as much as 8°c less than that in an exposed section upstream. Lower downstream, there were greater daily fluctuations with higher maximum temperatures but the minima were very similar to those upstream. Dr. Macan concluded that small rocky streams reach an equilibrium a few miles from the source such that the average water temperature is not very different from the average air temperature. Mr. Charles Smith has given me records for the River Test, at Laverstoke, between October 1959 and September 1960. The maximum temperature recorded was 19.5°c at midsummer and the minimum was 2.2°c in mid-January. The daily range was greatest in June but very seldom exceeded 4°c. Between November and March, the monthly average maxima were between 7.5° and 9.5°c and the minima were between 6° and 8°c. In the other seven months, the maxima were between 11° and 18°c and the minima were between 8½° and 13°c. There was less variation than in the lakeland beck and the water temperature seems nearly ideal for trout.

Lakes generally show thermal stratification in the summer. This is fully discussed in *Life in Lakes and Rivers* (Macan and Worthington, 1951). The upper waters of a lake may be warm and separated by a zone of rapid change from the lower waters which are cold. Fishes can swim freely between these two layers so that, under these conditions, it is difficult to assess the average temperature at which they are living. In Windermere, the large trout are always caught in deep water.

Winter temperatures in larger rivers and lakes in the British Isles are generally below 6°c (43°F) and it could be expected (from studies on appetite and growth) that trout would grow slowly or not at all at these temperatures. Trout may, however, feed actively in very cold water as Miss McCormack has observed in becks with a temperature of 0.4°c at night and less than 3°c by day. Niall Campbell found many trout growing fast in the newly flooded Loch Garry in March 1956 when the average water temperature was only 3.5°c (38°F). In spring, the water temperatures begin to rise and most trout begin to grow fast; in summer, temperature conditions fall within the optimum ranges for growth discussed above; in autumn, temperatures begin to fall and the trout cease to grow fast. Spring growth, however, generally begins before water temperatures have risen significantly and growth may cease in the autumn before the water temperatures have fallen below 8°c (46°F).

The annual cycle of growth can be related to climatic changes thus: increasing hours of daylight in February and March stimulate the trout to begin to grow rapidly and the temperature then rises to an optimum value. The late summer check is associated with decreasing hours of daylight at fairly high temperatures and in older fish the gonads mature in the autumn. The autumn growth peak observed in Llyn Tegid may be associated with the optimum temperature range at about 8°c. In winter, slow growth is associated with low water temperatures.

The annual physiological rhythm suggested above would enhance the effects of daylight and temperature. But Swift believes that his growth records—with two peaks of growth, in May and September—can be related directly to water temperature provided that rising and falling temperatures lead each to a different association between temperature and growth rate. The food supply also varies seasonally in quality and quantity (see pp. 189, 196) and this may well affect the growth of trout in nature, making it difficult to establish a correlation between changes in light and temperature and the observed growth.

We have already described how temperature affects the

development of trout eggs (see p. 77). It is interesting that the optimal range for development of eggs, 7 to 12°c (45 to 53°F) is more restricted than that for survival of older trout. Extremes of cold and heat are more lethal to eggs than to older fish. Ideal conditions for the development of eggs are waters with winter temperatures of about 10°c (50°F) so that it is not surprising that many trout hatcheries are built beside springs.

Table 17. Lengths (in inches) of brown trout at the end of the first three years of life from three small moorland streams—

Age	Upper Tees Westmorland	R. Rhydwen North Wales	Walla Brook Devonshire
end of year 1	1·9	2·5	2·9
2	3·8	4·1	4·6
3	5·3	5·1	6·1

We must consider whether differences in water temperature can account for the differences in growth rates which we have found among British trout. In general, winters are longer and summers less hot in northern Scotland than in southern England. From what we suspect about the *general* correlation between temperature and growth, we might expect that trout from similar waters would grow faster in Devonshire than in Caithness. But figures for the River Dart and the River Forss are very similar (see table 14 and map III).

The tributaries of the upper River Tees are subjected to an almost arctic climate whereas similar moorland streams in north Wales and on Dartmoor have less extreme climates. Table 17 gives growth data showing quite large differences in length at the end of the first year between trout living in three streams.

Average temperatures and monthly maxima and minima may well be misleading since they suggest gradual variation whereas there may be very large diurnal fluctuations. A temperature recorder in Kingswell Beck during hot summer weather revealed that the minimum daily temperature was less than 13°c (55½°F) but the maximum rose as high as 23°c (73½°F). This amount of variation in twenty-four hours must subject fish to considerable stress. It may perhaps cause lowered appetite; it certainly means a higher maintenance requirement and consequently less food available for growth. Small rivers flowing over impervious rocks, such as the Dart and the Forss, may show much greater diurnal variations in temperature than a spring-fed river such as the Lambourn; this may perhaps explain why young fry have such different rates of growth in these two types of river. Scales from different parts of the Rivers Test and Itchen have characteristic and different patterns of wide and narrow circuli, suggesting a very constant rate of growth. It is impossible to identify annuli so we cannot tell how fast the fish have grown. Fish living farther downstream show annuli which, though typical enough, sometimes consist of a very few circuli. Scales from fish from moorland streams have well-marked annuli suggesting a clear contrast between summer and winter growth.

Water Chemistry

There is an amazing diversity of scenery within the British Isles and we have already referred in the first part of this chapter to the contrasts between the swift streams rushing down the slopes of rocky mountains in Scotland and the slow-flowing rivers winding across the flat plains of the Fens. The physical differences between these types of water are partly due to the geological structure of the country and we are fortunate in the variety of geological formations which we can observe around us. The rocks differ in their hardness and in the ease with which they can be weathered by rain, frost and sun and dissolved away or disintegrated into boulders, gravel and mud. With these differences go differences in chemical composition, and the waters which flow over and from different rocks consequently differ in their chemistry. It is clear, as Southern (1932) stressed in a most interesting and wide-ranging paper, that there is an association between geological formations and the size and growth rates of trout living in the waters above them. But there is still a great deal of doubt and argument about the meaning of this association. In general, growth is good in "hard," alkaline waters and it is poor in "soft," acid waters.

The "hard," alkaline waters are derived from lime-bearing rocks, which are not hard at all from the point of view of weathering; the distribution of these is shown in map IV. In Ireland, much of the central plain is of carboniferous limestone while the surrounding hills are of granite and other non-calcareous rocks. In Great Britain, there is some carboniferous limestone in the Scottish lowlands and in the Pennines but most of the lime-bearing rocks are to be found south and east of a line drawn between the mouth of the River Tees and the Severn Estuary but excluding Devon and Cornwall. If map II is compared with map IV it is clear that the rocky, mountainous areas of Great Britain consist mainly of non-calcareous rocks while the lime-bearing rocks are generally associated with rolling "downs" and fertile plains. There is a marked contrast in the topography of the running waters of the two zones and some, also, in that of still waters—since the mountain lakes are often deep, narrow and tortuous while lowland lakes are broad and shallow and surrounded by agricultural land. Rainfall is especially high in mountainous areas and is higher in western than in eastern districts; so there are differences between the rates of flow of streams and their liability to flooding and spates. There is a contrast, too, in average temperatures (map III), which are higher in the south and east than in the north and west. We have already concluded that topography may be an important environmental factor affecting growth, and that the *differences* in average temperature found in British waters are unlikely to have marked effects but temperature *fluctuations* may be very significant. We shall now discuss whether there are

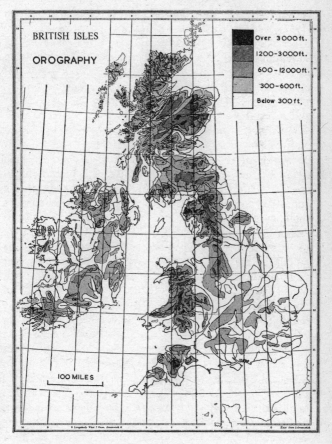

II.   Orography of the British Isles

differences in growth which can be attributed to the
chemical differences between waters.

Map v showing the growth of trout in the British Isles
is remarkable for the patchiness of the records. Most of
these come from Ireland, the Lake District, parts of Scotland and Wales and the chalk streams of Hampshire and

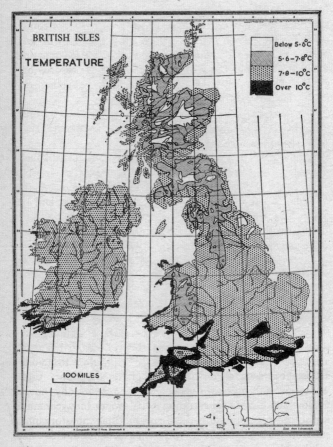

III. Average temperatures of the British Isles

neighbouring counties. These are, of course, the principal parts of the country where people fish for trout: fishermen in the blank areas of the map are mostly devoted to "coarse" fishing. There is a correlation with topography, for coarse fishes thrive in the more slowly-flowing rivers (see map VII) and seem to be more successful than trout.

Even in lowland districts, however, trout in gravel pits and reservoirs may do very well when protected from competition. We cannot quote figures for the growth of trout under these conditions, though it resembles that in the chalk streams. There are some areas where records of good and poor growth come from waters close together, as in the west of Ireland and parts of Scotland.

The principal chemical differences between waters from lime-bearing rocks and non-calcareous rocks are in:

(1) the amount of calcium,
(2) the amount of carbonates and bicarbonates in solution,
(3) the total amount of dissolved salts,
(4) the pH (or acidity or alkalinity) of the water, and
(5) the amounts of organic matter in solution.

"Hard" waters contain high quantities of calcium carbonate and bicarbonate. These compounds cause "temporary hardness," which is measured by the water chemist by its effect of dispersing the foam of standard soap solutions. Other salts of calcium and magnesium may be present (causing "permanent hardness"), so the total salt concentration is high. Acid waters have a pH of less than 7 (the neutral value of the chemist) and alkaline waters have a pH greater than 7. Usually a water which is hard is also alkaline, because the bicarbonates act as buffers to acidic substances such as dissolved carbon dioxide; but a soft water is not necessarily acid. Soft waters usually have a low total salt concentration. Acid waters may contain dissolved organic matter: it is possible that these organic substances cause their low pH (high acidity), but this has still to be properly investigated.

Water chemistry data are not easy to come by and we are grateful to those who have provided the information used in making map VI. The values plotted there are those for "total hardness" (temporary plus permanent). Most of this "hardness" is usually temporary hardness due to calcium carbonate, and it is expressed as the equivalent amount of calcium carbonate as parts per million (ppm) of

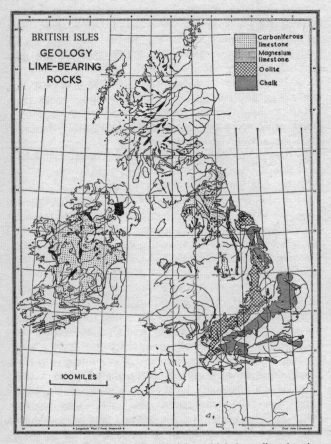

IV.   Geology. Regions of British Isles which have lime-bearing rocks

water by weight. As water samples are most usually ana-
lysed because their composition is of interest to water
undertakings or to industrial consumers, the geographical
distribution of our information is quite different from that
for our map of trout growth. There are plenty of figures
for the south and east of England and for the Midlands

and southern end of the Pennines. Thanks to those who have been interested in a possible relation between trout growth and water composition, we have quite a bit of information about trout waters also, but there are gaps where we should welcome further information.

When map VI is compared with map IV it is clear that the chemistry of the water is related to the rocks from which it is derived.

In constructing our maps for water hardness (VI) and for trout growth (V) we have used five categories in each and represented them by different symbols. We have figures for both hardness and growth for certain districts, though usually the two do not come from *exactly* the same locality. These are compared in table 18, where the five growth categories are represented by letters *a* to *e* representing increasing average lengths at the age of three years and the five hardness categories are represented by letters A to E to show increasing amounts of calcium carbonate in solution.

The eleven districts in table 18 are listed in an order which represents approximately increasing growth *and* increasing hardness, showing that there is an interesting association between the two. Some rivers rise among non-calcareous rocks and then flow over lime-bearing strata farther downstream so that their waters increase in hardness. There is an increase in the average growth made by the trout (see districts 6, 7 and 8) but this might be ascribed to topographical changes. The remaining eight districts fall into two clear groups: in 1 to 5 inclusive, growth is category *a, b,* or *c* and hardness is category A or B while in districts 9, 10 and 11, growth is category *e* or *d* and hardness is category C, D or E. Maximum growth may occur when hardness is category C but categories A and B of hardness are not associated with growth greater than category *c*. These figures suggest strongly that there is a threshold of hardness at about 150 ppm of calcium carbonate, above which the trout may grow at maximal rates, but below which they are limited in their

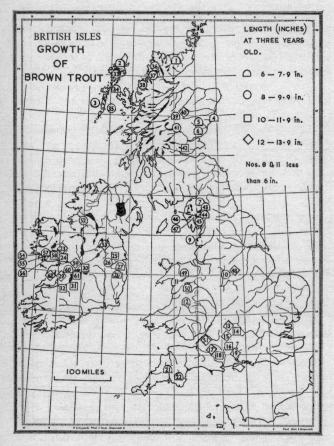

V. Growth of trout, expressed as length attained at 3 years old, in various waters of British Isles. The numbers in the symbols refer to localities listed in appendices III and IV

early growth and likely to be less than ten inches long at three years old, sometimes much shorter. The groups contrasted in Table 18, include lakes and rivers so the differences are not simply a consequence of topography.

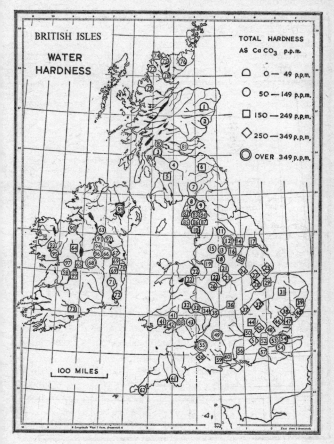

VI. Total hardness, expressed as parts per million of Calcium carbonate, of various waters. (The numbers refer to the names of the waters, see appendix VIII)

We can thus assume an association between water hardness and trout growth. The latter appears to be limited if the value for the former is less than 150 ppm of calcium carbonate; at higher hardness values, trout may display

Table 18. The association between water chemistry and trout growth as illustrated by maps V and VI—

Growth categories average length at end of third year		Water hardness categories calcium carbonate in solution	
up to 6 inches	a	0 to 49 ppm	A
6 to 7·9 inches	b	50 149	B
8 9·9	c	150 249	C
10 11·9	d	250 349	D
12 inches and over	e	more than 350 ppm	E

District or River	Growth category	Hardness category
1. Devonshire (Dartmoor) rivers	b	A
2. River Wye (S. Wales border)	b	A
3. River Dee (N. Wales border)	a/b	A to B downstream
4. Lake District tarns and lakes	a/b/c	A/B
5. East coast rivers (N. Scotland)	b	A/B
6. River Liffey, Ireland	b to c to d	A to B/C downstream
7. River Shannon system, Ireland	b to e	B to E downstream
8. River Derwent, Derbyshire	c or e	A to D downstream
9. Rivers Kennet and Thames	e or d	C/D
10. Hampshire and Dorset rivers	e or d	C
11. River Avon (Bristol) and Blagdon Lake	e	E

maximum rates of growth. It seems from the data from British waters that growth is not proportional to hardness but that there is a threshold value of hardness determining whether good growth can or cannot occur.

After writing the first version of this chapter, I (M.E.B.) visited the Freshwater Fisheries Laboratory at Pitlochry and learnt some very interesting facts about Scottish lochs, especially from Mr. Niall Campbell. None of their local waters has as much as 150 ppm of dissolved calcium carbonate; indeed, the marked differences among them are mainly associated with the acidity of the water. Where streams rise from peat bogs, the water, usually yellow or brown, may have a pH lower than 5.5; the calcium content is usually less than 20 ppm as calcium carbonate. Other streams rising from "hard limestone" may have a low calcium content but are alkaline or neutral and colourless. There are many artificial lochs formed by damming streams for it was fashionable to make a trout pond near a house;

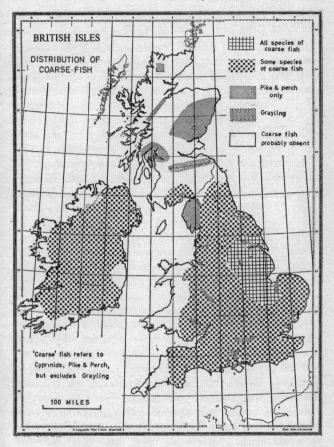

VII. Distribution, much generalised, of coarse fish, i.e. non-salmonids, in British Isles

often they served, and still serve, as domestic water supplies or yield some hydro-electric power. The water type of these lochans depends on the nature of the inflowing streams and on whether the surroundings are boggy or not. Trout growth in acid water is generally not as good as in

T.—F

neutral or alkaline soft water. Acidity is technically difficult to measure so it is difficult to quote figures.

There are several possible reasons for a relation between
growth and water chemistry. First, the composition of the
water may directly affect growing trout; secondly, the composition may directly affect the plants and invertebrate
animals, but the fish indirectly through their food supply;
thirdly, the composition may limit the distribution of competitors or predators, such as roach and pike, and thus
lead to variations in the size of trout populations and so
in their average growth; fourthly, the composition of the
water may be irrelevant, where topographical features
depending on the rocks may lead to differences in food
supply or in fish populations and so to differences in growth
rates. All these effects can be mixed simultaneously in
varying degrees so the situation may be very complicated.

Now if water composition can affect trout growth directly
we might expect to be able to demonstrate this experimentally. The main difficulty is that natural hard and soft
waters seldom occur together sufficiently near laboratories
for them to be used in parallel experiments. It is possible
to prepare artificial hard and soft waters but these might
differ from natural ones in ways affecting the fishes'
growth. Swift, using soft, neutral Windermere water and
hard, alkaline water from near Kendal, has shown that eggs
developing in soft water give rise to alevins which (when
they have used up their yolk and are ready to feed) are
significantly smaller than alevins of the same family grown
in adjacent tanks containing hard water. This is the result
we would expect, because alevins in soft water (with its
lower salt concentration) should need to do more osmotic
work, and thus expend more of their yolk supply on
maintenance and less on growth, than alevins living in hard
water. This should be true, also, of fry and older trout,
which we should expect to grow less well in soft water
if all other factors were equal.

Direct evidence that water composition may affect
growth comes from a comparison of growth in the highly

artificial conditions of hatcheries where the aim is to make the fish grow as well as possible. Most trout hatcheries are in districts where the water is hard. We can compare growth at the Freshwater Biological Association's hatchery at Wraymires, near Windermere, with that at the Bristol Waterworks at Blagdon: trout at the former average three inches at the end of one year while Blagdon trout average four inches. Eggs from these two hatcheries grown at Wraymires gave yearlings of identical size, so the difference should be environmental, but there are differences in average temperature between the two hatcheries which make it difficult to assess accurately the effect of water composition.

Calcium plays an important part in many physiological processes and is a necessary element in the formation of bony skeletons. Bicarbonates and carbonates provide a buffer system which means that changes in the amount of dissolved carbon dioxide or ammonia in water alter the balance between these two salts, but do not alter the pH. The pH may have considerable effects on trout membranes, such as gills and gut lining, and it may affect the red pigment, hæmoglobin, of their blood. But this sort of effect is only likely if the water is very acid or very alkaline. The organic substances giving the yellow colour to bog water are poorly known and may have all sorts of effects. There may be subtle differences between waters corresponding to differences in "trace" elements in the soil. Iodine in solution may have physiological effects; its absence in drinking water is associated with goitre in parts of Derbyshire, for instance. There are few analyses to show how the iodine content of British waters varies, and the few experiments with trout have given inconclusive results and have failed to demonstrate an important effect of this substance on growth.

There are various ways of making waters artificially hard and soft. A naturally soft water can be made hard by adding calcium chloride in solution: Wingfield (1940) treated soft Aberdeen water in this way and grew eight-month-old trout with or without the added calcium and found no real differences between the two groups. One method of softening a natural hard water is to use the zeolite (or Permutit) process, often used for domestic supplies; in this, the water runs through a column of zeolite and the calcium ions are replaced by sodium ions. This makes the water soft to the soap test; it contains quantities of sodium carbonate and bicarbonate and is thus alkaline and well-buffered with high total salt content. Pentelow (1936) used this sort of soft water and compared the growth of eight-month-old trout in it and in untreated chalk-stream water. He found no significant differences in growth, but that it was difficult to keep the fish alive in the softened water. Pentelow also found that eggs could be fertilised equally successfully in the two waters and that they hatched equally successfully.

One of us (M.E.B., unpublished) tried a series of experiments with various artificial waters using fry which had been hatched in Cambridge tap water and were ready to feed. Cambridge tap water is a hard water which has been partially softened by the Permutit process, so that its pH is about 7.7 and it contains 125 ppm of calcium carbonate and also sodium carbonate and bicarbonate.

This tap water was modified in five different ways: (1) Using the Permutit process, all the calcium ions were replaced with sodium to give an alkaline water with high carbonates and total salts but no calcium. (2) This completely softened water was mixed with a small amount of untreated tap water so that about one tenth of the usual amount of calcium was present together with the high sodium, carbonates and total salts. (3) Another softening process manufactured by the Permutit company (the Zeo-Karb process) was used to produce a water in which the sodium and calcium ions had been largely replaced by hydrogen ions; because of the ion exchange, this water contained much dissolved carbon dioxide which would have killed the fish, but this was removed by passing the water through an aspirator through which was bubbled a vigorous supply of compressed air. This water therefore contained about one tenth the usual amount of calcium, low carbonate and low total salts. (4) A calculated amount of hydrochloric or sulphuric acid was added to tap water to replace the carbonates and bicarbonates with chlorides or sulphates, the dissolved carbon dioxide being again blown off in an aspirator. This water then contained high calcium and sodium and total salts but no carbonates. It was intended that the pH should be about 6.2 but the fish produced ammonia and maintained a pH of 7.2 in the tanks. (5) The last water was prepared by diluting tap water with glass-distilled water so that the amounts of calcium, sodium, carbonates and total salts were reduced to thirty per cent of those present in untreated tap water. All these waters were based on Cambridge tap water and presumably contained the same trace elements.

One positive result was that fry were not able to survive in the fully-softened water where all the calcium had been replaced by sodium. Very small fry all died within two days but batches of older fish which had been reared in untreated tap water survived up to seven days, the majority dying on the fifth day after feeding well on the first two days. Pentelow, using older fish, had great difficulty in keeping them alive in this sort of water. Since trout fry survived and grew well when a small amount of tap water was added to the softened water (water (2)), the lethal effect was presumably the result of the absence of calcium and not the high level of sodium. There were no marked differences between the survival of fry in the other waters.

When the rates of growth for three months of the fry living in tap water, and in the four modified waters in which they survived well, were compared, there were only slight differences. Reducing drastically the amount of calcium reduced the growth rate slightly with a threshold effect between 12 and 34 ppm of calcium carbonate. Sodium ions when present in higher proportion than calcium ions slightly depressed the growth rate; the amount of carbonates and bicarbonates seemed to make no difference. The highest values of dissolved calcium were, however, only 125 ppm which is less than the threshold deduced earlier in this chapter, so the control water was not really hard by our present standard.

Water with a low pH was not investigated and there was no alteration in the organic constituents, so these experiments certainly do not prove that there is no effect of water chemistry on growth rates of young trout. The practical difficulties in running this type of experiment can be seen to be considerable!

When trout migrate from fresh water into the sea, they move into water with an increased total amount of salts in solution, particularly of sodium and chloride ions, but sometimes a decrease in the amount of dissolved calcium. Sea trout grow much faster in the sea than in fresh water and brown trout show this increase if they move into brackish water or the sea. Skrochowska reared sea trout entirely in freshwater and found that their growth rates and utilisation of food were very similar to those of brown trout under the same conditions. When thirteen years old, the largest male was about 19 inches long and weighed about $2\frac{1}{2}$ lb. while the largest female measured 17 inches and weighed about 2 lb.; they had spawned annually since they were two and three years old respectively. Skrochowska released pond-reared sea trout, brown trout and hybrids between sea and brown trout, all two years old, into a river; about four per cent were recaptured later. Some had migrated into the Baltic Sea which is less salt than seas round the British coasts. Skrochowska's figures for the hybrid sea $\times$ brown trout (table 19) illustrate how rapidly trout grow in this sea. One brown trout also migrated into the Baltic; after six months in the sea, it was the same size as the two-and-a-half-year-old hybrid trout which had grown as well as pure-bred sea trout in the sea. All these two-and-a-half-year-old trout were larger than pure-bred sea trout reared for thirteen years entirely in freshwater. Of course, there are very marked differences in food supply available for fish in the sea and in freshwater and much

Table 19. Average sizes of brown trout × sea trout "hybrids" after different periods spent in the Baltic Sea. (After Skrochowska, 1952)

Age (years)	Period in the Baltic Sea (months)	Length (inches)	Weight (pounds)
$2\frac{1}{2}$	7	20	3
3	12	$27\frac{1}{2}$	7
$3\frac{1}{2}$	18	31	10
4	24	29	$11\frac{1}{4}$

of this striking difference in growth must be due to this— but it is possible that the change in salt concentration also stimulates growth.

To assess whether the food supply varies between hard and soft waters means considering in detail the variations in feeding habits of trout in different waters and at different seasons. This is done in chapter 8 and we will anticipate matters here by stating only that there are some differences in feeding habits (i.e. the use of small crustaceans, p. 193) that might be significant.

Some aquatic organisms occur only in waters where the calcium content is high: these include many crustaceans and molluscs which need calcium to build exoskeletons and shells. Dr. D. S. Tucker has shown that there is a threshold value in small ponds near Reading of 63 ppm of calcium carbonate above which the fauna (other than insects) is much more diverse than in softer waters. This value is less than half the apparent threshold for good trout growth and higher than the suggested threshold between acid and neutral soft waters (20 ppm). Tucker experimented with flatworms in acid peaty water and found that they died in less than six hours—but could survive for at least 120 hours if the same water was diluted with three times its volume of distilled water and thus became less acid. He concluded that there is some substance, perhaps an organic humic acid, which is lethal to many animals in the concentrations found in bog water. These animals can survive when the substance is diluted. Campbell considers that the amount of winter food is deficient in acid lochs compared with neighbouring neutral lochs, all with soft water. There are great differences in the date at which fish start growing actively in spring and this may be related to the food supply. There are differences in the species of insects and other invertebrates present; snails are usually absent from acid water but the shrimp *Gammarus lacustris* has been introduced into many acid lochs and can survive in acidity down to pH 3. Thus it is possible that trout have more difficulty in finding adequate food in natural soft waters than in hard waters although there are many organisms which appear to be good food which occur widely in both types.

Another experimental approach to the problem of trout growth is through the "fertilisation" of soft, acid waters. This process is equivalent on the field scale to the use of artificial waters in the laboratory, for chemical substances are added to small lakes (tarns or lochs) and subsequent changes in plants, invertebrates and trout are observed. The bearing of these experiments on fishery management is discussed in chapter 10.

Fertilising water is analogous to the process of manuring land in farming; its object is to increase productivity by adding substances which are absent or in short supply but considered to be beneficial to the growth of organisms. In farming, the direct effect is on the plants; the animal stock usually benefits through increased production of fodder, though in some places there may be a direct effect of trace elements on it. In water, also, the added substances affect the water plants directly; and an increase in plant production should lead to an increase in the invertebrate fauna, finally to better growth of carnivorous animals such as trout. However, there may be a direct effect of substances in the water on both the invertebrates and the fishes. The substances added to trout waters are usually agricultural fertilisers, usually containing calcium, nitrogen and phosphorus, and sometimes potassium, in a variety of combinations. The results are often difficult to interpret even when there has been adequate sampling before and after treatment.

The Freshwater Biological Association investigated Three Dubs Tarn, a fish pond of four acres near Windermere; this has a natural trout population maintained by spawning in two of its inflowing becks. Its water is very soft (about 3 ppm of calcium carbonate) with much dissolved organic matter. Bonemeal was added in April in 1937, 1939, 1941 and 1944; it dissolved slowly, and alkalinity determination gave 19.5 ppm of calcium carbonate four months after the first treatment. Dr. Macan observed that after the first two applications the fauna of the bottom mud had increased significantly. For instance, the pea mussel *Pisidium* was ten times as abundant, and the spread of the alga *Nitella* probably allowed some larval insects to increase their range so that the mayfly *Cloëon*, for instance, became more abundant.

The growth of the trout was studied by reading scales from fish caught mainly by annual seine-nettings in spring, some by angling. There were clear differences from year to year, perhaps related to fluctuations in the population. The fish have a characteristic pattern of quite good growth in their first two years, with a decrease in the third year and a steady decline thereafter; they probably spawn at four years old. There were instances of significantly increased growth immediately after the applications of bonemeal; after the first treatment all year classes showed better growth but later there was no consistent trend. Two-year-old fish were about two inches longer in years near the end of the observations than at the beginning but older fish showed less increase in average length. Frost and Smyly (1952) suggested that the increase in bottom fauna might have provided more food for the smaller, younger fish but might not have helped the larger ones; the tarn is deficient in suitable food for these older fish. Thus, this experiment showed that the addition of fertiliser on this scale to this type of pond did not produce larger fish for the angler.

The Freshwater Fisheries Laboratory, Pitlochry, have investigated many lochs—using various combinations of fertiliser and observing the levels of plant and animal communities before and after the application. In the fishless Loch Kinardochy, the bottom fauna increased significantly and the numbers of the shrimp *Gammarus* at one sampling site were 21.7 per square foot before, 89.6 in the year following fertilisation, and 133 two years later. In small lochs holding slow-growing trout in the Scourie district of Sutherland, there was some improvement of growth in all the treated lochs, but the time before this became apparent and the time during which it persisted varied. It became clear that fertiliser must be applied regularly to maintain good growth. After fertilisation the trout remained relatively small even though there had been marked improvement—thus, three-year-old fish averaged nearly 10 oz. in Daimh Mhor in 1957 compared with 4½ oz. in 1954.

We discuss the relationships between trout and other fishes in chapter 9. Since a difference in fish fauna is one of the differences between hard and soft waters, we must refer to it here. There is a greater variety of fishes in hard waters where the normal fauna includes a large number belonging to the family Cyprinidæ (coarse fish). Where the water flows slowly, or is still, it seems that trout cannot compete successfully; good trout fishing is only possible if coarse fishes are restricted in numbers. Trout can grow very well in hard waters but their survival in numbers sufficient to satisfy anglers depends on human control of the other fishes. In soft waters, on the other hand, there are few competing species, which probably have little effect on trout growth. Many soft waters contain only trout, for instance many of the small lochs and tarns of Scotland and the Lake District.

When there are no competing species of fish, there may be very large numbers of trout. Such populations may be

stunted because (it is suggested) they are overcrowded:
too many trout compete for a limited food supply. Pentelow
(1944) suggested that natural soft waters often include
vast areas of gravel ideal for spawning sites, while trout
populations living in hard waters often have much restricted spawning facilities so that their annual recruitment
may be less.

We shall discuss in chapter 9 how the behaviour of trout
limits the numbers that live in a stream. If there is over-
production of eggs, there will be a very great mortality of
young fry—reducing the population to the maximum tolerable number: but this number may still be so large that
individuals cannot grow fast because of mutual disturbance and limitation of food supply. We know very little
about the behaviour of fry in still water. They may be less
aggressive than normal, particularly if the water is coloured
as it is in many peaty lochs. Campbell has recorded surprisingly good growth in some soft water lochs. Some
which have no spawning burn are stocked with unfed fry,
and it is possible that wild fry move into the other lochs
very early. Fry in lochs need to expend less food on energy
required to maintain station (and perhaps also less on
aggressive behaviour) than those in streams, but they still
need to seek their food. By living in lochs they also
avoid exposure to high and fluctuating temperatures, which
may explain why they grow better. Table 21 includes
several examples of this good growth which we shall discuss
in more detail later.

Frost and Smyly (1952) found that the rate of growth of
trout in Three Dubs Tarn probably varied inversely with
the population density. They suggest that differences in
growth between trout in this tarn, Yew Tree Tarn and
Windermere may be related to differences in population
and in available food supply. Yew Tree Tarn is much the
same size as Three Dubs but is probably very heavily
populated because of its excellent spawning facilities;
minnows are present, also, to compete for food. Windermere is, of course, very much larger than the others, with

a greater variety and size of food organisms, but its trout spend at least their first year in feeder streams where their diet is more restricted. All these water bodies contain very soft neutral water and the lengths of trout in them are given in table 20.

Table 20. Lengths (inches) of brown trout of various ages from two tarns and a lake in the Lake District—

Age	Yew Tree Tarn	Three Dubs Tarn	Windermere
end of year 1	2	$3\frac{1}{2}$	$2\frac{1}{4}$
2	$4\frac{1}{2}$	7	$5\frac{1}{2}$
3	$6\frac{1}{2}$	$8\frac{1}{2}$	$8\frac{1}{2}$
4	$7\frac{3}{4}$	$9\frac{1}{2}$	$11\frac{1}{4}$
5	$8\frac{1}{2}$	$10\frac{1}{2}$	14

In experimenting with reduced populations, it is essential to control the recruitment of fry as well as to cut down the number of older fish. Where only the population of older fish is reduced, results are very disappointing. Thus, in a mountain tarn in Norway, Dahl noted that the total weight of trout per area remained the same when a crowded population was cropped at a high rate as with a low rate of cropping, but the proportion of young, faster-growing fish increased. The maximum size attained remained much the same, as did the average condition (K) of the trout.

Campbell has shown that control of recruitment can lead to substantial improvement of trout growth in neutral lochs. The control is achieved either by planting known numbers of unfed fry in lochs where there is no natural spawning, or by restricting access to spawning burns so that the number of unfed fry produced is severely limited. Some relevant figures are quoted in table 21. In Fincastle Loch and Loch Lanish, similar chemically, the marked difference in trout size attained in three years' growth is probably the result of differences in population density. Mr. Campbell told me that he has regulated the recruitment of fry into Fincastle Loch at different levels over a period of years, and has found a marked association between his estimate of the population and the average weight of fish caught by anglers. The greater the recruitment, the higher the population and the poorer the subsequent growth of trout.

Table 21. Length (inches) of brown trout at the end of their third year in small Scottish lochs which differ in water hardness and in spawning facilities. (After Campbell, 1961)

Loch	Hardness ppm	Length (inches)	Sample size	Spawning facilities	Stocking with unfed fry
Lanish	78	14·2	11	none	light
nan Ealachan	27	12·8	19	poor	none
Borralie	109	12·6	15	poor	annual
Unnamed	<1	12	3	none	none
Fincastle	61	8·7	168	good	none
Glutt	<1	8·3	9	none	occasional
Strathkyle	4	8·1	163	good	none
an Daim	44	7·4	100	good	none

In acid lochs growth may be very good, but the density of trout must be extremely low. Thus growth is good in the very soft acid waters of Unnamed Loch—where only three fish have been caught recently by anglers and fleets of gill-nets set on two nights caught nothing. In Glutt Loch however—which is also very soft and acid with a low trout population—nets in one night caught eight fish which, at three years old, were only 8 inches long. An example of spectacular growth at very low population density in soft neutral water is provided by the four brown and five speckled trout left, by mistake, in Scale Tarn (near Windermere) close to Three Dubs Tarn and very similar to it. At 2+years old, two of the brown trout measured 14½ and 15½ inches in length and weighed 1½ and 1¾ lb. respectively.

We have not found good examples of growth at different

population levels in hard waters. It is possible that natural recruitment in these always yields fewer fry than the number which would mean competition limiting growth.

Southern (1932), in his discussion of the differences between trout growth in acid and alkaline waters in Ireland, showed that the trout living in these waters differ in spawning history as well as growth rate. We have already discussed in chapter 6 how the observed association between slow growth, early maturity and short life in soft waters could be the result of natural selection. The age of maturity is determined genetically and the types of life history of wild trout in different waters are well adapted relative to the natural growth rate in them. Selection must account for the fact that slow-growing, early maturing fish produce relatively larger eggs than do fast-growing, late maturing trout. The small trout of soft waters all produce fewer eggs at each spawning than do the larger older trout of hard waters. Since it seldom spawns more than two or three times, each small fish must lay many fewer eggs in its life than each large one. If it be true that soft waters are overcrowded because of over-successful spawning, then (since each individual small fish produces few eggs) their spawning populations must be vastly more numerous than those of hard waters. Slow growth in soft waters seems to be environmentally determined. It is possible, indeed, to alter the environment so that fish resident in soft water will grow faster until they are ready to spawn but, since they naturally mature when small, it is unlikely that any such treatment will make them grow as large as can those typical of hard waters.

We should like to be able to say exactly why trout usually grow faster in hard than in soft waters but there is as yet no simple answer. The low level of calcium and the presence, sometimes, of organic acids may affect the soft water trout directly or through their food supply, but the topography of trout waters differs in calcareous and non-calcareous districts and this affects spawning facilities and territories for small fish. The nature of the rocks also determines whether streams run off the surface or are spring fed. Spring fed streams must show less fluctuation in water level and water temperature than the others. All these differences may influence the growth rates of trout and the existing situation is the result of an interaction of all these factors.

It is possible to produce fast-growing trout in soft waters but this involves either regular expenditure on mineral fertilisers or being content with a small number of large trout and many hours of unsuccessful angling. Many soft water rivers, of course, are famous for salmon and sea trout. It might be worth encouraging these fish and trying to eliminate the resident small brown trout. Meanwhile, many soft waters (both neutral and acid, including innumerable tarns and lochs) offer to anglers the possibility of catching large numbers of small trout in surroundings of great natural beauty away from crowds and traffic. This may well be sufficient compensation for the absence of specimen fish.

Chapter Eight

The Trout's Food

The troughte . . . he is a right deyntous fyssh and also a right fervente-byter. *Dame Juliana Berners*, 1496

The food and feeding habits of the brown trout have long claimed the attention of the angler and the field naturalist. Their observations differ widely in kind and value and are usually recorded in angling books and periodicals. To these records, often much scattered, have been added in recent years results of the investigations in field and laboratory of fishery scientists. Thus we have now much and varied information on the food of the trout.

In spite of these many records, great gaps still remain in our knowledge. We cannot present a complete picture of how and why trout food varies in quantity and quality from place to place and from time to time. Trout caught by angling may represent a biased sample of feeding fish because the angler chooses his lures to suit his idea of what the fish will try to eat. Diet changes during the year because some foods are of limited and seasonal occurrence: stomachs collected, for instance, during a summer angling holiday give but little real information on the feeding of trout. Feeding habits differ with the time of day so stomachs of trout caught only during the evening rise give only a limited picture. Moreover, the number of stomachs examined is often small. There are remarkably few series of observations covering all seasons and including trout caught by methods which ought not to select those with special feeding habits. For this reason, critical comparisons are difficult to make. Our generalisations, based on limited data, may well be revised after future investigations.

We have already considered the physiology of feeding in chapter 1; now we will look at what a trout eats and its feeding behaviour in river and lake. Some results of examining stomach contents of trout from different waters are given later (p. 288), and the method of assessing such contents is described in the appendix VII.

The trout is essentially carnivorous. Most of the animals it eats are aquatic; a few are terrestrial. The aquatic invertebrates on its food list are usually insects, molluscs and crustaceans. The insects may be either aquatic for the whole of their lives, as are water boatmen (Corixidæ) and beetles (Coleoptera), or only in their nymphal or larval and pupal stages—the adult "hatching" (emerging) from the nymph or the pupa to become a terrestrial insect—as are the mayflies (Ephemeroptera), stoneflies (Plecoptera), alder-flies (Neuroptera), dragonflies (Odonata) and two-winged flies (Diptera). The most important of the Diptera are the blackfly or reed smut (*Simulium*) and the non-biting midges (Chironomidæ). Trout feed on all stages of all these insects. The aquatic molluscs eaten are snails (Gastropoda) and the small pea mussels (Lamellibranchiata). The crustaceans include larger animals such as the crayfish (*Astacus*), the freshwater shrimp (*Gammarus*) and the water slater or hog louse (*Asellus*); microscopic crustaceans, often called "water fleas," (Cladocera and Copepoda mainly) are found in still waters where they often form the greater part of the zooplankton, which in a few lakes includes the large shrimp *Mysis*. The phantom larva *Chaoborus* is a planktonic larval Dipterous insect. The remaining aquatic invertebrates which the trout eats are "worms" including bristle worms (Oligochæta), flatworms (Turbellaria) and leeches (Hirudinea). Vertebrates found in the food are mainly fish, some-

---

[1] Mayfly connotes to anglers only one genus of the Ephemeroptera, namely *Ephemera*, the large "Mayfly." In this book, "mayfly" covers all genera of the Ephemeroptera. The sub-imago of these is known to anglers as the "dun" and the imago as the "spinner."

times frogs and newts and their tadpoles. Some of the food organisms are illustrated in figs. 19 to 21.

The terrestrial organisms found in trout stomachs are mostly insects and include many kinds of Diptera, some aphids and tree bugs (Hemiptera), and some land beetles. Animals such as earthworms, slugs, woodlice, spiders and even mammals (mice) are eaten by trout in time of high water, particularly when rivers are in flood.

The trout is not normally a vegetarian. Weed fragments, moss capsules, etc., found in trouts' stomachs are probably taken while catching animals. Trout from a Welsh lake, however, have been recorded as containing semi-digested water plants. The stomach of one caught in the River Brathay was full of *Nostoc*, a round gelatinous alga—perhaps the fish had mistaken it for a mollusc, which *Nostoc* closely resembles in appearance.

The newly hatched alevin feeds on its yolk sac for some weeks (see chapter 4); when the yolk is almost gone, the small fry emerges from the gravel and begins to feed. Since the alevin uses yolk more slowly when the water is colder, the dates at which fry begin to feed vary from place to place and from year to year. Generally, the start of feeding is at any time between March and May.

The feeding habits of trout fry were observed from early April to August in Black Brows Beck. This small stream near Windermere is about six to eight feet wide and normally about six inches deep. In a pool about ten feet long were a dozen or so fry, about an inch long when they were first seen. The fry which were separated from each other by three or four inches, were poised in mid-water and had definite stations (see chapter 9, pp. 218-22). The larger individuals were stationed where the current was stronger, at the tail of a little run where the water swirled round a stone, while a smaller fish occupied a shallow tiny backwater. Each kept to its own territory and chased away any intruders. Every now and then a fry would dart to right or left, presumably to intercept some object drifting down with the current. Frequently a fry would rise to the surface,

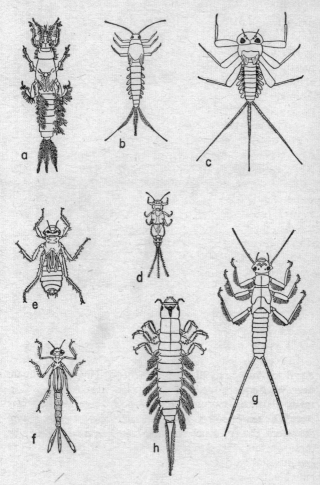

19.   Invertebrates eaten by trout: larval aquatic insects. Mayfly nymphs a-d ; a. *Ephemera* (24 mm) burrowing, b. *Baëtis* (8 mm) swimming, c. *Ecdyonurus* (12 mm) stone clinging, d *Caenis* 8 (mm) in slit. Dragonfly nymphs e. and f. (17-50 mm) primarily weed dwelling, g. Stonefly nymph (5-25 mm) among stones, h. Alderfly larva (17 mm) mud dwelling

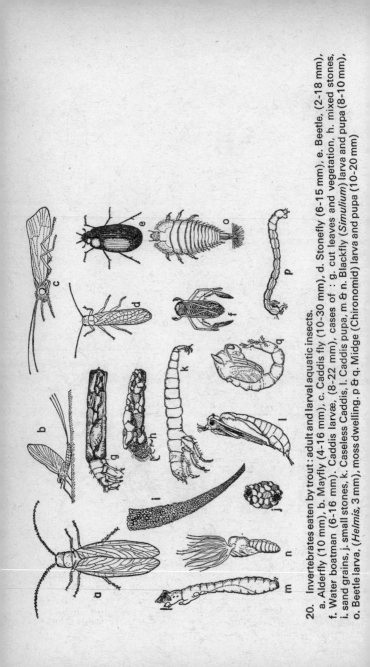

20. Invertebrates eaten by trout : adult and larval aquatic insects.
 a. Alderfly (10 mm), b. Mayfly (4-16 mm), c. Caddis fly (10-30 mm), d. Stonefly (6-15 mm), e. Beetle, (2-18 mm),
 f. Water boatman (6-16 mm). Caddis larvæ, (8-22 mm), cases of : g. cut leaves and vegetation, h. mixed stones,
 i. sand grains, j. small stones, k. Caseless Caddis, l. Caddis pupa, m & n. Blackfly (*Simulium*) larva and pupa (8-10 mm),
 o. Beetle larva, (*Helmis*, 3 mm), moss dwelling. p & q. Midge (Chironomid) larva and pupa (10-20 mm)

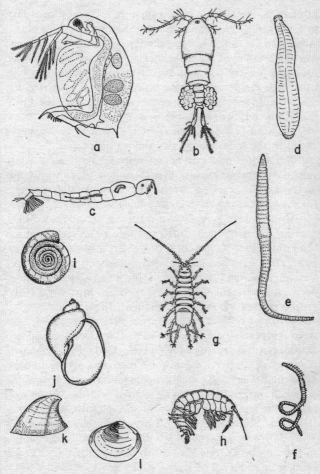

21. Invertebrates eaten by trout: belonging to various groups Zooplankton a-c; a. Cladoceran *Daphnia* (2.5-3.5 mm), b. Copepod *Cyclops* (1.5 mm), c. Planktonic insect Phantom larva (9 mm), d. Leech (50 mm), e. Bristle worm (60-80 mm), f. Tubificid worm (8 mm), g. Water Slater (*Asellus,* 8 mm), h. Shrimp (*Gammarus,* 10 mm), i. Ramshorn snail (5.7 mm), j. Wandering snail (11 mm), k. Freshwater limpet (5 mm), l. Pea mussel (3.5 mm)

often with the same downstream turn of an older trout, to catch some object that came floating down over its head. After a sortie to the surface, the fry returned to its station where it swallowed or, sometimes, spat out its capture. The food of these fry was thus the "living drift" in the stream, aquatic or terrestrial animals which were being carried by the current, submerged or on the surface, past the little fish. Only on two occasions was a fry seen to attempt to "nose out" an organism from the bottom of the beck and then the food animal was moving about.

From August onwards, the fry were seldom seen at their stations, probably because they were now more wary and disappeared at one's approach. They were certainly present for they darted out from cover when disturbed. They were occasionally seen poised in the stream, feeding, as when younger, on the "living drift" and sometimes seen hunting food organisms. As a trout grows older, it tends to become more of a food seeker, probably because it spends more time in pools and quiet waters, but the habit of feeding on what is brought by the current, either in mid-water or on the surface, persists throughout its life.

Samples of fry and yearlings from Black Brows Beck and from Kingswell Beck, north Westmorland, were examined throughout the year by McCormack (1962). Fig. 22 shows the stomach contents of fish which measured between 1 and $2\frac{3}{4}$ inches. They fed mainly upon larval aquatic insects, especially midge larvæ, mayfly nymphs (chiefly *Baëtis*) and caddis larvæ; they also ate other dipterous and beetle larvæ and shrimps—terrestrial organisms were negligible. The relative importance of the different organisms differed in the two becks, this is probably related to Black Brows being a soft water (12.7 ppm $CaCO_3$) and Kingswell a hard water (160 ppm $CaCO_3$). Some of the animals eaten are large so the fry do not select small food; they do sometimes spit out morsels which they have seized, so they do exercise some selection. The diet of a few fry I examined from the River Brathay (Windermere) and the River Forss (Scotland) is much like that found for Black Brows Beck.

The food of thirty-five small fry, less than 1 inch long, which had only just begun to feed in Black Brows Beck contained many midge larvæ (about sixty per cent of their diet) and the rest consisted of mayfly nymphs, shrimps and springtails (Collembola). There is no evidence that these very young fry select special foods for their first meal nor do they choose the smaller organisms.

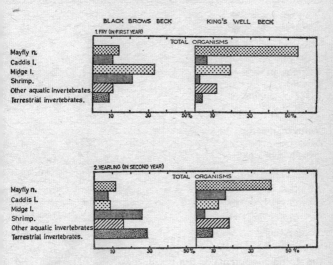

22.   Food of trout, fry and yearlings, in two becks. Different food organisms expressed as a percentage of the total number eaten. (McCormack, 1962)

In the food of trout in their second year of life (1+fish, 2½ to 5 inches long) in Black Brows and Kingswell Becks mayfly nymphs, caddis larvæ, midge larvæ and shrimps were the main items still but the proportion of midge larvæ was much less than in the diet of fry. Earthworms and terrestrial insects made up one third of the animals eaten by yearlings in Black Brows Beck but were seldom eaten in Kingswell Beck.

Table 22. Invertebrates eaten by trout compared with those in the bottom fauna

A In still water (Three Dubs Tarn, Frost & Smyly, 1950)	% number eaten	% number in bottom fauna
Midge l.	11·5	60·1
Midge p.	23·8	—
Mayfly n.	10·6	7·0
Caddis l.	24·7	2·0
Caddis p.	—	—
Stonefly n.	—	—
Beetle a.	+	+
Blackfly (Simulium)	—	absent
Dragonfly n.	3·0	2·1
Alderfly n.	8·2	0·8
Water boatmen	1·4	4·8
Mites	+	2·0
Pea mussels	16·2	19·4
Shrimps	+	+
Worms (Oligochætes)	—	1·1
Leeches	—	+

Older trout eat much the same kinds of animals as younger fish but take a greater variety of bottom living organisms, both larvæ and adult. More species are taken from each group (as from mayflies and caddises) and molluscs and vertebrates, chiefly fish, may be included in the diet. On the whole, older trout eat more surface food of aquatic origin, such as caddis flies, blackflies, winged midges and the duns and spinners of mayflies. We shall discuss later how the kinds and proportions of different animals eaten as food vary in different places and at different seasons.

First let us consider where the food animals come from. Ideally, we should compare the results of a complete faunal survey with an examination of stomachs collected at the same time and place but this is rarely possible.

Table 22 (continued)

B Running water (R. Don, Aberdeenshire, Neill, 1938)	% number eaten	% number in bottom fauna
Other Diptera l. (*chiefly midges*)	+	20·6
Other Diptera p. (*chiefly midges*)	1·2	1·6
Mayfly n.	19·0	35·8
Caddis l.	0·8	2·7
Caddis p.	1·5	1·2
Stonefly n.	+	1·1
Beetle l. and a.	+	2·5
Blackfly l. and a.	75·4	21·3
Dragonfly n	—	—
Alderfly l.	—	—
Water boatmen	—	—
Mites	—	+
Snails	+	+
Shrimps	1·1	0·9
Worms	—	11·0
Leeches	+	+

Table 22 gives two lists of animals found in trout stomachs and of the invertebrate animals found in the bottom fauna of the water in which the trout were caught. It shows that trout in a river and in a lake feed on a variety of animals, and that those eaten are of much the same kind in the two environments and mostly belong to the invertebrate bottom fauna. There is a close but not exact correspondence between the list of animals present in the stomachs and in the bottom fauna. This is partly because trout eat terrestrial animals and also aquatic animals which do not live on the bottom, such as zooplankton in lakes. But it is clear that the *greater* part of the trout's diet consists of animals which live on the bottom of stream, river or lake.

What makes trout eat these organisms? The feeding

behaviour of fry strongly suggests that movement (either of the organism itself or imparted to it by flow of water) is the characteristic which makes an animal "food" to these little fish. Later on, when the young fish seek food among stones, movement is probably still the most important attribute which indicates that an object is edible. Older trout probably respond to a number of visual properties of the animal as well as to its movement. A mayfly nymph looks different from a shrimp, and there are differences in shape and colour between different species of mayfly and also differences in the way all these animals move. A trout whose stomach is not full is likely to attempt to feed if it sees an object with the visual characteristics of a food animal. The artificial "wet fly" is sometimes intended to resemble in shape and size an organism on which the trout are feeding but by "working" his flies, the angler increases the resemblance by giving them the movement which is so important in stimulating the trout to feed. The "dry fly" usually has a much closer resemblance to the natural food animal than the wet fly and the angler does not usually give it movement so this implies that visual characteristics are important in the trout's recognition of this food. Some food animals, such as the freshwater limpet attached to its stone, seem to show little or no movement and must be recognised by some other attribute. It seems that sometimes trout will only feed when they see objects conforming to a detailed and specific visual pattern while at other times they will chase any object, regardless of its shape, provided that it is moving.

In table 22 some animals are found more, others less frequently in the stomachs than in the fauna. The use that a trout makes of a given species can be expressed in the "forage ratio":

$$\text{Forage ratio} = \frac{\text{Average percentage of species A in stomachs of trout}}{\text{Average percentage of species A in bottom fauna}}$$

This ratio is high for some species and low for others. The species with high forage ratios are usually conspicuous while the others are not: a completely concealed species has a forage ratio of o. The habits and life history of the animals in the community must thus be considered when assessing the value of the bottom fauna as food for trout. Allen realised this and used the term "availability factor" instead of forage ratio; we prefer the latter because it implies that it is the feeding behaviour of the fish which determines whether it is more or less likely to eat certain animals. Neill used the expression "coefficient of accessibility" and assessed this from his knowledge of the biology of the food animals; his coefficient varies in a similar way to the forage ratio.

The forage ratio of any species depends on its habit, size, appearance and life history. Animals which live in exposed positions and are active or conspicuous, or both, have a high forage ratio; for example, nymphs of the mayfly *Baëtis* and larvæ of the blackfly *Simulium*. Caddis larvæ with hard, strong cases can be easily seen by trout, but only larger fish can swallow them; so their forage ratio is generally low. Animals which live in exposed positions but are inactive or inconspicuous, like some stonefly nymphs and some midge larvæ and limpets, have a medium forage ratio, whereas those living in sheltered positions, such as net-spinning caddis larvæ (e.g. *Hydropsyche*), nymphs of the mayfly *Caenis* and various larval Diptera and shrimps, have low forage ratios. However, when the *Caenis* nymph emerges into the adult, which anglers call "the fisherman's curse," it leaves the shelter of silt and becomes visible to the trout and its forage ratio becomes high, as witness the trout stomachs packed with *Caenis* nymphs after a "hatch" of these mayflies on a July evening. Animals with a forage ratio close to o are those which normally burrow, such as bristle worms, some species of pea mussels *Pisidium* and the Mayfly nymph *Ephemera*; the latter's forage ratio turns high when the adults emerge.

Allen gives arithmetical values for forage ratios for salmon parr in the River Eden which would probably also apply to trout.

Forage ratios show that the primary factor determining what the trout will eat is probably the availability (accessibility) of food species. Yet fly fishermen are familiar with the sight of a trout rising persistently to one particular species of "fly," perhaps the dun of a mayfly *Baëtis*, whilst another fly, perhaps the blackfly *Simulium*, is equally abundant and available on the water but is ignored. An autopsy of such trout might show that ninety per cent of its stomach contents are *Baëtis* and only ten per cent *Simulium*, and that it was evidently not feeding at random but was selecting the dun and not the blackfly. Allen (1941) discussed selection in the feeding behaviour of salmon parr and found that it was apparent when stomachs contained many food animals but when there were only a few animals in the stomach there had been random feeding. Fish feeding vigorously tend to select; those that have just begun to feed or are feeding slowly feed at random.

The ability to select and concentrate on a single species of food animal is of value to trout because it enables it to exploit a transitory but abundant food supply such as that made available by a "hatch of fly." Many aquatic insects emerge or metamorphose at definite and limited times of year; the "rise" of the mayfly *Ephemera* is an obvious instance. Many emerge at particular times of day, such as the Yellow Evening Dun (*Ephemerella notata*), which does so just before dark. Large numbers of animals are simultaneously exposed to the hazards of moving from an aquatic habitat to air; chief among these hazards is the hungry trout which takes full advantage of this abundant food supply.

When the selected animals are blackfly larvæ, the trout concentrates not on a transitory source of food but on one which is relatively permanent. The value of selection may be that the trout uses its energy more economically by repeating the same movement many times to snap up larvæ instead of changing its feeding movements for different kinds of animals. The full stomachs of trout so feeding testify to the efficiency of this method.

When two kinds of fly are equally numerous on the water and a trout chooses only one or the other, it must be responding to a highly specific visual stimulus. The dry fly anglers' theory of exact imitation is based on this assumption. When no animal is particularly abundant, the stimulus needed to start feeding is likely to be much less specific and the trout will then take any animals which are available more or less at random.

To summarise the relationship between the trout's diet and the animals in its environment, we can say that the trout is an unspecialised carnivore which feeds mainly by sight. It eats a greater proportion of those animals which are easily captured and conspicuous than those which are concealed or difficult to obtain. At times, however, the fish may feed exclusively on one species even though others are equally available.

Tables of stomach contents and other published records show that the main constituents of the trout's diet in river and lake are animals which live on the bottom either permanently or for part of their lives. Seasonal changes in the diet, shown in tables 23 and 24, are primarily expressions of changes in the kinds and numbers of bottom living invertebrate animals; but other sources of food may be exploited at certain seasons or in certain waters.

In the River Liffey, at Ballysmuttan (see table 23), aquatic insect larvæ are the main food throughout the year. There are few molluscs and no large crustaceans so the permanent bottom fauna contributes little to the diet. At Straffan, farther downstream, the diet is similar, but there are differences in the degree to which particular insect groups are exploited—thus stonefly nymphs are more frequently eaten at Ballysmuttan. These differences can be associated with the relative abundance of the different insects in the fauna at the two places (see table 32). At Straffan, certain members of the permanent bottom fauna, such as snails, cray-

Table 23. Seasonal food. River Liffey, Ballysmuttan.
Percentage composition of the food of trout during each month. The + indicates less than 1 per cent

Food organism	Month and number of fish examined											
	Jan. 9	Feb. 33	Mar. 18	Apl. 28	May 20	June 33	July 49	Aug. 37	Sept. 39	Oct. 37	Nov. 19	Dec. 18
Mayfly n.	2	+	—	3	6	34	34	8	13	8	5	6
Stonefly n.	90	75	74	28	10	2	15	8	+	6	46	64
Caddis l. and p.	4	13	16	4	7	5	7	22	14	15	22	13
Midge l.	2	+	+	38	29	31	9	33	27	8	4	5
Blackfly l. and p. (Simulium)	2	+	+	4	10	18	+	+	9	+	+	8
Various Diptera l. and p.	+	8	6	16	9	+	+	+	7	+	4	3
Beetle adult	+	4	4	+	15	4	8	+	5	10	+	+
Beetle l.	—	+	+	+	+	2	5	+	+	+	4	+
Snail	+	+	+	+	+	+	+	+	+	+	+	+
Worms	+	+	—	+	—	+	—	—	+	—	—	—
Fish	+	+	—	—	—	+	—	—	—	—	—	+
Surface insects—aquatic origin	—	+	+	5	10	4	15	12	10	16	9	+
Surface insects—terrestrial origin	+	+	—	2	4	+	7	16	15	37	10	+

Table 24. Seasonal food. Windermere.
Percentage composition of the food of trout during each month (based on Allen, 1938)

Food organism	Jan.	Feb.	Mar.	Apl.	May	June	July	Aug.	Sept.	Oct.	Nov.	Dec.
Month and number of trout examined	58	23	34	27	46	32	18	9	11	9	69	10
Permanent bottom fauna:												
Water Slater (*Asellus*)	15	16	1	8	4	—	1	—	1	1	54	65
Shrimp (*Gammarus*)	71	41	12	8	25	4	1	—	10	19	17	29
Snail (*Lymnæa*)	4	24	8	6	2	1	11	4	4	33	4	—
Temporary bottom fauna:												
Midge pupæ	—	+	54	2	2	—	+	1	+	—	—	—
Stonefly (*Nemoura*) nymphs	+	3	6	31	4	—	—	—	—	—	+	1
Caddis (*Leptocerus*) larvæ	1	+	1	5	15	37	36	—	2	3	+	+
Char eggs	—	—	—	—	—	—	—	—	—	—	13	—
Surface food: (Largely terrestrial)	—	1	2	22	53	32	25	93	73	2	2	—

fish, shrimps and slaters, are frequently eaten in winter and early spring.

In Windermere, changes in the type of food eaten correspond closely to seasonal changes in the bottom fauna (see table 24). Between October and February, the trout feed principally on snails, water slaters and shrimps; these are present in stomachs throughout the year, but most numerous in winter. In the spring, the trout eat aquatic insects, chiefly stonefly nymphs, caddis larvæ and midge pupæ. These insect larvæ are numerous throughout the winter but they are small and only become large enough to attract trout in spring. The stonefly *Nemoura* emerges in March, April and May and midge pupæ ascend to the surface then so these are particularly available to the trout. In summer, from May to July, the larval caddis *Leptocerus* is a characteristic food and it has probably reached its largest size then. In late July, another caddis, *Limnophilus*, is eaten as its pupæ emerge at dusk. Trout feed on char eggs in November and December when these fish spawn in shallow water.

The seasonal diet shows clearly the importance of abundance, as well as availability, in determining the kind of organism the trout eats. Adults of aquatic insects are eaten at the surface of the water at certain times of year. Trout living in lakes seem to feed less on this type of food than do those in rivers, probably because there are greater numbers of these insects per unit area in rivers than in lakes. Moreover, a river's flow tends to concentrate this food, which may be dispersed widely over a lake. If there is a very heavy "hatch," as during the emergence of the Mayfly *Ephemera* on a lake, the numbers may be sufficient to form local concentrations which certainly attract the trout. In rivers aquatic insects are more varied in species and more numerous than in lakes, so the season for surface feeding is longer because the times of emergence of the various species may cover many months. There will thus nearly always be some "fly on the water" to encourage surface feeding.

Lakes with salmonids and some coarse fish

9 *Above,* Windermere, English Lake District, looking north. This deep lake has sandy and silty bays as well as rocky shores. Its main drainage area is mountainous but its water is richer in nutrient salts than that of Wastwater (Pl. 5) because there is more good agricultural land and a much greater human population round its shores. Trout, char, perch and pike are the typical species; salmon pass through; no cyprinids except the minnow. *Below,* Lough Derg, Co. Tipperary. This is a shallower lake, in richer land, with many more silted bays and water much richer in nutrients. Although there is good trout-fishing here, pike and perch thrive; the pollan and cyprinids such as bream and rudd, are also present

Man-made lowland lakes

10 *Above,* Filby Broad, Norfolk. This very shallow lake lies in flat, rich, agricultural country, with shores silted and fringed with reeds. These are cyprinid waters *par excellence;* pike and perch are also present. No trout. *Below,* Eye Brook Reservoir, near Corby, Northants, formed by damming a small tributary of the River Welland. In good agricultural land, its shores are silted and weedy. If this were a natural lake, it would be a cyprinid water, and roach are in fact very numerous; but it is managed so that there is excellent fishing for both brown and rainbow trout

Mountain trout streams
11 *Above,* Mossburn, tributary of the River Tees, at Moor House, Westmorland. This small stream flows through bleak country at an altitude of 1,800 ft. Trout and bullheads are the only fish present. *Below,* Upper River Liffey at Ballysmuttan, Co. Wicklow—a typical acid-water locality, at 700 ft. This river rises in granite mountains and flows through peat bogs, moorland, and rough pasture. Trout are the only fish present

12 Trout and grayling zones in the Yorkshire dales. *Above,* River Swale above Stonesdale. *Below,* River Wharfe at Bolton Abbey. The river is wider here and the gradient is less steep; the countryside, though hilly, is better farming land so the water is probably richer in nutrient salts. Trout are present at both places but grayling are to be found at Bolton Abbey but not **at Stonesdale**

13   Trout-with-salmon rivers of the north-east and south-west. *Above,* River Tweed near Melrose, Roxburghshire, flowing through a wide valley with fertile pastures, occasional large trees and woodlands. *Below,* River Barle from Tarr Steps, Somerset. This tributary of the River Exe rises on Exmoor and then flows through a steep-sided, wooded valley typical of many small rivers in south-western England

A limestone trout stream

14 River Dove near Thorpe Cloud, Derbyshire. This famous trout stream flows over mountain limestone which it has dissolved to form a gorge. The clear water has a high calcium content and water plants grow luxuriantly. The trout grow well; grayling are also present

A chalk trout stream

5   River Itchen at Winchester, Hampshire. This is a typical southern stream
fed by springs in the chalk downs. There is a good flow of clear water with a
high calcium content and water plants grow very well. Trout grow well;
grayling are present too

Lowland rivers
16 *Above,* River Avon, near Christchurch, Hampshire. Here the river
meanders through rich agricultural country and is fringed with rushes and
other emergent vegetation. Salmon and sea-trout pass through but the river
is famous here as a coarse fishing water with large barbel and chub and
also pike, perch, dace and roach. *Below,* River Arun, near Arundel, Sussex.
The river here is tidal but the water is fresh. The bottom is muddy and the
banks are fringed with reeds. Bream, roach, chub, dace, pike and perch are
present and sea-trout pass through

Surface feeding on terrestrial insects varies greatly from water to water. It seems to be least frequent in waters where there is a relatively rich bottom fauna, such as Blagdon Lake, Lough Inchiquin (Co. Clare), Malham Tarn, the River Itchen and the River Liffey at Straffan; it is more frequent in less productive waters, such as Windermere, Wise Een Tarn, the upper River Tees and the River Liffey at Ballysmuttan. Of course, the fish may take terrestrial insects incidentally when they are feeding on surface food of aquatic origin. For instance, twenty out of fifty-four trout caught on dry fly on the River Fergus between June and September contained terrestrial insects but the bulk of their stomach contents were Sherry Spinners *Ephemerella ignita* and probably the trout were primarily feeding on these mayflies (appendix VII).

When floods in rivers or the filling up of reservoirs make terrestrial animals such as earthworms, slugs and caterpillars available, these are eaten avidly by the trout regardless of the poverty or abundance of the aquatic fauna.

The diet of trout in lakes may include planktonic crustaceans, water fleas, particularly the cladocerans *Daphnia* and *Bosmina,* and occasionally a few copepods such as *Cyclops* and *Diaptomus.* Zooplankton has been recorded from trout in many British lakes, in Norway, and elsewhere. Allen's seine-caught Windermere trout had eaten very little zooplankton but in forty-one trout of about ¾ lb. caught in one-inch gill-nets during summer months it was the main food eaten. Trout caught on the wet fly may be full of zooplankton, as were fifty-five fish caught in Lough Inchiquin by Southern between April and September (see appendix VII, p. 289. All these were about 12 oz. in weight and larger trout caught at the same time were *not* feeding on zooplankton so perhaps trout in lakes at about this size pass through a phase when they feed on zooplankton. Southern found that trout in Lough Atorick had not eaten zooplankton—but he examined only twenty-two stomachs and they were of rod caught fish.

The absence of planktonic crustaceans from the stomachs of trout in moorland fishponds such as Yew Tree Tarn, Three Dubs Tarn—and particularly Wise Een Tarn, which has been well sampled at all times of year—is rather surprising, since the water flea *Bosmina*, especially, may be very plentiful in the water; similar planktonic cladocera also may be absent from stomachs of trout in Blagdon Reservoir. These small crustaceans are not filtered from the water but are caught individually so that a trout must expend much time and energy to fill its stomach with them. The trout in the tarns had however fed freely on the cladoceran *Eurycercus lamellatus* which lives among weeds and is large, slow-moving, and usually very abundant. It must be far easier to capture than the smaller, more active pelagic water fleas even when these are equally abundant. The importance of size is also emphasised by the predominance of the larger cladoceran species *Bythotrephes* and *Leptodora* in the diet, when trout feed on zooplankton in lakes containing these two species. Thus in shallow, weedy waters, such as the moorland fishponds and in Blagdon Reservoir, trout which feed on microscopic crustaceans utilise the easily available weed-living *Eurycercus* instead of zooplankton in the open water.

There remains to be considered one other source of food usually present in both river and lake, namely fish. These vary in seasonal habits, abundance and availability. In May and June, the trout in Lough Derg feed on perch fry which are then present in enormous numbers. The trout in Windermere eat minnows when they are spawning in May in the lake and the inflowing River Brathay; they also feed heavily on elvers in spring when these run up the River Leven into the lake. They gorge themselves on char eggs in November but do not attack the spawning fish.

The fish species usually recorded from trout stomachs are perch, sticklebacks, minnows, gudgeon, loach, bullhead, eel, young salmon and trout. The forage ratios of these differ, s with other types of food. Fish which form shoals, either permanently or occasionally, such as perch, sticklebacks and minnows, are more frequently eaten than solitary species. Typical trout waters do not usually hold a variety of cyprinid species, such as roach, rudd, and bream, but even where some of these are present, as in the River Cam and Shepreth Brook, the trout do not eat them. Trout have, however, been seen feeding heavily on roach fry in Eye Brook Reservoir, where these are present in very large numbers.

Trout eat fish only when they have reached a certain size, but this size varies from place to place. Thus in Windermere, trout less than twelve inches long seldom eat fish, but fish usually form a large part of the diet of larger trout. In the upper River Tees, however, half the fish examined which weighed more than $2\frac{3}{4}$ oz. had eaten fish (bullheads) and fifteen fish weighing less than 8 oz. had eaten fish at Straffan; but forty large fish, twenty inches or longer, from Loch Tummel were not predominantly piscivorous. Thus, though big trout are more likely to eat fish than little ones, there is no hard and fast rule about the extent to which trout are piscivorous nor the size at which they become so.

Large trout are often accused of cannibalism. There is no doubt that trout do sometimes eat trout; but the word "cannibal" is often used to describe eating fish of any species, so the extent of this habit is often overestimated. Authentic records of trout eating trout are uncommon and piscivorous individuals probably find other fish species easier to capture. However, when circumstances make trout an easy prey, they are eaten; for instance, thirty-five alevins were found in a ten-inch trout taken from Black Brows Beck in March. The trout which had eaten salmon smolts in Loch Tummell illustrate this, too.

Food supply and growth

The seasonal cycles in the growth of wild trout have some
times been attributed to the different amounts of food
either present or eaten during the different seasons. These
cycles also occur, however, in hatchery ponds where there is
no shortage of food. There appears to be no lack of food
in nature either; for instance, in the River Liffey, the
aquatic insect larvæ, particularly midge larvæ which form
the bulk of the moss fauna (see table 32), are almost
equally abundant throughout the year; and in Windermere members of the permanent bottom fauna are actually
more numerous in winter than in summer months. The
winter fauna differs qualitatively from that present in the
summer and this may possibly be important.

Low temperature seems to have little effect on the feeding of trout. They will take a lure when the water temperature is 4°c (39°F) and have been found with full
stomachs when the temperature has not exceeded 3°c. Half
the trout caught at Ballysmuttan in November, December
and January had stomachs which were three-quarters full
of food. But, since digestion is slower at low temperatures, the frequency with which fish refill their stomachs
is likely to be less in winter. Even though there is plenty
of food available, digestion, assimilation and growth are all
slower because the water is colder in winter than in
summer.

The growth of trout differs as between river and lake,
between reaches of any one river and between hard and
soft waters, and it is common practice to attribute these
differences to the quantity and quality of food animals
present. We will now consider the food supply in different
waters, especially the main source of the trout's food, the
bottom fauna, in the hope that some generalisations may
emerge about the part played by food supply in determining rates of growth.

Trout which spend all their lives in running water
seldom grow as fast as those living in lakes with similar

geological surroundings or water chemistry: the lake trout spend only one, two or at most three years in streams before moving into still water. Obvious examples of this in the Lake District are the trout in Raise Beck and in Three Dubs Tarn while in Wales there is the same contrast between trout in Llyn Tegid and the nearby River Rhydwen. To evaluate the part played by food in producing these differences, we need to know the amount and kinds of bottom animals per unit area of a river and a lake in similar geological surroundings. Comparative data of this kind are difficult to obtain. Moreover, since the numbers of trout present vary very greatly, as does their age and size range, simultaneous estimates of trout populations are necessary as well as qualitative and quantitative surveys of the bottom fauna.

Trout grow remarkably well in man-made lakes when these are newly filled. This growth is certainly related to the unusual food supply (which includes terrestrial animals such as earthworms). It seems likely that a lake usually produces less bottom fauna per unit area than a river and therefore less trout food. In Denmark, the River Susaa held twice the number of invertebrates per square metre as Esrom Lake.

We will begin by discussing the invertebrate bottom fauna of rivers. As already described in chapter 7 (pp. 124-32) the stream bed may be basically stony (eroding) or silted (depositing); and trout are usually more numerous where the bottom is stony. Table 12, p. 131, shows that the bottom fauna is different on these two types of substrata and it is more varied when it is eroding. Weeds may grow on both types and hold their own fauna of invertebrates. Table 25 is based on data from the Yorkshire Rivers Wharfe, Aire and Nidd and shows the kind and number of animals found in different habitats of an eroding stream bed. The numbers are highest in the vegetation (mosses and blanket weed) growing on stones; the great number in mosses is due to the presence of very many midge larvæ. Among stones, the cemented (i.e. very stable) bottom

Table 25. Average number of organisms per square metre on different types of eroding river bed in Rivers Aire, Nidd and Wharfe, Yorkshire. (Based on table 3, Percival & Whitehead, 1929)

	Loose stones Number	%	Stones cemented to bottom Number	%	Small stones and gravel Number	%	Blanket weed (Cladophora) Number	%	Loose moss Number	Thick moss Number	%	Potamogeton on stones Number	%
Mayfly n.	1144	34	682	17	475	14	4662	11	23648	6566	30	3450	1
Stonefly n.	165	5	160	4	25	+	50	+	763	965	1	3196	1
Caddis l.	1281	39	1868	46	900	27	2779	6	3604	34009	5	2930	1
Beetles a.	63	2	422	10	1300	39	1930	4	5314	24531	7	530	+
Midge l.	558	17	192	5	200	6	17625	40	36812	145500	46	203200	83
Blackfly l.	71	2	—	—	—	—	—	—	712	2400	+	27200	11
Snail and limpet	—	—	574	14	125	4	—	—	153	—	+	266	+
Oligochæte worms	8	+	62	2	300	9	17325	39	2876	196800	3	—	—
Shrimp	16	+	—	—	25	+	12	+	2760	780	4	—	—
Mites	10	+	100	2	25	+	—	+	3140	20400	4	3200	1
Average total per square metre	3316		4060		3375		44383		79782	431951		243972	

has the greatest number but there are large numbers present even in the unstable stony bottom.

In the stony reaches of a river, there may be patches of silt and deposits of silt and mud may be quite extensive in pools and reaches with slow flow. One of the stations on the River Wharfe, at Ulleskelfe, differed markedly from the others because there was a deposit of silt about half an inch thick and here all the kinds of invertebrates adapted to life in rapid water (stoneflies, many mayflies and most caddis flies) were absent but there were many pea mussels and snails such as *Lymnaea* and *Neritina*. Some idea of how the invertebrates from stony and muddy substrata differ in kind and relative representation in the fauna is apparent from comparison of the percentage composition of the fauna in the River Lark at Lackford where the bottom is stony and at Ichlingham where it is muddy.

Table 26. Percentage composition of the bottom fauna of different types of substrata in the River Lark. (Data based on Butcher, Pentelow and Woodley, 1931)

	Lackford Stony substratum	Ichlingham Muddy substratum
Shrimp	73·0	—
Water Slater	—	5·7
Mayfly n. (*Baëtis*)	4·5	—
Alderfly n.	—	3·4
Midge l.	3·2	7·2
Pea Mussel	—	43·0
Snails	6·3	—
Leeches	8·4	16·1
Oligochæte worms	—	14·7
Other organisms	4·6	9·0

These examples show that small bivalves, leeches and tubificid worms tend to predominate in the silted regions of a river from which mayflies, stoneflies and caddis flies are absent. In the Lark the number of animals per square metre is about 500 for a muddy, and 3000 for a stony bed so that these two types of substrata show quantitative as well as qualitative differences.

The Tuel Aa, a tributary of the Danish River Susaa with a stony bottom, holds an average of 16,556 bottom living animals per square metre, weighing about 7 oz. of which $\frac{1}{2}$ oz. is contributed by molluscs whereas in the Forest zones, where the Susaa River has a muddy substratum, there are 15,248 animals per square metre, weighing about 22 oz. of which 21 oz. is due to molluscs. Thus there are fewer individuals in the muddy bottom and the fauna is less varied. Considered as trout food, even if the difference in quantity may be immaterial, differences in quality may be of considerable significance because the forage ratios of animals living in the substratum, such as worms, pea mussels and mayfly nymphs like *Caenis* and *Ephemera*, are very low. These animals are virtually unavailable as food to the trout.

The invertebrate fauna of stream vegetation has already been mentioned (p. 130). Mosses and rooted plants give food and shelter to many animals and are therefore sources of much trout food. There are few assessments of numbers and little is known about the relative contributions to the trout's food supply by different kinds of plants. Aquatic mosses are certainly a good source of food in that they provide both abundance and variety of aquatic insect larvæ, particularly midge larvæ (see table 32). What rooted plants can produce may be judged from the 243,797 invertebrates on *Potamogeton* (pondweed) (see p. 130). Table 27 gives data on the fauna in samples of water parsnip (*Sium erectum*) mare's tail (*Hippuris vulgaris*) and water buttercup (*Ranunculus*) from the northern chalk stream, Driffield Beck (Whitehead 1930). All three weeds harbour mainly animals which have a high forage ratio. The buttercup fauna includes many midge and blackfly larvæ, the water parsnip fauna is nearly one third composed of shrimps; most of the snails are on the mare's tail.

From these studies of the invertebrate fauna of a trout river in terms of the supply of trout food, we can draw

Table 27. Percentage composition of fauna in three types of vegetation. (Whitehead, 1930)

	Water Parsnip (*Sium erectum*)	Mare's Tail (*Hippuris vulgaris*)	Water Buttercup (*Ranunculus*)
Mayfly n.	10	25	16
Caddis l.	3	3	2
Midge l.	9	16	43
Blackfly. *Simulium* l.	—	—	27
Snails	—	24	—
Shrimp	28	14	8
Water Slater	1	1	—
Worms	12	7	1
Leeches	1	2	2
Flatworms	2	2	—
Total animals	3164	3876	4220

some general conclusions. Trout food is likely to be more abundant in reaches of a river that are stony than in those silted or muddy, since animals in the first habitat are more varied, possibly more numerous and certainly more available to trout. Within a stony river, the reaches with the greatest amount of food will have loose and cemented (stable) stones and a plentiful supply of aquatic mosses together with occasional beds of water weeds. The reaches likely to contain least food are those where the stones are loose and easily shifted by the current; an unstable substratum of this kind shelters relatively few animals. A sandy, gritty bottom can be relatively barren and poor in trout food, although not always so.

We have already mentioned that trout fry in a river feed on living drift and this is also eaten by older trout. This drift consists partly of emerging insects, such as midge pupæ, caddis pupæ, "hatching" mayflies and stoneflies, and partly of bottom living animals which have become detached from the bottom, such as blackfly larvæ, midge larvæ, other insect larvæ and shrimps. Since the drift represents part of the fauna from upstream, it is richer where there is an abundant and varied fauna than where this is poor and sparse; it is also richer where there is a stony rather than a silted bottom since animals buried in silt are unlikely to be dislodged and swept downstream. In Walla Brook, Dartmoor, Mrs. Horton calculated that the mean value of drift flowing over one square yard of bottom was about ¾ oz. per year—almost enough to satisfy the food requirements of the rather small trout living there.

Elliott (1965) has studied drift in a Dartmoor stream and he has found that there are more aquatic invertebrates, chiefly nymphal and larval insects, in the drift at night, especially during the three hours after sunset, than by day. "It follows from this that the accessibility to salmonids of many members of the bottom fauna may be much greater than has been believed hitherto, provided that the fish are actively feeding by night." Trout can be seen rising at night and will take an artificial fly after sunset so there is good reason to suppose that they can take advantage of the drift then. In fact, Elliott has examined trout stomachs and has found that they certainly do feed during the early hours of the night, at least in summer.

The number of animals in the drift is not simply related to the density of the bottom fauna but depends to some extent on the rate of discharge of the stream. Mayfly and stonefly nymphs are especially common in the drift at times of year when they are growing rapidly, perhaps because competition among them for food is greatest then.

Living drift is sometimes compared with zooplankton but it is really very different. Animals in the plankton spend all their time there and often have adaptations enabling them to keep afloat; plankton can only survive in still water or in very large rivers such as the Nile. Animals in the living drift are only temporarily water-borne and must, if not eaten, either settle on the bottom again or emerge into the air. There must be a constant renewal of the drift from upstream. This means that either there is a flourishing resident population upstream, as usually when shrimps form part of the drift, or that some of the animals must move actively upstream either in the water, as some mayflies do while still nymphs, or by flying when they have become adults.

We have now established a relationship between different types of substratum and the amount of bottom fauna or potential trout food. We can proceed from this to estimate the proportions of eroding and depositing substrata and of weed beds in various rivers and from them to deduce the potential richness or poverty of the food supply for trout. In table 28, we have arranged various rivers in categories with different food supplies because of their different types of bottom. There is a good association between our guess about the probable amount of food available for trout and the growth rate as shown by the length attained by three-year-old trout in these rivers. Growth is faster where we would expect to find a richer food supply.

We suggested in chapter 7 that trout grow better in hard than in soft water: so we have divided the rivers in table 28 into those with hardness greater or less than 150 ppm of dissolved calcium carbonate. We shall consider the significance of differences between these categories later.

In lakes, as in rivers, the bottom fauna is an important source of food for trout and table 13 (p. 135) gives some idea of the animals composing this. The kind and number of animals present depends, as in a river, on the type of substratum and whether it is eroding or depositing, and on the depths of water.

Topographically, a lake can be divided into the littoral zone, down to about six feet, the sublittoral zone, from six to forty feet deep, and the profundal zone below this. In most lakes where trout are found, the littoral zone has a stony substratum, though it may be sandy; the sublittoral is usually muddy, but may be gritty and sandy near its upper limit; the profundal zone has a muddy bottom. Reliable data on the actual numbers of animals per unit area in these zones and on different types of sub-

Table 28. The growth of trout in rivers, as shown by their length in inches at the end of their third year, in relation to topography, food supply and hardness

Topographical category	Potential food supply	Soft water (<150 ppm CaCO₃)		Hard water (>150 ppm CaCO₃)	
unstable, eroded	poor	Raise Beck	5·7	None known to us	
		R. Liffey (Ballysmuttan)	6·0		
		upper R. Forss	<7·9		
stable, eroded	good	R. Liffey (Kings R.)	6·6	R. Liffey (Straffan)	9·6
		upper R. Dart	7·0	(Rye Water)	11·3
		lower R. Forss	>8·0	R. Fergus	12·1
stable, eroded, with weeds	very good	lower R. Dart	7·6	Nether Avon	good
		R. Bela	9·5	Windrush	good
eroded, depositing, with weeds	very good	None known to us		R. Itchen	12·0
				upper R. Test	13·0
				R. Kennet	13·4
depositing, with weeds	good	None known to us		lower R. Test	13·0
				Kennet Canal	13·5
depositing, without weeds	very poor for trout	None known to us		None known to us	

stratum are difficult to find and many studies allow us only to obtain an idea of the relative proportions of the different kinds of animals.

Table 29 gives a general picture of the distribution of bottom living animals in Windermere. Caddis larvæ and mayfly and stonefly nymphs, together with snails, form the greater part of the fauna in the stony littoral region. Some midge larvæ are present, there are probably more shrimps than the figure of three per cent suggests, and water slaters are certainly also present. Below the littoral zone, midge larvæ contribute one third of the total fauna; other aquatic insect larvæ form only a small proportion of the total fauna except for the mud-living mayfly *Caenis*; there are few snails but many pea mussels. The profundal fauna consists essentially of midge larvæ, pea mussels

Table 29.   Percentage numerical composition of littoral, sublittoral and profundal fauna in Windermere.

(Density data for profundal not given by Humphries (1934) but "common" indicates over 60% of a collection of animals)

Animals	Littoral 1–5 ft.	Sublittoral	Profundal
Caddis l.	46	2	—
Mayfly n.	6	19 (*Caenis*)	—
Stonefly n.	2	—	—
Alderfly l.	—	5	—
Midge l.	15	30	Common
Phantom l.	—	—	Common
Molluscs			
Snails	23	6	—
Pea mussels	—	27	Common
Shrimp	3	2	—
Worms (Oligochætes)	1	4	Common
Leeches	1	4	—

Data for littoral zone based on Moon (1934) tables IV and V, for sublittoral on table 5 and for profundal on table 2 of Humphries (1936).

and bristle worms, with phantom larvæ in the water above. Thus, the shallow water produces a more varied invertebrate fauna than the deeper water. The faunistic zonation in Loch Lomond is very similar, but the limits of the zones are deeper than in Windermere, with the sublittoral starting at twelve feet and extending down to eighty feet. There is, of course, a fairly gradual transition between them so the limits are artificial. It is difficult to estimate the numbers of animals present. In the littoral zone, Moon recorded values ranging from 100 to 1300 animals per square metre on a rocky exposed shore, and the numbers gradually decrease as the water becomes deeper; for the sublittoral in Wray Bay, Humphries recorded 883 individuals per square metre at ten feet, 110 at thirty feet and only thirty at forty feet, and Weerekoon estimated that there were only twenty-five animals per square metre in deep water in Loch Lomond. The profundal zone in Llyn Tegid is much richer.

When the diet of the trout in Windermere (see table 24, p. 191) is compared with the data on the bottom fauna, it is clear that most of the invertebrate food comes from the littoral and sublittoral zones; their feeding grounds therefore lie between the shore and about thirty feet depth of water. The experience of anglers confirms that the trout live in this region, at least until mid-June. The animals living in this region are those that are most available to the trout since most of those in the profundal zone burrow in the mud. The midge larvæ, however, come out of the mud at night and so become available as food for trout.

Investigation of stomach contents shows that most of the food comes from the shallow littoral and sublittoral zones; these produce the greatest number and weight of invertebrate animals and these animals are those most available to the feeding trout. Thus the store of food in a lake will depend largely on the amount of shallow water, as Dahl also concluded from studies of Norwegian lakes. A lake with a large area of shallow water, especially if this is stony rather than muddy, will produce more trout food than a lake with only a narrow littoral zone. Thus compared with Wastwater the relatively larger area of Windermere covered with shallower water may be in part the reason for the trout growing faster in Windermere.

The shallow area is also the place where rooted plants and mosses grow and these provide another "substratum" supporting invertebrate animals and making this area even more productive of trout food. In Windermere the shallow water area is not very extensive and there is little weed growth except for swards of lakewort (*Littorella*); these hold an abundant fauna. Shallow lakes such as Loch Leven and Blagdon Reservoir contain many and varied plants which support many and varied animals. We may therefore conclude that lakes which are wholly shallow or have extensive areas of shallow water will provide an abundant and rich food supply for trout. This will be greater if the bottom is stony (but with some silt or mud for plant roots) than if the bottom is all mud; the supply of food will be enhanced by the presence of swards or beds of weeds.

Having thus established a relationship between the type of substratum and the amount of food available for trout in lakes, we can proceed to classify lakes, as we did rivers, according to topographical features. We have first estimated the relative amounts of shallow and deep water and have then considered the type of substratum and the amount of weed growth in the shallow water. From these estimates we have deduced whether the lake is likely to provide a rich or poor food supply for trout as shown in table 30. On the whole, there is a good association between our estimate of the type of food supply and the growth of the trout as shown by their length at the end of their third year. We have, as with rivers, divided the lakes into those with water more or less hard than 150 ppm of dissolved calcium carbonate.

In chapter 7, p. 160, we gave reasons for concluding that trout growth in the British Isles reaches very high rates only where the amount of dissolved calcium exceeds 150 ppm as calcium carbonate. We have therefore divided the rivers and lakes in tables 28 and 30 into those with hard and those with soft water using this value as the limit between them. It is clear from these tables that growth is better in the hard waters even where we expect the food supply to be equally rich, judging by topographical features. In investigating the relationship between topography and water chemistry we have been unable to find examples to put into some of the possible categories in our tables; we know no soft water rivers with high proportions of depositing substrata and of weeds, nor any hard water river with an unstable eroded bottom. Among lakes, we know of none with hard water where the littoral zone is as restricted as it is in Wastwater. There are, however, a number of topographical categories, which we believe also to be categories with different food supplies, to which we can assign both hard and soft waters. In all of these, growth is better where there is more than 150 ppm of dissolved calcium carbonate. To what extent is this due to differences in the amount and kinds of animals available as food for the trout?

There certainly are qualitative differences between the faunas of hard and very soft waters. Molluscs are usually absent in acid waters and less common in soft than in hard waters. Shrimps are characteristic of hard waters but they are quite often numerous in soft waters and can live in acid waters too. Some mayflies are common in both soft and hard waters, though on the whole there is greater variety of species in soft waters. Stoneflies are characteristic of soft waters, caddis flies are more varied in hard waters, and midges occur abundantly in both. Generally speaking there is a greater variety of organisms in hard than soft waters. Table 31 gives the bottom fauna of eroded rivers of varying degree of hardness from Driffield Beck, which is a chalk stream, to Afon Hirnant, a very soft moorland stream, and illustrates qualitative differences between the two types. Hynes comments: "As the hardness

Table 30. The growth of trout in lakes, as shown by their length in inches at the end of their third year, in relation to topography, food supply and hardness.

Topographical	Potential food supply	Soft water (<150 ppm CaCO₃)		Hard water (>150 ppm CaCO₃)	
Deep with almost no shallow water	very poor	Wastwater	6·1	None known to us	
Deep with some shallow water	good	Llyn Tegid	8·5	L. Inchiquin	12·1
		Windermere	8·5		
More shallow water than deep:					
Littoral stony	good	Granabhat I.	8·6	L. Derg	11·6
		L. Atorick	7·0	Malham Tarn	11·2
Littoral very weedy	very good	Boisdale I.	9·3	L. Glore	12·1
		L. Leven	11·1	L. Rea	13·8
				Blagdon Res.	13·9
Littoral silted	poor	Strathkyle I.	8·0	Sunbiggin Tarn	11·3

of the water declines a number of changes occur. Worms, shrimps, molluscs and finally chironomids tend to decline in importance, to be replaced by various insects, particularly mayflies; and stoneflies increase steadily in importance." These are only general trends because the rivers will themselves be marked by individual topographical differences.

It is difficult to find comparable quantitative estimates of hard and soft water faunas. Mr. N. C. Morgan, lately of the Freshwater Fisheries Laboratory at Pitlochry, Perthshire, has some data on the standing crop of invertebrates in some Scottish lochs with different calcium content, which he has given permission for us to use and they are summarised here. Highland lochs with 0.5 to 14 ppm $CaCO_3$ have from 0.5 to 2.8 g. per square metre of invertebrates and showed an increase of number of organisms with an increase in calcium content of the water. Two lowland lochs surrounded by arable land with 36 to 51 ppm $CaCO_3$ had 37 to 40 invertebrates per square metre. On the other hand a loch at 1100 feet and among bogland with 50 to 70 ppm $CaCO_3$ had only about half this number of invertebrates. Thus this evidence suggests that the amount of bottom fauna increases with an increase in the calcium content of the water but that this relationship can be modified by other factors, e.g. altitude, nature of the surrounding countryside, etc. In two small Welsh streams, Jones found about one third as many more organisms per unit collection in the one with harder water, about 60 ppm of calcium carbonate, compared with the softer water one with about 8 ppm. In the upper River Tees, with "moderate" calcium in solution, Pentelow found 106 invertebrates per square foot compared with 2031 in the hard River Lark, but there are probably topographical differences between the last two. In Denmark Berg found 4180 invertebrates per square metre in Esrom Lake, which is highly calcareous, compared with only 600 per square metre in the nearby Gribsø Lake, which is both soft and acid.

Table 31. Percentage composition of faunas of various rivers arranged from left to right in order of decreasing hardness. (From Hynes, 1960)

Place	Driffield Beck Yorkshire Whitehead 1935	R. Avon Wiltshire Pentelow et al 1938	R. Dee Denbighshire Hynes 1960	Trout stream Northumberland Hynes 1960	Afon Hirnant Hynes 1960
Season of Investigation	All	All	Winter & Spring	Spring & Summer	All
Mayfly n.	3	5	53	37	28
Stonefly n.	—	—	5	28	51
Caddis l.	30	3	3	3	9
Midge l.	2	22	7	16	4
Blackfly l.	*	—	—	1	6
Other Diptera l.	1	—	—	—	—
Beetles a. and l.	2	2	3	6	1
Snails	—	16	1	1	*
Limpets	—	1	14	2	*
Oligochaete worms	27	—	8	1	*
Shrimp	32	3	1	—	—
Mites	*	—	1	1	—

This problem of the amount of trout food in soft and hard waters led Southern to plan a survey of the River Liffey, one of the objects of which was to estimate the kind and number of animals present in different reaches and to compare what was found in the fauna with what was eaten by the trout. Table 32 gives the percentage composition of the moss fauna at Straffan and at Ballysmuttan. The calcium content at Straffan (170 ppm $CaCO_3$) just exceeds 150 ppm but it is at best only about 10 ppm at Ballysmuttan; the river bottom where the moss samples were taken is eroding at both places but is more stable at Straffan than at Ballysmuttan. There are differences in the kinds of animals present in the moss with stoneflies and beetles very numerous at Ballysmuttan and mayflies and caddis larvæ more important at Straffan but midge larvæ are equally abundant at the two stations. Shrimps, water slaters and young crayfish are present only at Straffan (they are entirely absent from the fauna at Ballysmuttan) and snails, always rare in moss, are also found only at Straffan. It is, however, very striking that the total numbers of all organisms is much the same at the two places and so is the number of midge larvæ. Thus there seems to be the same amount of food present in the moss at the two places. When stomach contents are compared with the moss, however, it is evident that the forage ratios of the food species vary so that mayflies are eaten at Ballysmuttan more often than their representation in the moss fauna would suggest. Moreover the kinds of invertebrates more easily available to the trout (p. 187) are more numerous at Straffan. Thus although the amount of trout food in hard and soft water may be similar the qualitative differences must be taken into account when comparing the food supply in the two types of water (Frost, 1945). The food value of the different invertebrates may differ greatly but on this we have no information, apart from the biochemical studies of Geng (1925).

Workers at Exeter University have been investigating

Table 32. Percentage composition (based on average number of organisms per sample) of moss fauna in hard (170 ppm $CaCO_3$) Straffan and in soft (5-14 ppm $CaCO_3$) Ballysmuttan water

Food organisms	Straffan Per cent composition Moss fauna	Ballysmuttan Per cent composition Moss fauna
Midge l.	83·2	84·5
Midge p.	0·2	—
Mayfly n.	4·0	0·1
Caddis l.	3·7	1·2
Stonefly n.	0·1	2·4
Beetles adult	0·4	1·0
Beetle l.	1·6	7·9
Other flies (Diptera) l.	0·5	0·5
Blackfly l.	1·9	0·5
Threadworms	0·4	0·3
Oligochæte worms	0·4	0·3
Mites	1·1	0·9
Copepods	2·5	0·4
Crayfish ⎫	+	⎫ Absent
Shrimp ⎬	+	⎬ from
Water slater ⎭	+	⎭ fauna
Average no. all organisms per moss sample	13,343	12,260
Average no. exclusive of midge (chironomid) larvæ	2,233	1,900

trout rivers in Devonshire since 1955 and in 1964 Professor Harvey published a short survey of their results. The Walla Brook on Dartmoor and the Yarty in east Devon have pH values of 5.9—6.8 and 7.5—8.2 respectively; the latter flows over some limestone while the former is entirely a moorland stream. The mean density of the fauna in Walla Brook is about 2000 per sq. m. compared with about 5000 per sq. m. in the Yarty, a proportion of $1:2\frac{1}{2}$. This represents a considerable difference in the amount of food available and trout in the Yarty average

9 inches (23 cm.) when three years old while those in Walla Brook are only 6 inches (15 cm.) long at this age. There are other differences between the two rivers which may also contribute to the differences in growth rate.

Recently (1968, 1969) Dr. Egglishaw has investigated the amount of plant detritus in streams near Pitlochry and has shown that nearly all the common species of animals in the bottom fauna are more numerous where there is more detritus. This statement is true of different types of bottom within one stream and also when comparing similar streams which have different amounts of detritus because they flow past different sorts of vegetation. Dr. Egglishaw also found that the number of bottom invertebrates in nine small burns could be correlated with the amount of dissolved calcium in the water but there was not necessarily more detritus present in the waters with more calcium. He explained this paradox by showing that plant material decomposes faster when there is more calcium in the water so that there is a more rapid turnover of the detritus which can thus support a greater number of animals. The processes of decomposition have not been fully investigated and it is possible that some variable associated with the calcium content—perhaps the amount of bicarbonate—may actually determine the rate of breakdown of detritus.

Our estimates of the number of animals present in different types of water have all been of the stock, the actual number present at one time, or an average of this quantity at several times. Allen pointed out that in the Horokiwi River the level of abundance of the bottom fauna at any one time was too low to provide enough food for all the trout for a year; he estimated that the stock must have renewed itself at least eightfold during the year. The potential food supply is increased by the growth of bottom-living animals and by their reproduction. Many of these animals have an annual life cycle reproducing at a certain season, the young growing (often with seasonal changes in rate), reaching maturity the following year and then dying. Sometimes there are two generations in one year, perhaps in the spring and the autumn; some species may have many generations in one year, probably during the summer with little reproduction in the winter. There are also species in which the life cycle is longer than one year. Dr. Macan has found that the dragonfly *Pyrrhosoma nymphula* usually spends two years as a nymph when it lives on lakewort but three years when it lives on sedge in Hodson's Tarn; when nymphs were exceptionally abundant, they took three years to grow large enough to metamorphose even on lakewort. This may reflect differences in the food supply available for these carnivorous nymphs. The freshwater limpet *Ancylus* breeds annually in Scotland, but has a small second generation in the autumn in the Lake District; it seems that populations which live farther north or at higher altitudes breed later in the year than those living farther south or at lower altitudes and the later they breed, the less is the probability that there will be a second generation in the autumn. The limpet feeds on algæ encrusting stones and its growth depends on that of these plants which depends in turn on temperature and on daylight.

Many of the animals which are common in soft waters have life cycles which take one year or longer, as for instance stoneflies and mayflies. Midges may breed more often and so may some species of shrimps and the latter are more characteristic of hard than of soft waters. It is quite likely that production, the growth and reproduction of all the animals, is higher in hard than in soft waters. This would mean that there would be more food available for trout in hard waters; it might be the result of a direct effect of water chemistry on the invertebrates or an indirect effect through their food supply which is ultimately the mosses, rooted plants and algæ growing in or near the water. We can only conclude that there are qualitative differences between the faunas of hard and soft waters, that there may also be quantitative differences, and that these may play some part in determining the different rates of growth of trout in topographically comparable waters with more or less than 150 ppm of dissolved calcium carbonate.

Sea trout grow faster in the sea than in freshwater, though we are not specially concerned with them in this book. We must, however, consider the "slob" trout, which are brown trout living in estuaries. These usually grow very well. Their food must consist of brackish water invertebrates which differ in species from those of freshwaters; there are few insects available but many crustaceans and molluscs, especially bivalves. A dock of 500 acres with brackish water with twenty per cent salinity was recently stocked with four-inch brown trout. After eighteen months, some measured fourteen inches and thus had grown very well. Their stomachs contained the crustacean *Sphæroma* which was present in the water in enormous quantities. The fish were not at all crowded and the water was warmed to some extent by effluent from a power station, so several factors may have contributed to their good growth.

This chapter has dealt with what the trout eats at different seasons, in various places and at its different size stages. We have, however, found no simple explanation in terms of food supply of why trout grow at different rates in different waters. There are some instances where the growth rate is fairly obviously related to the amount of food present, as in the different zones of the Horokiwi River where more crowded trout were associated with a smaller stock of bottom fauna and grew at slower rates. The extraordinarily good growth of the few trout left in Scale Tarn when it was cleared of fish probably reflected the very abundant food supply. Even in these two cases, however, other factors were also involved; in less well-documented cases it is very difficult to determine the relative importance of food supply and of other factors. We still need quantitative surveys of the aquatic fauna and of the food eaten by trout at frequent intervals throughout the year for several different waters of varied types. When these are available, we hope it will be possible to make general statements confidently about trout growth in terms of the natural food supply.

Chapter Nine

The Biological Environment

The relationship between the trout and the other fish of its environment, particularly other trout, must be considered in the light of the basic needs of any fish, namely somewhere to live, food, and the right conditions for reproduction. If any of these requisites are insufficient to meet the demand at any one time we may reasonably assume that there will be competition for them. We may conclude that this competition is indeed a fact if there is evidence that growth or survival (or both) is adversely affected.

The brown trout is a territorial animal, that is, it has an area that it defends. The ideal territory in running water is where the current is not excessive, where food is obtained with least effort and where there is good cover from enemies and little disturbance from other trout. As soon as a fry begins to swim upwards in an aquarium, it adopts a station, at any level in the water. This becomes a fixed base to which it returns after an excursion into its surroundings and from which it chases any other fish; the fry has in fact established a territory, even though this is small and rather ill-defined. Some fry begin feeding earlier than others and therefore establish their stations earlier, grow a little better and become bigger than those which start feeding later. But when the larger fry are removed the smaller fry grow much faster and when larger fry are added the smaller fry grow more slowly. The food supply in an aquarium is supposed to be unlimited, so it seems likely that it is the very presence of the larger fry that depresses the growth of the others. Thus the growth of an individual trout depends on its position in the "size hierarchy" which is set up in the tank. This situation, with its results, applies not only to fry but to older trout kept in aquaria.

In nature, as soon as fry have left the gravel and begin to feed, each adopts a station which it leaves only to dart after some passing food organism and from which it chases other fry. This defended area around its station is primarily a feeding territory and is fairly well defined. Those fry which begin feeding earlier than others probably get the best stations, with plentiful food and moderate current; those which begin to feed later have to be content with inferior stations where food is less easily obtained and the current is more disturbing. The fry in the good stations consequently grow better and become larger than those in the inferior stations, and soon a size hierarchy becomes apparent in a stream, as it does in an aquarium. In nature it is difficult to dissociate the effect of position in the size hierarchy (i.e. the depressing effect of the presence of bigger individuals on the growth of smaller ones) from the effect of the more restricted food supply associated with inferior stations. But it seems probable that among trout of the same age (whatever that age may be), from fry to old fish, the very presence of a larger individual depresses the growth of smaller individuals. Trout farmers recognise this when they "grade" the trout of any one age into groups where the larger are separated from the smaller, so that the latter may grow better.

As the wild fry grow they become more aggressive and try to expand their territories. Eventually big fish may force smaller fish to emigrate and colonise a different part of the stream (Kalleberg, 1958). Thus there is likely to be a maximum number of trout of the same age which can survive and grow in a given stretch of stream. That this should be so is the result of competition for a place to live and may not depend on the food supply. Recognition of this competition is very important when considering stocking policy (see chapter 10, p. 255).

Mr. Le Cren has experimented in Black Brows Beck,

using five similar reaches separated by screens. He put into these different numbers of alevins, from three to 234 per square yard, all derived from the same parents. He sampled the survivors later in the summer with an electric shocker and removed all of them in September. At the end of six months, there were about seven fry per square yard surviving in each reach, except where the original number was less than this. This appears to be the maximum tolerable population density for this particular stream. In this and other experiments it became clear that most of the high mortality in the densely stocked reaches occurred between twenty and forty days after the little trout began to feed—which is just when they are establishing territories. Fry dying from starvation were collected in the crowded sections. The growth was greatest in the most sparsely populated reaches, perhaps because aggression and mutual disturbance were least there. Thus, mortality in the first five months of feeding varied between seven per cent in the most sparsely stocked and ninety-seven per cent in the most densely stocked reaches and the individual fry were twice or three times as heavy in sparsely stocked compared with crowded reaches.

Kalleberg pointed out that a small trout only attacks to defend its territory when it sees an intruder. Territories are smaller and can be more numerous where the bottom is uneven or where there are water weeds or when the water is turbid, than over a level bottom in clear water; moreover as current speed increases fish keep closer to the bottom and individual territories become smaller and so may be more numerous. A moorland beck, with its rocky bed, frequent riffles and swift currents, should support a greater population of trout than a lowland river, with a more even stony bottom and gentler flow, unless such a river contains much weed which can allow more territories to be established.

The size of a territory depends on the size of the trout. That of a fry (o+) in Black Brows Beck is about 4×4 inches; in Kalleberg's tank a nine-inch trout defended four square yards. Territories thus increase in area with the age of the fish. However, as Kalleberg found, older (larger) fish tolerate younger (smaller) fish within their territories. This means that several age groups *can* live in one place: thus many fry and a few yearlings can also occupy the territory held by one two-year-old trout.

The effect of territorial behaviour is thus to disperse trout of the same size through a river. The same sort of behaviour occurs in ponds and lakes, although this has not been demonstrated clearly. The value of this to the species is in theory that the spacing of territories divides up the available feeding ground among that number of fish which can derive most benefit from it. It is clear that territories can vary in size according to the pressure of the competition, so that there must also be variation in the average amount of food made available to each fish. Hence the average growth rate differs in different waters, but in theory territorial behaviour should prevent overcrowding leading to starvation provided that the excess fish can move away. Where heavy overcrowding occurs, presumably the food supply is so small that no trout can obtain sufficient to grow big enough to drive their competitors downstream, with the result that many fish succeed in maintaining themselves on the borderline of starvation in very small territories. This situation is more likely to occur in rivers with rocky uneven bottoms than in those with even bottoms, since the former allow of more territories than the latter; so we can expect more intra-specific competition in upland than in lowland rivers.

Territory and hierarchy profoundly affect the life and growth of trout. If different numbers of trout are grown in equal volumes of water those fish which are very crowded do not grow as fast as the less crowded fish even when all are given more food than they can eat. This retardation may be due to mechanical disturbance causing greater use of energy and less appetite. In the stream tank, Kalleberg noted that when individuals were very crowded a certain number were able to maintain territories but the others were chased from place to place. When trout are overcrowded in nature it is difficult to dissociate the effect on growth of this disturbance from that due to restricted food supply, but the chief food of fry in their first year of their life (midge larvæ and mayfly nymphs) is usually abundant. Soft waters, with better spawning grounds than hard waters, are more likely to have all available territories occupied and a maximum tolerable population. Mutual disturbance is far more likely to occur in them than in hard waters where the population may be less than the maximum permitted by the territorial system. This may be one of the factors accounting for the poorer growth of fry in soft waters.

For populations of older trout less evidence is available on the connection between overcrowding and growth. But Allen found, in the Horokiwi, that the amount of bottom fauna (trout food) was least where the stock of trout was greatest so that the amount of food available for growth was least where trout were most numerous. The rate of growth was least in those zones of the river where the trout were most numerous and increased where the population density was less. Using Allen's results it is justifiable to explain the growth and size of crowded trout in terms of competition for food.

If the trout population of lochs is reduced by keeping recruitment to a low level, this leads to better growth. This may mainly be the consequence of an increase in the amount of food available to individuals, but it may also reflect reduced mutual disturbance.

Competition for food must vary with the age and size of the trout, with the seasons and in different types of water. The maintenance requirement is bigger proportionally for the smaller fish weighing less than 3 oz. (90 g.) and usually one and two years old. A large population of these require more food than the same weight of trout present in the form of larger fish. Therefore if the food supply is low, competition is likely to be greater among young and small trout than among older larger trout and where many of the population are slow-growing the duration of competition will be protracted.

It seems unlikely that competition can be severe among those of the older trout living in a lake which may feed on zooplankton. Among large, almost entirely piscivorous trout (particularly those in a lake), competition seems unlikely indeed for there are usually relatively few such trout in a population, and their food can be utilised very efficiently and should not be hard to come by in those waters which hold forage fish, like perch, minnows and sticklebacks.

The number of trout may be too many for the available breeding grounds, so leading to over-cutting of redds, spawning on unsuitable grounds, and thus to loss of eggs. This may be beneficial in so far as it reduces an over-crowded population but the reduction of the population may bring it below the level the water can efficiently maintain so that there is a waste of trout water. This could be the case in productive lakes, such as L. Owel, Co. Westmeath, which have few inflowing streams and therefore limited spawning grounds with the result that waters capable of supporting more trout are understocked. In understocked waters reproduction may be affected: the sexes may not meet, or there may be a dearth of females, to the extent that the stock may finally die out through lack of breeding potential. Undercrowded conditions may produce big fish (because of much food) but constitute a waste of this trout water.

In aquaria overcrowding has an adverse effect on the growth of trout but, paradoxically, undercrowding also caused slower growth. A few two-year-old trout in large tanks had small appetites and used their food less efficiently than when they were more crowded. They spent most of the time resting in their stations. There was very little contact between individual fish, which thus lacked a stimulus which could have led to better growth in more crowded conditions. There is no evidence that undercrowding depresses growth under natural conditions; for example two small tarns near Windermere were deliberately rendered fishless but each produced three brown trout of 1½-2½ lb. aged only 2+ years; this growth was far better than with a normal population.

The numbers of trout in different waters varies from few to many and it is generally true that the greater the population density the poorer the average growth of individual fish. In the British Isles, large numbers of trout are characteristic of soft waters, and particularly of upland rivers, which usually have excellent spawning grounds. Trout are aggressive individuals and guard territories within which they obtain much but not all of their food. The territorial habit should set a limit to the maximum number of fish of the same size which can reside in a stream and is probably an efficient way of sharing the available food among the population. Territories become smaller under crowded conditions so that the food supply is shared among a greater number of trout than in less crowded waters where territories are larger. Thus if the total amount of available food is the same, each of the more crowded fish has access to less than do individuals with larger territories. The more crowded fish will use more energy in defending their territories so the less crowded fish should grow faster on average unless the food supply is so great that it is not a limiting factor. It is therefore possible that the small average size of trout in soft waters is often the result of overcrowding and of competition for a restricted food supply in spite of the territorial behaviour of the young fish. This effect may be superimposed on a direct effect of chemical substances in solution (see pp. 151-70) and the water chemistry may also affect the food organisms.

The relationship between trout and other species of fish living in the same water depends on the degree to which their fundamental needs coincide; this will vary with the species of fish and will determine whether they can co-exist peacefully or must become competitors or prey or predators. The other fishes typically present in a trout river are salmon and sea trout so we will first consider the relationship between these fish and the brown trout.

Strictly speaking sea trout are not a separate species but a sea-going variety of the species *Salmo trutta* to which the brown trout belongs (see pp. 50-3). As it is impossible to distinguish the young stages (parr) of sea trout and brown trout we cannot assess the reactions between these two when young. Since salmon and trout eat the same animals and when spawning both make redds in gravel and at the same time of year, there is good reason for expecting competition between them also.

Among brown trout competition for territory leads to the dispossession and migration of smaller individuals so that they have to live in less favourable territories. Young salmon are very similar to trout in appearance so that where trout and salmon are mixed interspecific competition can occur. Since young trout are much more aggressive than young salmon they may drive the salmon away from the better territories. Overcrowding in a river holding both salmon and trout may prevent salmon establishing themselves at all.

Figure 23, which shows the food of trout and young salmon, is based on data from the Rivers Liffey and Forss; the former were collected over a longer period and from a much wider range of trout sizes than the latter. The diet of the two species was almost identical. One marked difference is that the winged stages of aquatic insects (mayflies etc.) figured much more in the trout's diet than in the salmon's; a much less obvious contrast, apparent from the Liffey data only, is that trout consumed more terrestrial insects and molluscs. Maitland's study (1965) of the River Endrick, which flows into Loch Lomond, has led to similar conclusions: trout ate relatively more terrestrial organisms and shrimps while salmon ate relatively more mayfly nymphs.

Trout and salmon parr in the River Teifi also had very similar diets as listed in detail by Thomas (1962) but the

T.—H

salmon perhaps stayed closer to the bottom, eating many limpets in late summer, while trout ate a higher percentage of terrestrial organisms and their diet also included fish and salmonid eggs.

Food organism	River Forss June and July 83 salmon 74 trout	River Liffey (Straffan) February to November 192 salmon 229 trout
Mayfly nymphs		
Stonefly nymphs		
Caddis larvae		
Beetle larvae		
Midge larvae and pupae		
Misc. aquatic insects		
Molluscs		
Weed-living Cladocera		
Winged mayfly, stonefly, caddis and alder fly		
Terrestrial animals (chiefly insects)		
Freshwater shrimp		

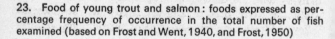

■ Brown trout   ▨ Salmon

23. Food of young trout and salmon: foods expressed as percentage frequency of occurrence in the total number of fish examined (based on Frost and Went, 1940, and Frost, 1950)

The close similarity of diet suggests that where salmon and trout are numerous (and in the same reach of river) competition for food is highly probable although its severity may be somewhat diminished by the trout's greater use of terrestrial organisms.

A comparison of growth of trout in rivers with and without salmon might reveal the importance of this interspecific competition—but the rivers must be similar in all other respects, and this makes choice difficult. Table 33 gives the lengths of trout of the same ages in the River Forss at Cnocglass (Caithness) with salmon present; in the

Table 33. Lengths (in inches, back-calculated from scales) of brown trout from five comparable rivers, two with salmon and three without

end of year	R. Forss (with salmon)	R. Liffey Bally-smuttan (no salmon)	Straffan (with salmon)	R. Bela (no salmon)	R. Derwent Derbyshire (no salmon)
1	2·4	2·0	3·4	3·3	3·4
2	5·2	4·6	7·2	7·0	7·6
3	7·9	6·0	9·6	9·5	9·7
4	9·2	6·9	11·7	11·7	11·6

River Liffey (Ireland) with salmon present at Straffan but absent at Ballysmuttan; and in the River Derwent (Derbyshire) and River Bela (Westmorland), both without salmon. The River Liffey at Ballysmuttan is, topographically, much like the River Forss at Cnocglass and the upper part of the Derbyshire Derwent—except that the Derwent contains more calcium in the water. At Straffan the River Liffey contains far more calcium in the water than at Ballysmuttan and differs topographically from this station; whilst the River Bela is not very hard but resembles the Liffey at Straffan in flow and type of surrounding country-side. There appears to be no relationship between the type of growth and presence or absence of salmon.

Trout may be predators on young salmon as well as competitors and Mills (1967) remarks because of this it is desirable to empty the stream of its existing stock of trout before introducing any young salmon, although many streams containing trout have been stocked successfully with young salmon. After partial clearance of eels and

trout of the Cottage River (a small stream in the west of
Ireland), the survival rate of planted salmon fry into
migrating smolts increased from 0.25 per cent to 1.7 per
cent (Rogers, Spence & West, 1965).

A typical trout lake resembles a trout river in that the
other chief fish characteristically present are salmonids.
These are characteristically the char (*Salvelinus alpinus*)
and whitefish (*Coregonus* spp.). Almost nothing is known
about the interrelationship of the trout and whitefish and
very little about that of trout and char in British waters
although there have been some studies in Norway and
Sweden. Such information as exists for Britain refers to
waters where other species of fish, usually perch and pike,
also occur, as in Windermere; so our discussion of the
relationship between trout and char will be based mostly
on this lake.

Char in Windermere, except at spawning time, live
usually in the deep off-shore water. Trout of the same
size are found in the littoral region, except during high
summer when they are seldom caught in shallow water
and are presumably off-shore. This difference in habitat
makes it probable that there is no competition for territory
between the species, at least in the sense of a place to live
in. The main food of the Windermere trout is bottom
fauna and the terrestrial insects which are blown on to the
lake, whereas the char feed to a very small extent on
bottom fauna and mainly on planktonic Crustacea (Frost,
1951). The large trout, living always in deep water, are
piscivorous. The little information available from other
British waters, such as Ennerdale Water and Coniston
Water indicates that the char is essentially a plankton
feeder, and so there is no competition with trout.

Char usually spawn on the shores of the lake, but in
England there are two known groups which spawn in
running water—the autumn spawning population of Windermere, and the char of Ennerdale Water. As in both these
instances, spawning is confined to a small part of the

river, competition for spawning places between char and trout is extremely unlikely.

Some typical trout rivers have another salmonid, the grayling (*Thymallus thymallus*), but the species is absent from Ireland. On the few data available it is difficult to determine if this fish competes with the trout for food and so affects trout fishing adversely. Grayling do not eat snails (so probably do no harm where these are abundant), but may be a nuisance where shrimps and caddis larvæ are the most important food organisms. The spawning habits of trout and grayling differ in certain ways that preclude competition for spawning grounds.

In many trout-holding waters the predominant coarse fish are the perch and pike; one or more of the small fish species —minnow, bullhead, loach, gudgeon and stickleback— may also be present, and the eel is almost always there. This kind of fish community is common on limestone formations but not confined to them (see map VII, p. 161). Since most information about the biology of the different species is available from Windermere, this lake will be taken as the example of a trout-perch-pike community. The food of the different species is summarised in table 34.

The overlap in the diet of many of the species makes it possible that interspecific competition for food may exist but this is not established as a fact. In the last twenty years the perch population of Windermere has been reduced to less than five per cent of what it was previously and the perch now grow better than heretofore. It is likely that this is due, in part, to there being more food for the four- to seven-inch perch, than when the invertebrate bottom fauna was grazed by enormous numbers of these fish. The brown trout feed on the same organisms but their rate of growth has not changed since the numbers of perch were reduced. The local anglers' opinion that "good trout" are now more numerous suggests that there may have been competition between trout and perch before the latter were reduced in number.

Table 34. Food relationships of fish in Windermere

Food organisms	Fish feeding on the organisms
fish } perch, trout, char, minnows, sticklebacks	pike
fish } perch, minnows, sticklebacks	large trout, large perch
zooplankton (*chiefly Crustacea*)	trout, char, minnow, young perch, young pike
bottom-living Crustacea (*water slater & shrimp*)	trout, perch, bullhead, char
larval aquatic insects	trout, perch, bullhead, minnow, char, eel, young pike
Mollusca (*snails*)	trout, eel
Algæ (*non-planktonic*)	minnows

In Windermere, the food of the minnow is only to some extent similar to that of the trout. But in the River Brathay it is wholly so. The diet of bullheads in both Windermere and the Brathay is very like that of the trout (Smyly, 1957). The food of the stone-loach in Esthwaite Water (the species is absent from Windermere) is largely chironomid larvæ and coincides to some extent with that of trout, and in the River Brathay the chief food items are the same for both loach and trout, although their proportions differ in some instances (Smyly, 1955). The diet of the stickleback in Windermere is planktonic crustaceans, but in a small Cheshire stream consists of chironomid larvæ, shrimp, and water slater (Hynes, 1950), so competition between this fish and trout is likely in the stream but not in the lake. In the River Cam gudgeon and trout both eat aquatic insect larvæ and crustaceans, but the gudgeon feed far more on midge larvæ and on shrimp than do the trout.

Minnow, loach, gudgeon and stickleback are all foods of the trout but the extent to which they are eaten differs with the water concerned, the season of year, the size of trout and other factors, so it is difficult to evaluate this aspect of the food web.

The following general conclusions are probably justifiable. In large lakes, such as Windermere, it is unlikely that the minnow, stone-loach, bullhead, stickleback and (when present) gudgeon rank as serious competitors for food with the trout. Well distributed over the littoral area of such waters, they are indeed often a source of food for larger trout. In running waters the small fish species may be numerous, and when this is so probably compete for food with the younger trout—particularly since they all frequent much the same kind of habitat, the shallow pools and reaches. Young trout do not eat these (or indeed any) fishes. Thus minnow, loach, bullhead, gudgeon and stickleback in any numbers are almost certainly undesirable in a trout stream and possibly also in any small lake which is primarily a trout preserve. Sticklebacks are chiefly plankton feeders in lakes and are thus unlikely to compete with trout there and are occasionally, as in Blagdon, an important food for larger trout.

Various coarse fishes may live in streams and rivers with the trout. Some of these—chubb, rudd, dace and bream— eat much the same food as the trout and so *may* compete with it. Roach vary greatly in diet and may eat either animals or plants. Hartley concluded that members of the community in a trout-and-coarse-fish stream drew, in varying proportions, on the constituents of a common stock of food; he was unable to say, on the data available to him, how the trout fared in comparison with the other fish.

In reservoirs and gravel pits, roach very often come into competition with trout. In Eye Brook Reservoir, trout feed on roach fry but do not always do so in other waters. When great numbers of roach survive however in a trout water they could probably affect the trout population adversely by their inroads into a mutual food supply; this may have occurred in Cheddar Reservoir, Somerset.

There is no competition for breeding places between trout, perch, pike and cyprinids because trout spawn at a completely different time of year from the rest and need a different substratum.

The pike eats invertebrates for its first few months only, and then becomes piscivorous for the rest of its long life. It is in many waters the major predator of trout. When the trout is part of a mixed community of fishes, including cyprinids and perch, there is evidence that it is preferred by pike to the other fish species, even when they are more abundant. Where, as in Windermere, there are large numbers of perch, the latter figure prominently in the pike's diet, but even so trout form an appreciable part of it.

The extent of predation may depend on the size of the water and be greater in the confined limits of a river than in the open space offered by a lake. In a large lake, the difference in distribution of pike and trout at some times of the year reduces the possibility of the trout being eaten. Some large Irish loughs, such as Corrib, Mask and Sheelin, hold both good trout and large pike. Their trout fishing improves after reduction of the pike population (chapter 10) showing that even good trout waters suffer as the result of the pike's predation. How great this may be is indicated by Toner's (1959) estimate that in Lough Corrib, 1170 pike together eat over forty-six tons of trout in a year.

Predation by the pike affects the structure of the population of trout as well as its total number. Pike tend to crop trout of a certain size more heavily than others. In Windermere the principal trout-eating pike are twenty-four to twenty-eight inches long and feed mostly on trout of eleven to fourteen inches, that is fish which are three, four or five years old. These fish are within the size range kept by anglers; moreover, the survival of fewer of these medium-sized fish means that there are fewer potential big fish, so that the pike's predation reduces both the total catch and the likelihood of anglers catching record fish! This proved preference of the pike for medium-sized trout disproves the popular notion that pike predation leads to increase in the average size of the trout because they remove the small and stunted individuals.

The eel occurs in all kinds of lakes and rivers, including those which are predominantly trout waters. How far is it the trout's competitor, predator or prey?

In both lake and stream, eels of all sizes (from five to twenty-four inches) eat mainly the invertebrate bottom fauna. The species taken are similar to those eaten by the brown trout, though not always quite so; for example, in Windermere snails form a greater part of the diet of eels than of trout. In the River Teifi, two fifths of the trout stomachs examined contained terrestrial organisms while eels ate none of these, but one quarter of the eel stomachs contained minnows compared with one in twenty of the trout stomachs. In the British Isles most eels spend from eight to twelve years in fresh water, so each individual may compete with several generations of trout. It seems reasonable to believe that competition is less severe in lakes than in streams where the feeding area of both species is more limited. Since eels seek cover, there are likely to be more of them in a weedy river with undercut banks and tree roots than in a bare stony river.

The alleged "winter hibernation" of the eel may provide some respite for the trout, though we have little evidence that eels entirely cease to feed in cold weather. Lake-dwelling eels certainly feed in winter: they are caught in seines in Windermere in November, December, February and March, with their stomachs filled with char spawn. Eels of running waters may be quiescent in winter as found by Thomas but Jones and Evans record many caught then that had been feeding actively.

The eel is usually regarded as an important predator of trout and young salmon. I have examined eels from various lakes in the English Lake District and from a few rivers. Practically none had eaten salmonid fish. Jones and Evans examined 498 eels from Welsh rivers and found the same as did Thomas in the Teifi. In the spawning areas of a river the eel is suspected of preying on the eggs and alevins of trout and salmon. Jones and Evans paid particular attention to this form of predation and concluded that it was negligible. I found no evidence of such predation in sixty eels from a local beck where trout spawn; Sawyer also found no such predation on eggs or alevins in a chalk stream. These examples exonerate the eels as a predator on trout eggs and alevins.

Examination of hundreds of stomachs of trout from fish of all sizes and caught at all times of the year has shown that trout seldom eat eels, but may feed heavily on elvers during a run.

The trout-eel relationship is a controversial subject but in general terms there can be no doubt that the food requirements of the trout coincide so closely with those of the eel that serious competition between the species is probable. Because of this (and considering that it has virtually no value as a forage fish) the eel is clearly undesirable in a trout water, particularly a running water.

Many kinds of birds eat the "flies" on which trout feed; swifts, swallows and martins hunt over rivers and to some extent so do warblers, wagtails and flycatchers. Black-headed gulls, which live much inland, take up stations on the shores of lakes. On Wise Een Tarn they eat the newly emerged duns of *Leptophlebia* and on Windermere the green drake, *Ephemera danica*. Shrimps and the larval stages of aquatic insects have been recorded from the stomachs of various species of water birds, e.g. the moorhen, dipper and the dab chick.

Berry (1936) reviewed the fish-eating habits of aquatic birds and found that the cormorant, black-headed gull and goosander cause serious destruction to young salmonids but the dab chick and kingfisher (particularly the latter) do much less harm to a trout fishery than is usually supposed. The heron is well known as a predator on all kinds of fish.

According to Berry the most destructive mammal is the water shrew which eats salmonid fry, alevins and eggs, a diet also enjoyed by the brown rat. Although the otter eats salmonid fishes, eels are equally important in its diet (Stephens, 1957). A comparatively new predator is the mink. a North American relative of our native stoat and weasel, which has been reared for its fur in "ranches" in Britain since about 1929. Some animals have escaped and have survived in the wild. The first recorded breeding of feral mink was in 1956 on the River Teign in Devonshire but since then populations have become established in Hampshire and Wiltshire, West Wales, parts of Scotland and probably elsewhere (Southern, 1964). The mink is mainly an aquatic animal and in America catches much of its food in the water. Although here it may raid chicken coops, there is now evidence that it eats fish so that it is a potential danger to trout waters. Stringent conditions are now imposed on anyone who wishes to keep mink in captivity and it is obligatory for an occupier of land, who knows that mink are at large on his property, to notify the Ministry of Agriculture, Fisheries and Food, who must take such steps as are necessary for their destruction.

Of all mammalian predators, however, the angler remains the most persistent and efficient and he would do well to remember this in his attempts to conserve his prey!

Parasites

Like all animals, the trout supports a population of parasites. Sometimes these are virulent or numerous enough to damage or kill the fish. Most of our knowledge of trout diseases is based on hatchery experience and rather little is known of the effect of parasites on wild trout. Very few wild trout are entirely without parasites. Sometimes healthy-looking fish in good condition may harbour surprising numbers; for instance, a group of plump-looking trout killed by insecticide in a tributary of the Wye each had thirty or forty spiny-headed worms (Acanthocephala) in their intestines. Big-headed, lank, dark-coloured trout often have large numbers of roundworms (Nematoda) in their guts and air-bladders and it seems reasonable to suppose that their poor condition is not unconnected with the many parasites. The heavy infections of trout in reservoirs near Cardiff, Dublin and Bristol with tapeworm plerocercoids (Cestoda) during and just after the War unquestionably damaged the fishing. Occasional epidemics of furunculosis (a bacterial disease) and white spot (caused by *Ichthyophthirius*, a protozoan parasite) have both led to heavy mortalities.

Parasites may live on the outside of the host. The leech *Piscicola* sucks blood so it may cause anæmia. The fish-louse *Argulus* feeds on blood, mucus and skin. The "ich" protozoan *Ichthyophthirius* burrows into the skin. Louse and "ich" may interfere with salt and fluid regulation, and allow pathogenic bacteria to enter the fish. The "ich" also lives on the gills and may cause great damage to the filaments and thus kill the fish. Small gill-flukes (Trematoda), such as *Discocotyle* and *Gyrodactylus*, attach themselves to trout gills by armoured suckers; when they are present in great numbers, there is obvious damage. Other small flukes live in the eye, e.g. *Diplostomum*, and cause "pop-eye" or opacity of the lens leading to blindness and starvation. These organisms are actually larval stages (metacercariæ) of flukes whose adults live in the guts of water birds, usually gulls. An earlier larval stage swims freely in water and seeks out a snail *Lymnaea* in which later stages multiply before cercariæ emerge to infect the trout's eye. The birds are infected by eating freshly dead or dying fish and the fluke's eggs pass out with their fæces and hatch in the water ready to infect another snail.

The trout's gut may harbour a variety of organisms. Among those commonly found in the intestine are small flukes (*Crepidostomum*), tapeworms (*Eubothrium*, very common in the pyloric cæca of Windermere trout), roundworms (*Agamonema*) and spiny-headed worms (*Echinorhynchus*). These "worms" are all adult in the trout but have larval stages which live in other animals—usually crustaceans—which are eaten by trout. Thus, *Eubothrium* has a procercoid larva which lives in the water-flea *Diaptomus* in Windermere; this becomes a plerocercoid stage in small fishes such as minnows and sticklebacks which eat the *Diaptomus*; and these fishes are eaten by the trout in which the worm becomes adult. Larvæ of *Echinorhynchus* probably live in the shrimp *Gammarus*. A variety of protozoans live in the gut, gall bladder and bile duct of trout and at least two of these, *Octomitis* and *Chloromyxum*, have caused mortalities in hatcheries. The roundworm *Cystidicola* is sometimes found in great numbers in the air-bladder of trout.

All the parasites mentioned so far have direct access to the outside world. There are also parasites which live in the body cavity, such as the plerocercoids of *Diphyllobothrium*. The adults are tapeworms living in the guts of birds or of mammals such as the otter and man, according to species. The life history is complicated: the egg hatches into a short-lived swimming coracidium larva which must infect a water-flea, *Diaptomus* or *Cyclops*, in which it changes shape and grows into the resting procercoid stage. The water-flea dies if these larvæ are numerous but is usually eaten by a fish. The parasite then burrows through the fish's gut wall and becomes a plerocercoid, which grows and becomes enclosed in a cyst—usually attached to part of the gut but sometimes in the body muscles. Trout with many cysts develop peritonitis and anæmia and die. In the recent epizootics near Cardiff, Dublin and Bristol, the affected trout each contained 100 to 360 cysts. The degree of infection increased with age and size and the trout usually died when three and a half years old, usually during the summer. The final host is infected by eating diseased trout.

Recently there have been outbreaks of the salmon disease "UDN" (ulcerative dermal necrosis) among mature brown trout in some lakes and reservoirs. These fish show the same signs as diseased salmon and generally they have contracted the disease either from infected salmon or sea trout or from the water through which diseased fish have passed. The cause of the disease is still (1969) not fully established. Some workers believe it to be a virus, others believe that bacteria are involved (including the myxobacterium *Chondrococcus* (*Cytophaga*) *columnaris*) while other workers believe that a fungus is the causative agent (a sterile type of *Saprolegnia* different from the usual *Saprolegnia ferax* which attacks damaged fish). The disease may be due to a complex interaction of pathogens but when the trout become heavily fungussed they almost certainly die. Immature trout are much less susceptible than fish maturing to spawn and the disease is characteristic of the autumn and winter months when the water temperature is low. In November and December 1967, 83 per cent of 158 breeding brown trout, which ran into a stream entering Windermere to spawn, died of the disease, and there were heavy mortalities in at least two southern reservoirs in the autumn of 1968. In one of these many rainbow trout also died, covered with fungus while running with eggs or milt.

Apart from "ich" and bacterial infections causing lesions, only *Diphyllobothrium* may be found in the muscles of trout. This is the only organism mentioned that might be eaten by man, who usually eats only the muscles. (In any case, none of the others would survive in or infect man.) The *Diphyllobothrium* species involved in the recent epizootics have *not* been *D. latum*, the species which is dangerous to men who eat raw fish in some parts of the world; there is still some argument about their exact identities but their definitive hosts are probably otters and waterbirds.

Disease epidemics are more likely to occur where trout are crowded together in hatcheries than under natural conditions where their behaviour patterns tend to disperse them. It is also, of course, easier to control epidemics in hatcheries where chemicals and antibiotics can be used, than in reservoirs, lakes and rivers. Since many internal parasites have several hosts during their life cycles, it is sometimes possible to prevent infection by eliminating one of the other hosts. But most hosts are food organisms and live in water with the trout making this sort of control impracticable. Even when the other host is a bird or mammal (which could theoretically either be destroyed or prevented from having access to the water containing the trout) there may be considerable practical (and some legal) difficulties in controlling it. Fish tend to gather parasites cumulatively, so that it is the oldest fish which are likely to be most heavily infected. Maintaining the balance of a trout population so that there are plenty of young fish helps to reduce the likelihood of epizootics of parasites (such as *Diphyllobothrium*) by spreading the infection over a greater number of individuals, each being relatively lightly infected, and by reducing the chances of the final host preying on heavily infected fish. Removal of the older fish (if they are caught at spawning time) should also help. All this means that it is in the angler's interest to fish a stock of relatively young and medium-sized trout in good condition, rather than a population weighted with old and biologically more dangerous fish.

It is to the disadvantage of a parasite that its host should die and prevent it from completing its own life cycle: long-established parasites often produce little apparent effect on their hosts. However, it is difficult to believe that the presence of parasites has no adverse effects and trout which are in good condition even though heavily parasitised would probably have grown larger and faster if they had not shared their food intake with the other organisms. Holmes (1960) comments that the fattest trout he has ever caught in Malham Tarn had no cysts of *Diphyllobothrium* in its body cavity. It weighed $3\frac{1}{2}$ lb. Fish of this size in the Tarn usually contain some (up to 100) cysts; some trout are probably killed every year by this parasite.

more urgent and important than ever and will be dealt with in this chapter.

Angling for trout takes place in both running and still waters. The techniques of catching trout may be divided into those in which an artificial bait or lure is used, as in fly fishing and sometimes in spinning and trolling, and those which depend on the use of a natural bait, as in dapping and worm fishing.

In fly fishing the lure ("fly") is an artificial representation of some trout food organism, usually an insect. In dry fly fishing, the artificial fly floats on the surface of the water and is intentionally cast to a rising fish. In wet fly fishing, the artificial fly is submerged and the angler usually though not necessarily "fishes the water" rather than casts to a particular fish. In nymph fishing the imitation of a larval aquatic insect is fished only slightly submerged and cast to a rising trout. Of these three methods wet fly fishing is the oldest, dry fly fishing is first mentioned in 1851 and nymph fishing dates from the beginning of the present century. The artificial fly is cast, a technique first mentioned in the seventeenth century, whereas the natural fly is dapped, that is, held on the surface of the water. In spinning and trolling the "bait" may be either artificial (usually an imitation fish) or natural. In spinning this bait is flung into the water and then wound in; in trolling the angler gently pulls the bait through the water while rowing.

Fishing for trout with rod and line and an artificial or natural bait has been practised since the twelfth century and is described as early as 1496 in Dame Juliana Berners' *The Treatyse of Fysshynge wyth an Angle*. The essentials of the equipment for angling for trout—rod, line, reel and cast and "baited hook"—have always been the same, although alteration in their pattern and usage has occurred over the past five centuries. Until the nineteenth century the favourite wood for the rod was hazel, thereafter hickory and greenheart, particularly the latter, were used. Around 1860 rods of six-sectioned split cane were introduced and these still are the most favoured, although to-day fibre-glass and steel rods are available. Up to the sixteenth and seventeenth centuries rods were one piece, but spliced and ferruled rods have been in use from the seventeenth century onwards. The length of the rod has tended to get smaller with time, and Charles Cotton's eighteen or fifteen footer would find few counterparts to-day. The reel is an addition to the trout angler's tackle which came into general use at the beginning of the eighteenth century, although as early as Walton's time it was used for salmon fishing. For centuries the fishing line was made of twisted horse hair, but in the seventeenth century silk lines came gradually into use. To-day lines made of nylon and other plastics are to some extent replacing those made of silk or cotton. For fly fishing the early cast was certainly of horse hair, although during the eighteenth century "Indian weed" a plant difficult to identify, was much in favour. Silk-worm gut, first mentioned in 1724, superseded horse hair, and to-day nylon is rapidly replacing gut in the fly-fisher's cast and is almost exclusively used for the spinning trace.

The trout angler's bait is artificial or natural. The fly-fisher uses imitations, in feathers, fur, wool, silk, etc., of organisms, chiefly insects, on which the trout feeds, and the copies may be in general or exact terms. Old and modern books on trout fishing deal with the identification of the natural insect and the pattern required to imitate it; incidentally much can be learnt of the habits of both the trout and its food animals from this literature. The artificial baits, mostly made of wood or metal, used in spinning and trolling usually imitate fish, both in form and action. Natural baits include fish, worms, maggots and some aquatic insects, and are presented to the trout by appropriate methods. Live aquatic insects are usually dapped, the best known perhaps being the sub-imago of the mayfly, *Ephemera danica* (green-drake), which is used on lakes, particularly on the large Irish limestone loughs. Other aquatic insects, such as caddis flies, as well as terrestrial insects like the rose beetle (bracken-clock) and the daddy-longlegs, are used for dapping. In north country streams the creeper—the larva of the large stoneflies *Perla carlukiana* and *P. cephalotes*—is used as a live bait, as also is the adult form of this insect.

Man has improved his methods of catching trout just when, through his own civilised activities, he is rapidly reducing the number of waters available for trout.

Water plays an essential part in our civilisation. In using it we often upset the balance of nature and make conditions in rivers and lakes less suitable for fishes. Lakes which are "regulated," because they are water supplies or serve power stations, often suffer violent changes of water level which naturally affect the plants and animals living in the littoral and sublittoral zones and reduce the potential food supply for trout. The depletion of water in streams (often abstracted for urban water supplies) may affect spawning grounds as well as food supply. The ponding of water above weirs may lead to the deposition of silt over a formerly eroding substratum. A drainage scheme may involve straightening and dredging a river and so altering it that there is neither food, nor shelter, nor spawning places for trout in it. It may take a long time for normal biological conditions to be restored.

Another important physical change results from the discharge of hot effluents from power stations or factories. Higher temperatures mean less dissolved oxygen in the water but the fish need more oxygen because their whole metabolism is raised, as explained in chapter 7. Since cyprinid fishes can survive higher temperatures and lower oxygen concentrations than can trout, heated water will favour coarse fishes. The temperature must also affect the invertebrate fauna, though probably some species will flourish while others disappear and the fauna as a whole may remain diverse and abundant provided that the water does not become too hot.

We usually group man-made chemical changes in waters under the heading "pollution." We shall consider this topic only very briefly. It is fully covered in an excellent book by H. B. N. Hynes (1960)—*The Biology of Polluted Waters*. Through most of this country now, domestic sewage and effluents from factories, gasworks etc., are treated at sewage disposal works before being discharged into rivers. The treatment is essentially a biological process of decay in which complex organic compounds are changed by bacterial action into carbon dioxide, water and mineral salts. Where the process is completed and the effluent is of excellent quality it will have an effect on a river comparable to the addition of mineral fertilisers to land. The salts encourage plant growth and this in turn encourages invertebrate animals to live on the plants so that the productivity of the river is increased. It is characteristic of productive rivers that the fish fauna contains many cyprinids in contrast to unproductive rivers where salmonids dominate the fauna, so high-grade sewage effluent will swing the balance in favour of coarse fishes.

If the effluent from the sewage disposal works is of poor quality, then the processes of decay, which should be completed in the works, continue in the river. The suspended solids in the effluent cause silting of the bottom, smothering plants and drastically reducing the number of invertebrate species which can survive. The organisms causing decay form "sewage fungus" blanketing all submerged objects with a slimy film and drifting downstream in unsightly masses. These organisms use so much oxygen that the water may become almost or entirely deoxygenated. Where this occurs, anærobic organisms continue the decay process but produce methane and evil-smelling hydrogen sulphide which bubble to the surface from the bottom of stinking black mud. When decay is complete, the river gradually acquires oxygen by solution from the air and the fauna recovers progressively downstream as the effects of the discharge diminish.

There is a very characteristic "pollution fauna" in rivers into which poor quality effluent is discharged. No animals can live in a totally deoxygenated zone but where there is a very small quantity of oxygen, millions of small red

Tubificid worms live in the bottom mud. Downstream, as the amount of oxygen increases, these are replaced by thousands of bloodworms, the red larvæ of the midge *Chironomus thummi*, which feed on bacteria in the mud and stir it up, aerating and dispersing it. Downstream again, the water slater *Asellus*, a detritus feeder, becomes very abundant, as do the leech *Erpobdella* and certain snails. Rooted plants can grow in shallows and gradually more plants and other animals appear and conditions return to normal.

Some cyprinid fishes can stand low oxygen concentrations and penetrate in to the chironomid zone where they find a rich food supply by grubbing in the mud; they probably have to seek water with more oxygen for part of the time. They are occasionally asphyxiated in hot weather or by waves of poorer effluent passing downstream. Trout have a fairly high oxygen requirement and cannot penetrate above the *Asellus* zone. When they live in this, as some do, they have very little margin of safety and may die in hot weather.

Rivers may be polluted by organic compounds, such as phenol and tar-acids, and by many inorganic compounds which are also poisonous. Even in these enlightened days, baths of cyanides are sometimes emptied down drains and produce devastating mortalities of fish in nearby rivers. Certain Welsh streams, contaminated from lead and zinc mines, offer classic cases of toxic pollution by metal salts. Toxic effects continued long after the mines stopped working because heavy rain washed small quantities of metal out of spoil heaps and this intermittent contamination prevented susceptible species of animals from establishing themselves. Streams with intermittent toxic pollution characteristically have a sparse fauna because it is depleted of susceptible species, which gradually reappear downstream.

Modern detergents, herbicides, insecticides and radioactive wastes are new hazards to life in water. If detergents are not fully broken down by passing through sewage disposal works, they cause unsightly foaming at weirs and reduce the rate at which rivers can take up oxygen from the air; they are surface active and may also harm plants and animals directly. Herbicides and insecticides used on land may be washed into rivers, kill the plants and insects and thus deplete the shelter and food supply for fishes. Some insecticides may kill fishes directly or affect their fertility, as they do birds and mammals on land. Some aquatic animals may accumulate these poisons, and radioactive wastes also, and so may become dangerous to other animals and to man.

To make the best use of available waters, some form of management is essential. Allen has listed three quantities that must be established before deciding how to alter the existing conditions in any water. These are:

(1) The *stock* which is the number and weight of trout present in the whole area at any given time. This means knowing the number of fish present multiplied by their average size, for each year class or age group.

(2) The *production* which is the amount of fish flesh grown during a given period. To estimate this we must know the weight of the stock on two different occasions separated by a reasonable time interval: the difference in the two weights is the production, i.e. the amount of trout flesh produced. This production of trout flesh is going on all the time but not all of it survives so it is possible to obtain only an approximate value of the actual total weight of trout flesh produced *during* the period. Usually the number of fish at the second occasion is lower although the total weight is greater because by then most of the surviving trout have grown bigger.

The term *production* denotes the amount of trout flesh made by all the fish as they grow. Production as used by Allen, in this strict sense, should not be confused with the term "production" so often used as a synonym for "productivity" which, in practice, really means the crop or yield.

(3) The *crop* which is the number or weight of trout removed by man during any given period.

Fishery management will be considered in terms of the stock, production and crop of trout waters. First, we may see how these three factors vary during the life span of a trout. Allen deals with this matter in detail, and a brief summary of his findings is expressed diagrammatically in fig. 24. In the figure the height of the column is proportional to the total weight of trout *produced* to that age, and it is divided into the amount which remains alive (the *stock*) and the amount which has died naturally or through being taken by anglers (the *crop*). The total amount of trout flesh produced during the life of the year class *rises throughout this life*, rapidly at first and then more and more slowly as is indicated by the increasing height of the columns. But *the proportion* of the amount of fish flesh produced *which is still surviving* at any one time (e.g. at the end of each year) and which forms the stock follows a different course: during *early* fry life the proportion of the trout flesh produced which survives is small, but as the mortality rate diminishes in the later fry and yearling stages, the proportion that survives rises to form about one third of the total production to date. Some time during the second year the weight of stock begins to decline because survivors are fewer and their growth rate is slower. The amount of new fish flesh produced is inevitably less and the proportion which survives as stock decreases, a process which continues until none of the year class stock remains. Cropping, i.e. anglers' catch, begins in the second year of each year class's life when the amount of production alive as stock is already beginning to fall. The anglers' catch increases in the years following, when both the production of trout flesh and the proportion of it surviving as stock are decreasing.

It may appear that this analysis of the life of a population of trout in terms of stock, production and crop is of purely theoretical interest; but, as Allen pointed out, the "realisation of the difference between the actual quantity of trout present in the stock at any time, and the amount [of trout flesh] which has been produced in obtaining

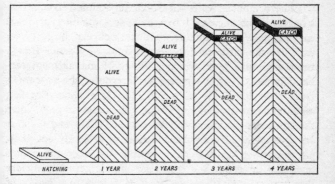

24. Stock production and crop. As the trout in a year class grow, the total weight of trout flesh which they have formed increases continually, at first rapidly, and then more slowly. The total weight of those still alive, on the other hand, only increases for a time, and then decreases again as the fish die off. In the Lower Waters of the Horokiwi most of the angling catch is taken in the second and third years. In the figure the height of the columns is proportional to the total weight of trout produced up to that age (production), and they are divided in proportion to the amounts which remain alive (stock), or have been taken by anglers (crop), or have died natural deaths. (Allen, 1952)

that stock is of great practical importance." We shall illustrate this by showing how fishery management policy depends on manipulation of the stock, the production and the crop of trout.

A sport fishery aims to provide the angler with as large a total weight of fish as is possible from the water. The weight of stock, which may be in terms of many small or few large fish, should therefore be the maximum the water is capable of carrying. To attain and maintain this it is first necessary to have some idea of the amount of trout flesh present. This can be estimated from regular nettings (especially if the fish have been tagged), from trapping spawning runs, and from anglers' records, provided these are expressed as per unit effort and are collected over a period of years. The value of such estimates for indicating whether or not the water is carrying its optimum amount of trout is much increased by knowing something of their age and growth, when the existing stock can be assigned to a size-age category (after the manner of Hartley (1947) for coarse fish) from which a policy of management can be deduced. The five categories are fish which are (1) large and young, (2) large and old, (3) medium size for medium age, (4) small and young, (5) small and old. When the trout are predominantly of classes (1) (2) and (3) and are present in fair numbers the stock is probably adequate for the water, but if there are only a *few* large and young or a *few* large and old trout this almost certainly means that the stock is too low. If it is found that class (4) trout predominate, the stock is too low, unless fish are present in large numbers, and if class (5) predominates and fish are numerous it is almost certain that the stock is greater than optimum for the water. Of course the terms "large" and "small" mean different lengths in different waters, but for any particular water they have relative meanings which are of value.

If the stock is adequate the aim of management is to keep it so. If the stock is too low or too high the aim will be to adjust the number of fish to the carrying capacity of the water by increasing or reducing it respectively.

Increase of the stock may be achieved by adding trout directly to the water or by reducing predators so that more of the existing stock survives, either as greater numbers or as larger individuals. The first practice, usually referred to as "stocking," is the more common. Before adding trout to waters where they are already present (as is often done) it should be remembered that there is a definite risk that increased competition for food may cause a reduction in growth rates and there will be increased competition for territories. Let it first be well established that the water *is* understocked and let an eye thereafter be kept on the effect of the additions on the growth and number of trout.

Fish used in stocking are mostly hatchery reared, though

sometimes wild trout are transferred from an overstocked to an understocked water. Miller (1958) in Canada, investigated the effect of the presence of a resident population on the survival rate of the stocked trout (brown, cut-throat and rainbow) and also the differences in survival between hatchery reared and wild fish. Briefly he found that the survival of the introduced fish was probably much lower when they were planted in streams already occupied by trout than when planted in troutless streams. When wild trout, semi-wild trout (i.e. fry reared for the first five months in a hatchery and then for several months in a stream) and trout straight from a hatchery were put into a stream already having a resident population, the first type showed the best survival, the second the next best and the last the worst. Miller concluded that when *any* trout, hatchery or wild bred, is planted into a resident population it has to compete with the resident fish for a living place or food, or both, and is at first in a state of constant muscular activity which results in accumulation of lactic acid in the blood. Such fish may succumb to acidosis and they may also exhaust stores of some metabolite and die of starvation. Hatchery reared trout have never been faced with the problem of finding a living place and these die in greater numbers than planted wild or semi-wild trout: the latter have been exposed to natural selection in a stream before planting and are thus better able to face the competition from the resident trout. Miller gives two useful suggestions to the fishery manager: (1) good survival of hatchery stock is likely when heavy fishing pressure has materially reduced the resident trout population; (2) when lakes are rehabilitated by poisoning or otherwise removing the resident populations, the desirable species should also be eliminated when this is not providing satisfactory angling.

Trout may be added to a water as eggs, or as fish ranging in size from fry to four-pounders. For more detailed information and practical advice, books on the management of trout fisheries such as Hills (1934), Coston, Pentelow and Butcher (1936), Peart (1938, 1956), Needham (1938), Sawyer (1952), Fort and Brayshaw (1961) should be consulted. These and earlier works deal with techniques of artificial propagation and the rearing of trout, etc., technical matters which are not considered here. It is, however, pertinent to note that a hatchery should be fed by a spring since this normally means that the water supply is constant, silt-free and of suitable temperature. Moreover if it be sited near a reservoir the compensation water from this provides an excellent rearing pond with a natural food for fry in the form of plankton washed out from the reservoir. When artificial propagation is on a small scale Kashmir and Vibert boxes containing eggs may be placed in a convenient stream and there is then no need for a hatchery.

Eggs for stocking are stripped either from wild or hatchery parents and are planted in a river a few hours after stripping (green eggs) or after partial incubation (eyed ova). They are put in artificially made redds, either directly into the gravel or enclosed in a Vibert or similar box before being buried. This is the least expensive method available of adding trout to a water. It is satisfactory in virgin waters or in tributaries inaccessible to spawning trout but where there are sufficient indigenous spawners these will lay far more eggs than can be "seeded" by man. So unless the introduced eggs are planted out in very great numbers, the number of sizeable trout arising from them is unlikely to augment the native population of the stream. Moreover heavy plantings of eggs do not necessarily result in more fry because this depends on the number of available territories (see chapter 9, p. 219).

The fish added to the water can be unfed fry, fed fry, yearlings, two-year-olds or of takeable size; all except the last must make some growth (months or years) and are subject to varying degrees of mortality before they can be caught. By takeable size, we mean fish bigger than the legal size limit, if there is one, or fish which anglers will be pleased to keep.

Results from the Horokiwi stream make it possible to give a general idea of roughly how many fish of a particular age will have to be planted to produce one *extra* takeable-sized fish in a water (not necessarily to add one more to the angler's catch). Assuming that the trout reaches takeable size at three years old then

    1250 fry

or   25 yearlings

or   5 two-year-olds must be planted to produce one takeable fish.

Stocking with takeable trout means that more anglers can be provided with trout fishing. It has become essential in many British waters, because of the greatly increased angling pressure. If the planting of takeable trout pushes the carrying capacity of the water above its optimum the intensive and immediate angling which usually accompanies it means that any ill effects are of short duration. Figures for the return to the angler are few. From a wide experience of stocking English waters Peart maintains that a large proportion of the stocked takeable trout are caught. Many angling clubs expect a return of at least two-thirds of the number stocked. Wise Een Tarn, a twelve-acre fish pond on the heights above Windermere, was stocked with ten-inch brown trout in two successive years. The recapture in the years of their release was 30% and 16%; a similar stocking with rainbow trout gave recoveries by anglers of 47% and 80%. It is difficult to assess accurately the value of stocking with takeable fish since it is affected by the intensity and season of angling. Returns are highest soon after planting because planted fish may move and so be lost to the fisherman. Myers, for instance, maintains that trout planted in rivers like the Lune, where floods occur, may drop downstream although they may "stay put" in a chalk stream.

There is no doubt that, to obtain maximum sporting value, the planted trout should be caught during the year of their release. In subsequent years they form an insignificant part of the catch of fish, in both stream and lake, as witness our own experience in Wise Een Tarn. Thus of brown trout stocked in Wise Een Tarn in 1955 and 1956 the total number killed from 1955 to 1958 was thirty-nine of the 1955 stock and ten of the 1956 stock; so that the cost of each fish killed of the 1955 stock was four times and of the 1956 stock seven times its purchase price.

In Britain, takeable trout are usually planted in the spring, before the open season for angling. Sometimes trout are added during the open season, a policy which has been found to give greater returns to the angler in U.S.A.

How the planting of takeable fish may affect the total catch is seen by comparing the proportion of planted to native wild fish in the catch. In the two years when takeable trout were added to Wise Een Tarn these formed 28% and 14% of the total annual catch. In much managed waters where native fish are few, the effect of planted trout on the catch will be much higher.

Finally how much does the planted takeable fish add to the angler's sport? In a heavily fished water or one where indigenous trout are few it may make all the difference between some sport and none at all! There are rather few data of catch per hour that show the effect of stocking on the angler's catch. Between 1955 and 1959 takeable brown trout were added to Wise Een Tarn in two years and then the catch per hour was 1.6 and 1.5 fish, but in the following three years when there was no stocking it was 1.3, 0.8 and 1.5. This suggests that the angler did not benefit very much from the stocking.

Where natural regeneration is poor and when time can be allowed for the fish to grow it is feasible to stock with unfed or fed fry. This should certainly add some trout to the water, since at least a few should survive to become takeable fish; but the real measure of the value of this policy lies in how much these added trout mean as *extra* fish for the angler and how much each of these extra fish has cost. Sawyer (1952) regards stocking with fry as a successful practice for, on the Upper Avon, Wiltshire, he found that after a period without stocking there was a big falling off in the rod catch in subsequent years whereas good catches were made when a year class which included planted fry became takeable trout. Nicholls (1958) points out that in north-western Tasmanian rivers, of every fifty-one trout taken by the angler fifty were the result of natural spawning. In the Horokiwi each year 15,000 fry are added to the 500,000 naturally produced, but of the 300 trout caught each season by the angler "not more than ten of these had been added by the liberation; the other 290 would have been caught in any case" and each of these extra fish cost between 10s. and £1. This analysis certainly casts doubt on the view that it is more economical to stock with fry than with larger fish simply because the initial monetary outlay is so much less.

Because of heavy mortality (sometimes up to 94%) among fry during their first three or four months of life great numbers of unfed fry must be planted in the hope that some may survive. After these early months the death rate decreases to about 20%, so liberations of feeding fry later in the year might be more economical. As mortality among both types of introduced fry will be aggravated by the presence of indigenous fry (p. 251) allowance must be made for this when estimating the numbers to add to a stream; their best survival can be expected from troutless streams. There is however a limit to the value of stocking with very large numbers because of the territorial behaviour which limits the number of fry which can live in any water.

Fry are usually liberated in spring (if planted in October they are called yearlings in Britain, fall fingerlings in U.S.A.). There seems little justification for delaying their planting till May or June on the assumption that there will be more fry food available, since faunal surveys have shown that this is not true, but they may survive better because older; we have no information about the relative value of autumn and spring plantings.

Because trout are strongly territorial (p. 218) the number which can survive in any particular water will vary with the type of stream. Kalleberg (1958) found that territories are smaller and therefore crowding greater where the stream bottom is uneven, where there are water weeds or where the water is turbid, than where there is a level bottom in clear water; individual territories become smaller with an increase in current speed so that faster flowing reaches can hold more fry than the slower flowing ones.

The value to the angler of stocking with yearling or two-year-old fish is the proportion of these trout that are caught and the number of years over which they provide fishing. In November, 1948, Mr. Cecil Myers marked 255 brown trout yearlings (ten months old, six inches long) and released them in Blagdon Reservoir. In the next five years 73 of these trout were caught by anglers, 4 in 1949, 48 in 1950, 16 in 1951, 3 in 1952 and 2 in 1953, after spending one, two, three, four and five years in the lake respectively. These figures show that there was quite a high return spread over several years. These data refer to stocking in a lake where, unlike a river, migration could not deplete the number stocked. There are no pike in Blagdon, which is rich in trout food and certainly not over-populated, so there would have been presumably little loss of the stocked fish through predation and competition. Mr. Charles Oliver found for Eye Brook Reservoir that when takeable fish were released in the autumn, 40% were recaptured in the following fishing season compared with 70% recaptured from takeable fish released in the spring. Nicholls released 1000 yearlings at each of ten sites in the North Esk River, Tasmania, and calculated that this added 20 takeable fish, spread over two years, to the natural population of 150 takeable fish per annum near each site. Since anglers caught about 44% of the takeable fish each year, this means that fewer than one in a hundred of the stocked fish were caught. This return is much less than that obtained at Blagdon.

The planting of trout is expensive but it is a practical method of maintaining the population at a definite level and in many hard-fished waters it is the only such method. The same end may be achieved indirectly, by ensuring that there is adequate natural recruitment to the population. This can be done by legislation which protects breeding fish, by close seasons, by building fish ladders to ensure that the spawners reach all available spawning grounds, and by making sure that drought and floods do not reduce the potential of these grounds. When spawning grounds are inadequate, improvement of existing ones by raking may help to overcome the deficiency; it is possible to restore spawning grounds by cleaning up suitable gravels which have been rendered useless by becoming silt-covered or packed hard; Sawyer has shown what can be done in this way and with excellent results.

Control of predators and of competitors is part of the policy of many organisations concerned with conservation of trout fisheries. The Inland Fisheries Trust of Ireland has, since 1951, netted and trapped pike (and perch to some extent) in many Irish loughs, both great and small, with the aim of improving the trout fishing. To-day many more trout, both large and small, are seen in these waters than heretofore, more fish enter spawning streams and anglers report better fishing.

Since 1944 pike have been taken out of Windermere by winter-set gill nets, and perch have been removed since 1940 by traps. The pike is the chief predator on trout and char in the lake and the perch probably compete for food with trout. There is documented evidence of a marked increase in number and size of the char. The comments and catches of anglers suggest that the trout fishing has also improved in quality and quantity though there is no formal scientific proof of this yet.

In New Brunswick, control of eels and of bird and mammal predators led to better survival and increased yield to the angler of planted yearling speckled trout in Crecy Lake, whereas these remained low in the neighbouring Gibson Lake where no control measures were applied (Smith, 1952). Survival of fry of sockeye salmon in Cultus

T.—I

Lake, British Columbia, was more than three times greater after removal of predatory fish.

So far we have been considering waters in which the stock of trout present is below the optimum for the water, the remedy being to add trout, directly or indirectly. But should the trout be small, old and numerous (category 5 on p. 250), it is almost certain that there are too many of them and the remedy is to take them out.

The numbers of trout may be reduced (1) by removal of restrictions on bag and size limits, a policy strongly advocated by Hartley (1947) for the reduction of the often encountered populations of stunted coarse fish; (2) by netting—although nets, as well as removing the unwanted small old fish may also take out the desirable small young fish; (3) by trapping trout during their spawning run or limiting spawning by shutting off some spawning streams (both reduce future additions to the stock); and (4) by the introduction of trout-eating species of fish, notably pike.

To introduce predators, particularly pike, as a method of reducing trout numbers seems a dangerous policy, even in theory. In Windermere the smaller pike eat few trout and predation on trout is almost entirely by big pike and these select the larger and older trout (see chapter 9). In these circumstances it would appear that the pike would not reduce the too numerous small trout—thereby giving the desired result of an increase in size of the remaining ones— but they would unfortunately remove the few larger fish of the stunted trout population. (Incidentally there are no grounds for the belief that pike select "sickly" fish.)

Campbell's work on Scottish lochs (see pp. 172-3) has shown how effective limitation of spawning facilities may be in improving growth. There are probably large numbers of soft, neutral lochs where quite simple measures would reduce the number of eggs produced each year and thus lead to better angling.

On the whole the removal of unwanted trout is best done

by man, preferably by angling, for he knows what he wants and can suit his methods to his requirements.

So far we have considered how to manage a trout fishery by manipulating its stock; we will now discuss management by manipulating production. The aim is that the amount of trout flesh grown in a given time shall be maximal, the increased production being expressed either as bigger or as more numerous trout, or both. To achieve optimal production man must create or maintain those environmental conditions which ensure good growth, a high survival rate and adequate reproduction of the trout; to this end he may alter the physical, chemical and biological environment. Policy must be based on sound knowledge of the biology of the trout, particularly of the factors which affect its growth.

It is easier to alter the physical environment in running than in still waters. The primary aim is to control the rate of flow so that resting places for trout are made, water is conserved in times of poor flow, and in times of spate the effects of the water's violence—the scouring of spawning beds and wash-out of invertebrates—is reduced. The current can be used to improve the stream by building up banks on which aquatic plants can become established, thus increasing shelter for the trout and its food organisms. Alternatively silt and sand may be shifted by the current so that the gravel, which can hold a greater number and variety of invertebrates than the silt, is exposed for colonisation by trout food organisms. The current may be used to break up a cemented substratum so that it can be used for spawning. Any methods of altering the physical environment to ensure sufficient spawning grounds are means of increasing the production of future trout flesh. By deflecting the flow to the shady side of the river, the water temperature may be kept lower and so more favourable for trout during hot weather. Methods of altering the physical environment are given in books dealing with river management.

The fertilisation of fresh waters to increase the production of table fish is a centuries old custom, but its application to sport fisheries is modern. We have already referred to experiments with fish ponds by the Freshwater Biological Association and the Freshwater Fisheries Laboratory (see pp. 169-70). These have shown that it is essential to continue adding the fertiliser at intervals since each application has only a transitory effect. The improvement in growth of the trout has been variable and not very impressive. These ponds all held very soft water and it is possible that the fertilisation of ponds which are more productive to start with might have greater and more worthwhile effects.

Alteration of biological features of the environment may increase the production of trout. Trees and shrubs on the river bank provide shelter and shade and so increase the number of "lies" for trout. Fallen leaves provide food for detritus feeding bottom-living invertebrates and so encourage their numbers and hence increase the food supply of the trout. This is also increased because trees and bushes shelter the water from the wind and so prevent aquatic and terrestrial insects being blown away from the river and lost to the trout, and also because insects may drop from them into the water. Too much terrestrial vegetation may result in excessive water abstraction, which is to be avoided. The biological environment may be improved by planting and fostering those aquatic weeds which are known to harbour an abundance of aquatic insect larvæ (chapters 7 and 8). Even when this is not known it is well to encourage some submerged aquatic vegetation because it provides a living place for certain trout food organisms and also a shelter for the trout itself. In some waters, such as chalk streams, however, there is normally too much weed, which interferes with angling and drainage and so has to be cut. This must be done carefully so that only "useless" weeds are removed.

An obvious method of altering the biological environment is to add trout food organisms to the water. Many anglers regard this as the most effective method of increasing the production of trout flesh. Snails, shrimps, mayfly nymphs and other invertebrates collected from other waters, or bought at no small cost, are turned into river or lake. It is usually better to encourage the species of animals already present in the water. This can be done by altering stream conditions to suit them, and by various other devices, such as the provision of "fly-boards." Species which have become absent or rare may be reintroduced: on the River Test, at Stockbridge, the Mayfly (*Ephemera danica*) has been successful in this way, but of the caddis flies, the caperer (*Sericostoma personatum*) was only partially successful and the grannom (*Brachycentrus subnubilis*) a failure. In most cases the introduction of new species, not represented at all in the water, is probably of very little use but it may be valuable in man-made or man-altered waters. For example, snails have been usefully added to reservoirs, and species of *Gammarus* have been put into small, artificial Scottish lochs. Some species can become established permanently, or at least for a long enough time to provide useful food; in the latter case, it is necessary to continue adding the animals, perhaps every year, and to examine trout stomachs to make sure that the fish are really benefiting from the additions. The accidental introduction of a species is sometimes very successful, as, for instance, that of the large snail *Vivipara* into Scale Tarn where it is well established and forms a fair proportion of the trout's diet. These trout grow better than those in neighbouring tarns but they are also far less crowded.

Reduction of predators leads to increased production by ensuring the survival of a higher proportion of the trout flesh produced. If the reduction of parasites is possible, it should lead to improved growth as well as greater survival. Reduction of competing fish species (p. 224) is also advisable so that production of *fish* flesh becomes primarily production of *trout* flesh. In practice this is not always easy to achieve. Eels are most easily removed by trapping the elvers "running" up the river, and other fish competitors can usually be caught in nets and traps.

The purpose of managing stock and production is to obtain as great a weight of trout as is possible from the water. The aim, in theory, of manipulating the crop is to enable the angler to take as much as possible of that weight. To achieve this he should crop at an age when the stock of each year class, the total weight of trout flesh produced which is still alive, is at its maximum and this will be at a time when the trout are still numerous and when the fish are growing well. Although this theoretical aim can sometimes fulfil the anglers' requirements, namely to catch a fair number of trout of reasonable size, in practice this is not always so. Thus in fig. 24 the weight of the stock is maximal during the second year of life. Theoretically this is when the trout should be cropped, but at this time they are young and too small to provide sport, or to have reproduced themselves. In practice it is often necessary to delay taking the trout for a year or more beyond the theoretical cropping time so that the angler can catch larger but fewer trout and the fish have a chance to spawn at least once. There is a real danger that the size limit may be fixed too high. If it is, much production is lost because of the death of some trout and slower growth of the survivors in the extra years; the anglers' catch will be less in number and weight of fish than it would have been had the size limit been lower. It is justifiable to raise the limit if the fish are small and young and not very numerous, but should they be present in large numbers the limit is better lowered, so that their numbers are decreased and the remainder have a chance to grow to a larger and more acceptable size. How the angler benefits from correct adjustment of the size limit is dealt with and aptly illustrated by Allen (1952), his illustrations are reproduced in fig. 25.

The growth rates of trout vary greatly from one water to another. So does the angling pressure. Ideally, then, a separate size limit should be fixed for each lake or river. But even if this is not possible and legislation has to be made on general lines, it is obvious that some knowledge of the age and growth of the trout of the area concerned is essential.

The usefulness of size and bag limits vary greatly from water to water. That the angler benefits from a bag limit is based on the assumption that by limiting his catch trout are "saved" for another fisherman. In some "big trout" waters, such as some south country chalk streams, stocking and management are framed to meet a known angling pressure and the demand is for large (if few) trout; here size and bag limits are automatically part of the policy. In the Horokiwi, where fishing pressure is light or moderate, only about one third of the takeable fish are killed by anglers and the rest die from natural causes so that "the effect of the bag limit is to cause wastage of two-thirds of the fish." Where the majority of the fish are small and old then the time of maximum production is obviously passed and it is advisable to abolish limits altogether. Trout which are small and numerous may all be young and therefore still at a size when production is potentially high. If such a water is heavily fished, limits may be essential to allow the trout to grow larger. There may be natural limits set to the anglers' efforts, especially on large lakes, by the behaviour of the trout. Thus in Windermere, the trout leave the shallow fishable waters in late June, and in some large limestone loughs in Ireland, for example Lough Derg, trout rise freely only when the Mayfly *Ephemera danica* is emerging, so fly fishing, at least, is confined to a few weeks in May and June. In big lakes, too, weather conditions may make suitable fishing grounds inaccessible at times and topography restrict their access, therefore limiting the anglers' efforts. Limiting rod-days is usually difficult to enforce but it is possible to close a whole water or part of it to all angling for a period of varying duration. This has been done on some Kenya trout streams, as in the Thiba River, where eight months closure had the

RIGHT

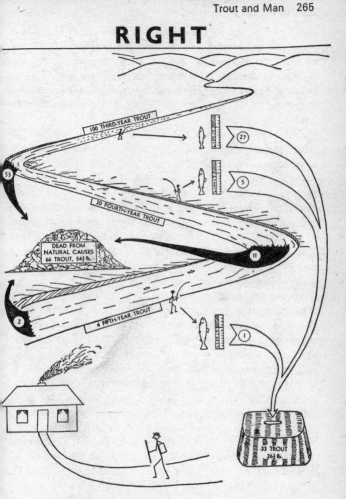

100 THIRD-YEAR TROUT

27

5

20 FOURTH-YEAR TROUT

53

DEAD FROM
NATURAL CAUSES
66 TROUT, 54½ lb.

11

2

4 FIFTH-YEAR TROUT

1

33 TROUT
26½ lb.

25. The effect of the RIGHT size limit. The same trout stock with the correct size limit. From the same original number of fish (100 in their third year) the anglers are able to take three times as many, weighing more than twice as much as when the limit was too high. The amount wasted by natural deaths is correspondingly less. (Allen, 1952) effect of building up the stock of rainbow trout. There was a marked increase in the number and weight of trout per acre and an increase of 5 oz. in the average weight of the fish, so that more and larger fish were available to the angler (Copley, 1953). Here angling pressure was preventing young fish from growing larger than the minimum size limit.

The close season in the British Isles is a device for protecting spawning fish when they are very vulnerable to poachers. A size limit may be necessary to ensure that some fish survive to spawning size. The close season also allows opportunity for stream improvement and other activities without the danger of spoiling an angler's sport. Moreover, trout are not palatable when ripe or just spent.

The use of restrictions on fishing to produce an optimum crop for anglers should be directly related to the conditions in each water; such restrictions may be either essential or useless depending on circumstances.

Throughout this chapter we have been concerned with the trout-carrying capacity of a water and it would seem pertinent to give some values for this, expressed as the number or weight, or both, of the stock of trout per unit area for different types of water. Unfortunately few figures are available and these provide very little information for comparison of the "productivity" of different waters. Allen gives the stock of trout in the Horokiwi stream, New Zealand, as 200 lb. per acre (the different six zones of that river ranged from 110 to 393 lb. per acre). Two small streams flowing into Lake Ellesmere, Tasmania, held between 40 and 135 lb. per acre and the number of yearling fish per 1000 yards varied from 44 to 490 (Nicholls, 1958). In Walla Brook, Dartmoor, Mrs. Horton found between 5 and 20 lb. of trout flesh per acre and the number of yearling fish varied between 600 and 1250 per 1000 yards; few of these fish exceeded 6½ inches in length. In the North Esk River, in Tasmania, there were about 45,500 takeable fish at the beginning of the season. More than half of these were three years old but 900 were six years old; the total weight of trout was at least 52 lb. per acre. In the Kenya Highlands, the Thego River supported 140 lb. per acre and the Sagana River 200 lb. per acre in 1949; the Kiringa River held only 36½ lb. per acre before closure but the stock had risen to 129 lb. per acre after twenty months with no fishing. These Kenya figures are for rainbow as well as brown trout.

There appear to be few records for the "productivity" of lakes. Loch Kinnaird Mill Dam has a "standing crop" of 50 to 60 lb. per acre. Wise Een Tarn, with predominantly brown trout, a few speckled trout (*Salvelinus fontinalis*) and occasional additions of rainbow trout, supports about 25 to 34 lb. per acre of all species, and 23 to 34 lb. per acre of brown trout only. For Windermere Allen (1938) estimated that there were of the order of 12,000 brown trout in the littoral zone of the lake. If this zone is taken as within two metre contour and the average weight of the trout there as about one pound then this part of Windermere has approximately 2 lb. per acre of brown trout. In Three Dubs Tarn, which is nearby and contains only brown trout, a rough estimate is 21 lb. per acre.

A very general idea of the productivity of a water, useful for comparative purposes, may be gained from the crop taken by anglers. In the British Isles figures are available for the annual yield of trout from some man-made lakes: Blagdon yields 5 to 6 lb. per acre, Chew Valley 11.5 lb. per acre, Weir Wood Reservoir (Sussex) 19.0 lb. per acre, Sutton Bingham (Somerset) 55 lb. per acre, Eye Brook Reservoir (Leics.-Rutland) 39 lb. per acre, the recently formed Grafham Water also about 39 lb. per acre, Ladybower Reservoir (Derbyshire) 2.4 to 5.2 lb. per acre and Lake Vyrnwy (N. Wales) about 1 lb. per acre. The famous trout fishing in Loch Leven yields 7 to 10 lb. per acre. Wise Een Tarn yields 8 lb. per acre after the addition of takeable fish and 5 lb. per acre when the cropping is of the indigenous brown trout only. As these figures have not taken into account the fishing effort that produced them they can only be of very limited value but may provide the angler with a guide as to the good or indifferent fishing he is likely to obtain on a water. The Kenya rivers yielded about 35 lb. per acre to the angler.

This last chapter has been concerned primarily with the conservation of the trout and trout waters. It is abundantly clear that such conservation depends for success on sound knowledge of the biology of the trout and of its environment.

But why conserve the trout? We may agree that *Salmo trutta* presents an interesting ecological study and—because of its relative simplicity of structure and physiology—is a useful laboratory animal. For neither purpose need it be conserved. The brown trout in the British Isles has practically no *economic value* as a food fish. There is no commercial fishery for it. It is not reared in ponds for the table. The only reason for conserving the brown trout is to provide trout angling. The value of this sport can only be appraised by its devotees, an appraisal which, though felt by many, only finds adequate expression in angling books written by masters of style like Lord Grey.

To-day the value of going fishing is appreciated more than ever. The need to conserve the waters where such fishing may be found becomes imperative. To lose the opportunity to "cast an angle on the brook" means more than the loss of catching a fish.

To devote a whole book to one fish might imply that we now know all about the species. This is far from true, but on the strength of what has been written we might describe the ideal trout and the ideal trout water.

The ideal trout is quick growing, late spawning and free rising. The ideal trout water has the physical, chemical and biological conditions which make for optimum growth: it harbours no competition—so that all the food available is turned into trout flesh; no predators—so that the angler can reap the maximum crop; and, finally, an abundance and variety of aquatic insects to ensure a "hatch" of fly at all seasons!

An ideal fish surely demands an ideal angler. Both Dame

Juliana Berners and Izaac Walton stressed the piety and virtue of such an one but the Prioress of St. Albans demanded also that he should have good manners and her precepts hold as much to-day as they did 500 years ago. She admonishes the angler that he must not break any man's hedge nor leave gates open. "Also ye shall not be to rauenous in takyng of your sayd game as to moche at one tyme: . . . whyche lyghtly be occasyon to dystroye your owne dysportes and other mennys also. As when ye have a suffycyent mese ye sholde coveyte nomore as at that tyme."

Appendix I

The Routine Examination of Trout

The date, place, and manner of capture are noted.

The *length* is measured in centimetres (cm.) or inches (in.) from the mouth to the fork of the tail (some workers measure to the caudal peduncle and call this "standard length").

The *weight* is recorded in grammes (g.) or in pounds (lb.) and ounces (oz.).

Scales are removed from just above the lateral line in an area below the dorsal and adipose fins. Plenty of scales should be taken, either by scraping with a knife, or, when the skin is thick as in old spawning fish, digging them individually out of their pockets. The scales may be preserved in a special small envelope or in a seed packet or else smeared on to a piece of paper which is folded several times so that they are completely enclosed.

The *sex* cannot easily be determined from external features so the fish must be opened by slitting the belly from vent to throat. The presence of ovaries or testes (see pp. 65, 69 for description) then reveals the fish to be a female (hen) or male (cock). The *state of the gonads* should be recorded as one of the following: (a) immature—the fish has never spawned and will not "ripen" to spawn at the next breeding season; (b) ripening—it will spawn at the next breeding season; (c) ripe—it is ready to spawn at once or is spawning; (d) spent—it has spawned at the last breeding season; (e) resting—it has spawned in the past but will not spawn at the next breeding season. (See fig. 9.)

The whole gut should be removed and the *stomach* (the U-shaped organ, see fig. 1) either preserved in formalin solution or else opened and its contents examined at once or preserved in formalin for future examination. The *amount of food* may be noted as stomach full, $\frac{1}{2}$ full, $\frac{1}{4}$ full, etc.; the presence of food in the intestine may also be recorded but its contents are usually difficult to identify.

The *information* about the capture, the length, weight and sex of the trout should be written on the scale envelope if one is used. Where several fish are caught, each may be given a serial number for convenience in tabulating data. This should be written on the scale packet.

Age and Growth Determination from Trout Scales

The scales removed from the fish must be cleaned. This can be done by soaking them for about an hour in a weak solution (4%) of sodium hydroxide (caustic soda) or for a short time in household ammonia, and then rubbing each scale between thumb and finger or with a fine brush (not a needle) to remove the soft, coloured tissue.

There are various ways of making *permanent mounts* of scales: (1) press the damp scales on to a microscope slide (or mounting glass for colour transparencies), cover with another slide (or glass) and hold the two together with adhesive paper; (2) smear the slide with gelatine mountant and stick the scales on to this; (3) mount the scales in glycerin jelly under a cover glass. The first method is simplest and lasts longest. A permanent record can also be made by pressing an imprint of the scale on to thick $\frac{1}{8}$ inch celluloid sheets, using a jeweller's roller. *Only scales with perfect centres are any use* for age or growth determinations (see p. 90); all others should be discarded so it is worth examining scales briefly before making permanent mounts.

To determine *age*. it is only necessary to identify and count the annuli (see p. 90). A simple compound microscope, with one eyepiece and one objective giving a magnification up to twenty diameters, is very useful but a good pocket lens or a toy microscope may suffice. The slide with scales mounted on it can be treated as a photographic transparency and projected on to a screen or wall. Special projectors have been designed for scale reading (see Fort and Brayshaw (1961) for a full account).

To determine *growth*, it is necessary to measure the distance of the annuli from the focus (centre) of the scale and also to measure the total length of the scale from focus to edge, all along the same antero-posterior axis (see p. 89). It is possible to use an eye-piece micrometer scale in a microscope and record the measurements directly as units of this scale. The length of the fish when each annulus was laid down is then easily calculated (especially with a slide-rule) from the proportion:

length at end of year Y

$$= \text{length at capture} \times \frac{\text{distance from focus to annulus Y}}{\text{distance from focus to edge}}$$

Most workers, however, project the image of the scale on a table or screen, then place a strip of paper or cardboard in position as shown in fig. 14 and with a fine pencil mark off the end of each winter band. These measurements are now turned into terms of annual increments in length by means of the simple apparatus in fig. *a*. This is a sheet of paper graduated into equal parts (a piece of graph paper is best) and the parts numbered as centimetres or inches (the actual width of the part does not matter). Suppose the scale examined came from a trout of $15\frac{1}{2}$ inches and the slip had four year marks on it. Place the end of the slip, which was the centre of the scale, at 0 on the calculator then adjust the slip until the mark which denoted the edge of the scale is at $15\frac{1}{2}$, then read off the other four marks, these would come to say $4\frac{1}{2}$, $8\frac{3}{4}$, 12, $14\frac{3}{4}$ inches, lengths which represent the growth made by the trout in the first, second, third and fourth years respectively of its life, the last and fifth year's growth being that made between $14\frac{3}{4}$ and $15\frac{1}{2}$ inches.

The lengths obtained from both the procedures outlined above may need *correction* because both are based on the assumption that the scales grow in exact proportion to the growth in length of the fish and this is often not true (see p. 91). Corrections can only be applied to trout from the water for which they are calculated. Several fish (as many

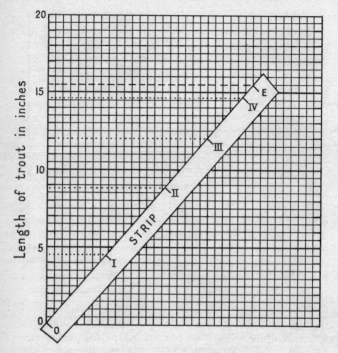

Figure *a*. Strip of paper marked to show the positions of the annuli on a scale (by lines at I, II, III, and IV) placed with the line marking the position of the centre (O) at zero of the calculator scale and the line marking the position of the edge of the scale (E) at $15\frac{1}{2}$ inches (the length of the fish at capture). The lengths attained at different ages can then be read as follows: at 1 year, $4\frac{1}{2}''$; at two years, $8\frac{3}{4}''$; at 3 years, $12''$; at 4 years, $14\frac{3}{4}''$.

as possible) of different sizes must be available for the water. The simplest method to use is as follows:

Measure one scale from each trout, recording the distance from focus to edge in arbitrary units and using the same units for every fish. Use a micrometer eye-piece or measure the projected image of the scale as preferred. Plot the lengths of the scales against the lengths of the fish using

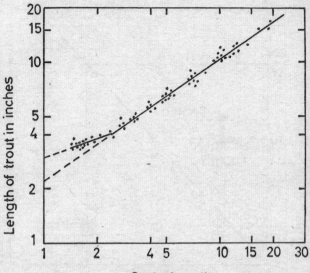

Figure *b*. Graph on logarithmic paper of scale length (in arbitrary units) against trout lengths in inches. The "best straight lines" have been drawn through the points by eye; the slopes of these represent the regression coefficients which are different for fish less than and more than 4 inches. [Based on imaginary data]

logarithmic graph paper (if this is not available, read the logarithms of the lengths using Four Figure Tables and plot these values on ordinary (arithmetic) graph paper). Draw a straight line as accurately as possible through the points on the graph (see fig. *b*). From this straight line, read off values of scale length for different body lengths (converting logs. back to ordinary numbers, if necessary) and plot these values on *arithmetic (ordinary) graph paper*. If these points fall along a straight line, then no correction is necessary.

If the points on the second graph fall along a curve, then the corrected length for any age can be found as follows:

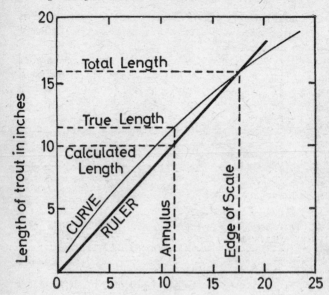

Figure *c*. Graph on arithmetic (ordinary) graph paper of scale length against trout length using the straight line for fish over 4 inches in Fig. *b*. The ruler is in position for calculating the corrections for a fish of 15¾ inches. For a back-calculated length of 10 inches, the true length is just over 11 inches. [Based on imaginary data]

Read the scales as usual (and they may come from fish not forming part of the original sample provided that they come from the same water) and obtain the uncorrected back-calculated lengths. Lay a ruler or straight paper edge against the second graph so that one end touches zero and the other crosses the curve opposite the length of the fish when captured. The true length for each back-calculated length can then be found by reading vertically upwards from the point marked by the ruler to the point on the curve, as illustrated in fig. *c*. If the same units of scale length are always used, then the true length can be read off the curve directly by using this measured scale length (focus to annulus).

For growth data it is usual to read five or more good scales for each fish and take the average values for back-calculated length at the end of each year of life. The data are set out as in the table below.

Table 1. Growth of trout as back-calculated from scales

Length in centimetres: figures in brackets denote annual increments

Age of fish (years)	1	2	3	4	Average for all fish	Range for all fish
Number of fish	6	25	15	8	54	54
Length after 1 year	5·5	5·4	5·7	5·0	5·5	3·9-7·8
		(5·4)	(5·9)	(6·0)	(5·6)	
Length after 2 years		10·8	11·6	11·0	11·1	8·5-13·0
			(2·6)	(4·5)	(3·6)	
Length after 3 years			14·2	15·5	14·7	12·4-18·3
				(2·3)	(3·1)	
Length after 4 years				17·8	17·8	15·1-19·7

Appendix III Rivers

Data from various authors for the growth of brown trout in the British Isles. Average length (in inches) attained at the end of each year of life as calculated from scales

Water	Age in years								No. examined	Age at first spawn	Authority
	1	2	3	4	5	6	7	8			
England											
19. R.Test (Hants.)	4·8	10·0	13·0	16·0	19·0	—	—	—	49	3,4	CJR 1938
R. Test Fast-growing	5·2	10·5	13·6	14·6	—	—	—	—	13	3	CSG 1935
R. Test Slow-growing	3·6	8·5	13·0	16·7	19·3	21·0	23·0	24·0	36	4,5	CSG 1935
16. R. Avon (Bulford) Fast-growing (Wilts.)	5·1	10·2	12·7	—	—	—	—	—	41	3	CSG 1935
16. R. Avon (Bulford) Slow-growing	3·8	7·9	11·1	12·8	13·8	—	—	—	49	4,5	CSG 1935
R. Lambourn (Berks.)	4·6	9·6	12·0	14·0	—	—	—	—	311	3	CJR 1938
13. R. Lambourn Fast-growing	4·7	10·0	12·5	—	—	—	—	—	—	3	CSG 1935
14. R. Lambourn Slow-growing	3·7	7·9	11·1	12·1	13·5	—	—	—	—	4,5	CSG 1935
17. R. Nadder Fast-growing (Wilts.)	4·7	10·5	13·4	—	—	—	—	—	—	3	CSG 1935
18. R. Nadder Slow-growing	3·6	7·5	10·8	12·5	14·0	15·4	—	—	—	4,5	CSG 1935
15. R. Kennet (Berks.)	4·5	9·5	13·3	15·7	18·7	—	—	—	106	3,4,2	CJR 1938
Kennet Canal (Berks.)	4·5	9·5	13·5	15·7	20·0	—	—	—	16	3,4	CJR 1938
20.*R. Stour (Dorset)	4·4	8·4	12·0	15·0	15·5	—	—	—	17	3	CJR 1938
22. R. Dart (upper) above Buckfastleigh (Devon)	2·4	5·0	7·0	8·6	9·6	11·3	—	—	27	3,4	CJR 1938
22. R. Dart (lower) below Buckfastleigh	2·4	4·7	7·6	9·6	11·1	13·0	—	—	62	3,4	CJR 1938
21.*R. Tamar (Inney & Lyd) (Devon)	2·3	4·5	6·9	8·3	12·0	—	—	—	20	3,4	CJR 1938
10. R. Derwent (Derbyshire)	3·4	7·6	9·7	11·6	—	—	—	—	15		WEF 1943 in litt.
9. R. Bela (Westmorland)	3·2	6·8	8·2	9·6	10·7	12·2	—	—	75		WEF 1960 in litt.
7. R. Eden (Cumberland)	2·1	5·0	7·8	9·6	11·2	—	—	—	49		KRA 1937 in litt.
8. Raise Beck (Westmorland)	2·1	4·4	5·7	7·0	—	—	—	—	54		WEF 1954 in litt.
63. Upper Tees (Yorks.)	1·9	3·8	5·3	6·5	7·8	8·5	9·4	10·2	171		DTC 1963

Water	Age in years 1	2	3	4	5	6	7	8	No. examined	Age at first spawn	Authority
Scotland											
1. R. Forss (Caithness)	2·4	5·2	7·9	9·2	9·4	—	—	—	64		WEF 1950
3. R. Howiemore (S. Uist)	2·4	5·9	9·5	12·5	15·1	18·1	—	—	15		GHN 1934
2. R. Gisla (Lewis)	2·3	5·0	7·0	8·9	8·6	10·4	—	—	20	4,3	CJR 1938
6. R. S. Esk (Angus) (Tidal)	1·8	4·3	6·7	8·9	10·7	12·2	13·4	—	152		GHN 1934
5. R. N. Esk (Angus) (Tidal)	1·8	4·3	6·7	9·0	10·6	12·3	13·9	—	51		GHN 1934
4. R. Bervie (Kincardineshire) (Tidal)	2·0	4·5	6·9	9·1	10·6	12·0	—	—	15		GHN 1934
Wales											
12. R. Ithon & Irfon (Tribs. of Wye)	2·5	5·5	7·7	9·8	10·8	—	—	—	27	3,4	CJR 1938
11. R. Rhydwen (Merioneth)	2·5	4·1	5·1	6·0	6·6	—	—	—	917		JNB & JWJ 1960
R. Lliw (Trib. of Llyn Tegid)	3·6	5·5	7·0	8·2	—	—	—	—	192		JNB & JWJ 1960
65. R. Teifi (Cardiganshire)	2·9	6·5	8·4	10·2	10·7	—	—	—	42		JDT 1962
Ireland											
27. R. Liffey, Ballysmuttan (Co. Wicklow)	2·0	4·6	6·0	6·9	7·6	8·0	9·0	—	366		AEJW & WEF 42
26. R. Liffey, Straffan (Co. Kildare)	3·4	7·2	9·6	11·7	12·6	13·5	14·6	—	242		AEJW & WEF 42
28. King's R. (Liffey Trib.) (Co. Wicklow)	1·8	4·9	8·1	9·6	9·6	—	—	—	78		AEJW & WEF 42
25. Rye Water (Liffey Trib.) (Co. Kildare)	3·7	8·8	11·3	14·0	—	—	—	—	26		AEJW & WEF 42
30. R. Shannon, Meelick (Co. Tipp.)	2·4	5·7	10·4	13·7	—	—	—	—	22	3,4	RS 1935
31. R. Shannon, Killaloe (Co. Tipp.)	2·8	7·1	10·3	13·6	—	—	—	—	14	3,4	RS 1935
32. R. Shannon, Limerick (Tidal)	3·1	7·1	10·7	13·8	15·7	17·7	20·6	21·4	85	4,5	RS 1935
23. Black R. (Co. Galway)	3·7	8·2	12·1	15·6	17·8	—	—	—	122		AEJW 1943
24. Clare-Galway R. (Co. Galway)	3·4	8·2	11·8	15·6	18·5	21·2	—	—	35		AEJW 1943
29. R. Fergus (Co. Clare)	4·3	8·7	12·1	14·9	17·5	—	—	—	204		AH 1957

*Arranged from published figures

Appendix IV Lakes

Data from various authors for the growth of brown trout in the British Isles. Average length (in inches) attained at the end of each year of life as calculated from scales.

Water	Age in years								No. examined	Age at first spawn	Authority
	1	2	3	4	5	6	7	8			
England											
45. Windermere (Lake District)	2·3	5·4	8·5	11·2	14·1	16·0	19·0	—	420		KRA 1938
43. Ullswater (Lake District)	2·2	4·7	7·9	9·3	10·5	—	—	—	67		GHS & EBW 1939
44. Haweswater (Lake District)	2·0	4·3	6·3	7·6	8·7	—	—	—	101		GHS & EBW 1939
44. Wastwater (Lake District)	2·0	4·5	6·1	7·9	9·4	10·0	—	—	47		WEF 1960 in litt.
46. Three Dubs Tarn (Lake District)	3·4	7·1	8·5	9·5	10·2	10·6	10·8	—	865		WEF & WJPS 1952
47. Yew Tree Tarn (Lake District)	2·0	4·4	6·3	7·8	8·4	9·1	—	—	121		GHS & EBW 1939
Wise Een Tarn (Lake District)	2·2	4·7	8·2	10·0	11·0	11·5	12·0	—	126	3,4	WEF 1960 in litt.
Sunbiggin Tarn (Westmorland)	3·2	8·1	11·3	13·5	—	—	—	—	17		WEF 1956 in litt.
64. Malham Tarn (Yorks.)	2·6	6·8	11·3	14·3	16·1	18·3	20·1	—	70		PFH 1960
51. Blagdon Reservoir (Somerset)	3·9	9·1	13·9	16·4	18·3	22·0	—	—	36		EBW 1941
48. Ladybower Reservoir (Derbys.)	3·4	7·6	9·7	11·6	—	—	—	—	15		WEF 1943 in litt.
Scotland											
42. Loch Leven (Kinross-shire)	2·3	6·5	11·1	13·3	14·6	15·1	—	—	30		EBW 1939 in litt.
38. Loch Maree (Ross & Cromarty)	2·4	5·6	8·3	10·5	12·4	15·1	—	—	318		GHN 1934
41. Loch Tummell (Perthshire)	2·5	5·3	8·0	11·0	13·2	15·7	17·2	—	233		RNC 1957
36. Altnacealgach (4 lochs av.) (Sutherland)	2·5	5·3	8·0	9·6	11·0	—	—	—	13	3,4	CJR 1938
37. Loch Beannach (Ross & Cromarty)	2·0	5·5	8·1	9·7	10·8	12·0	—	—	50		EBW 1939 in litt.
39. Loch Gamhna (Inverness)	1·6	3·7	5·7	7·1	7·4	—	—	—	45		EBW 1939 in litt
40. Lochan Mor (Inverness)	2·2	5·7	9·0	12·0	14·1	15·7	—	—	24	3,4	EBW 1939 in litt.
33. Loch Granabhat (Lewis)	2·6	5·3	8·6	10·3	11·2	—	—	—	21		CJR 1938
34. Loch Maddy (N. Uist)	2·4	4·8	7·4	9·3	10·5	—	—	—	48	3,4	CJR 1938
35. Loch Boisdale (S. Uist)	3·1	6·7	9·3	10·5	12·3	15·2	—	—	65	3,4	CJR 1938
35. Loch a Bharp (S. Uist)	3·0	6·3	9·4	11·6	14·3	15·2	—	—	19		GHN 1934
35. Loch Laga (N. Argyll)	2·5	6·4	9·1	11·0	12·0	13·5	—	—	29		RNC 1960 in litt.

Water	Age in years								No. examined	Age at first spawn	Authority
	1	2	3	4	5	6	7	8			
Loch Sligneach (N. Argyll)	2·9	6·9	9·0	10·6	11·9	14·4	—	—	33		RNC 1960 *in litt*
Fincastle Loch (Perthshire)	2·5	6·1	8·7	9·6	—	—	—	—	168		RNC 1961
Lochan an Daim (Perthshire)	1·6	4·6	7·4	9·2	—	—	—	—	100		RNC 1961
Strathkyle Loch (Ross & Cromarty)	2·5	6·1	8·0	9·2	—	—	—	—	163		RNC 1961
Loch Borralie (Sutherland)	3·6	9·1	12·6	15·8	—	—	—	—	15		RNC 1961
St. Mary's Loch (Orkney)	2·4	5·2	8·3	10·3	11·3	—	—	—	62		GHN 1933
Wales											
49. Llyn Tegid (Bala) (Merioneth)	3·6	6·0	8·5	10·5	12·0	11·6	—	—	327		JNB & JWJ 1960
50. Lake Vyrnwy (Montgomery)	1·8	3·9	6·8	9·0	10·3	11·6	—	—	10		EBW 1939 *in litt.*
Ireland											
61. Lough Derg (Co. Tipp.)	2·8	6·6	11·6	15·8	18·6	—	—	—	92	4	RS 1935
52. Lough Melvin (Co. Sligo)	3·1	7·5	9·6	12·0	15·3	—	—	—	37	3,4,5	AEJW 1952
59. Lough Rea (Co. Galway)	3·5	9·4	13·8	17·2	19·2	20·7	—	—	135	4	AEJW 1949
58. Lough Corrib (Co. Galway)	3·2	7·0	11·2	14·1	15·7	19·1	24·2	—	104	?4	AEJW 1943
60. Lough Atorick (Co. Clare)	2·3	5·4	7·0	7·9	—	—	—	—	53	3	RS 1935
56. Lough Bofin (Co. Galway)	2·6	5·3	8·2	8·5	9·1	—	—	—	81	?3	AEJW 1943
55. Loughaunierin (Co. Galway)	2·6	6·3	8·2	9·5	10·7	11·3	—	—	51		AEJW 1943
57. Lough Tawnaghbeg (Co. Galway)	1·9	4·5	6·1	8·0	8·7	—	—	—	29		AEJW 1943
54. Ballynahinch loughs (Co. Galway)	2·1	5·0	7·1	9·0	10·3	12·6	14·2	—	69		GHN 1934
Caragh Lake (Co. Kerry)	2·2	5·2	7·6	9·6	10·5	13·5	—	—	1114		ET 1956
62. Lough Inchiquin (Co. Clare)	4·3	9·1	12·1	14·4	16·0	18·2	20·2	—	257		AH 1957
53. Lough Glore (Co. Westmeath)	3·8	8·3	12·1	16·3	19·9	22·8	23·1	—	208		AH & MK 1958

Authorities for Appendices IV and V

KRA K. R. Allen. 1938. *J. Anim. Ecol.* 7. No. 2. 1937. *In litt.*

JNB & JWJ J. N. Ball & J. W. Jones. 1960. *Proc. Zool. Soc. Lond. 134.*

RNC R. N. Campbell. 1957. *Sci. Invest. Freshwat. Fish. Scot. No. 14.* 1961. *Salm. Trout Mag. No. 161.* 1960 *In litt.*

DTC D. T. Crisp. 1963. *Salm. Trout Mag. No. 167.*

WEF W. E. Frost. 1950. *J. Anim. Ecol.* 19. No. 2. Other data *in litt.*

WEF & WJPS W. E. Frost & W. J. P. Smyly. 1952. *J. Anim. Ecol. 21.* No. 1.

CSG C. S. Gerrish. 1935. *Salm. Trout Mag. No. 81.*

AH A. Healy. 1957. *Salm. Trout Mag. No. 151.*

AH & MK A. Healy & M. Kennedy. 1958. *Salm. Trout Mag. No. 153.*

PFH P. F. Holmes. 1960. *Salm. Trout Mag. No. 159.*

GHN G. H. Nall. 1930. *Fisheries Scotland, Salmon Fish. No.* III. 1933. *Fisheries Scotland, Salmon Fish. No.* VIII.

CJR C. J. Raymond. 1938. *Salm. Trout Mag. No. 93.*

RS R. Southern. 1935. *Proc. R. Irish Acad. 42B. No. 6.*

GHS & EBW G. H. Swynnerton & E. B. Worthington. 1939. *Salm. and Trout Mag. No. 97.*

JDT J. D. Thomas. 1956. *J. Anim. Ecol. 31.* No. 2.

ET E. Twomey. 1956. *Salm. Trout Mag. No. 147.*

AEJW A. E. J. Went. 1943. *Proc. R. Irish Acad. 48B. No. 12.*
1949. *Salm. Trout Mag. No. 127.*
1953. *Salm. Trout Mag. No. 136.*

AEJW & WEF A. E. J. Went & W. E. Frost. 1942. *Proc. R. Irish. Acad. 48B. No. 4.*

EBW E. B. Worthington. 1941. *Salm. Trout Mag. No. 100.* 1939. *In litt.*

Appendix V

How to Calculate Specific Growth Rates

(*using the data for Straffan and Ballysmuttan on the River Liffey*)

We shall assume that only tables of log.$_{10}$ are available and that the fry are 0.95 inches long when they start to feed (i.e. at age 0).

First, arrange the average lengths in order of descending age and write beside each the value of its logarithm, taken from an ordinary Four Figure Table.

	Straffan		Ballysmuttan	
Age	length	log. $_{10}$	length	log. $_{10}$
6	13·5	1·1303	8·0	0·9031
5	12·6	1·1004	7·6	0·8808
4	11·7	1·0682	6·9	0·8388
3	9·6	0·9823	6·0	0·7782
2	7·2	0·8573	4·6	0·6628
1	3·4	0·5315	2·0	0·3010
0	0·95	$\bar{1}$·9777	0·95	$\bar{1}$·9777

Next, subtract each log. value from the one above it and write the values down. *Finally*, multiply each of these by 230 (which is 100×2.3026) and the answer is G, the annual specific growth rate for length, as % per annum.

Straffan

	$Log._{10}Y_T - Log._{10}Y_t$	G
T = 6, t = 5	0·0299	6·9
T = 5, t = 4	0·0322	7·5
T = 4, t = 3	0·0859	20·6
T = 3, t = 2	0·1250	28·8
T = 2, t = 1	0·3258	75
T = 1, t = 0	0·5538	128

Ballysmuttan

	$Log._{10}Y_T - Log._{10}Y_t$	G
T = 6, t = 5	0·0223	5·2
T = 5, t = 4	0·0420	9·7
T = 4, t = 3	0·0606	14·0
T = 3, t = 2	0·1154	26·6
T = 2, t = 1	0·3618	84
T = 1, t = 0	0·3233	75

The figures can now be arranged to show:

Specific growth rate during the year:	0-1	1-2	2-3	3-4	4-5	5-6
River Liffey at Straffan	128	75	29	21	8	7
River Liffey at Ballysmuttan	75	84	27	14	10	5

Appendix VI

Specific Growth Rates

for length (expressed as % per annum) of brown trout from various waters in the British Isles (calculated from the data in appendices IV and V)

		Growth rate during year:					
		0–1	1–2	2–3	3–4	4–5	5–6
Rivers							
R. Test (Hants.)	fast-growers	170	70	26	7		
	slow-growers	133	86	43	25	15	8
R. Avon (Wilts.)	fast-growers	168	69	22			
	slow-growers	139	73	34	14	8	
R. Lambourn (Berks.)		158	74	22	15		
R. Kennet (Berks.)		156	73	36	16	18	
Kennet Canal (Berks.)		158	73	35	15	24	
R. Dart above Buckfastleigh (Devon)		93	73	34	21	25	3
below Buckfastleigh		93	81	34	23	15	16
R. Forss (Caithness)		93	72	42	15	2	
R. Gisla (Lewis)		88	78	34	21		
R. South Esk (Angus)—tidal		64	87	44	28	18	13
R. Rhydwen (Merioneth)		97	50	22	16	10	
R. Teifi (Cardigans.)		112	81	26	19	5	
R. Shannon at Meelick (Co. Tipp.)		93	87	60	28		
at Limerick—tidal		118	83	53	25	13	12
Black River (Co. Galway)		136	80	39	26	13	
R. Fergus (Co. Clare)		151	71	33	21	16	
R. Liffey at Ballysmuttan (Co. Wicklow)		75	84	27	14	10	5
at Straffan (Co. Kildare)		128	75	29	21	8	7
Clare-Galway River (Co. Galway)		128	89	37	28	18	13
Lakes							
Windermere (Lake District)		89	85	45	28	23	13
Haweswater (Lake District)		75	77	38	19	20	
Three Dubs Tarn (Lake District)		128	74	18	11	7	4
Yew Tree Tarn (Lake District)		75	79	36	21	7	6
Malham Tarn (Yorks.)		101	96	51	24	12	13
Blagdon Reservoir (Somerset)		141	85	43	17	11	18
Loch Maddy (N. Uist)		93	69	43	23	12	
Loch Boisdale (S. Uist)		118	77	33	12	16	
Loch Maree (Ross and Cromarty)		93	85	37	26	17	20
Strathkyle Loch (Ross and Cromarty)		97	89	27	14		
Lochan Mor (Inverness.)		84	120	50	16	11	
Fincastle Loch (Perths.)		97	89	36	10		
Lochan an Daim (Perths.)		52	106	48	22		
Llyn Tegid (Bala) (Merioneth)		133	51	35	21	13	
Lough Inchiquin (Co. Clare)		151	75	29	17	11	13
Lough Atorick (Co. Clare)		88	85	26	12		
Lough Derg (Co. Tipperary)		108	86	56	31	16	
Lough Rea (Co. Galway)		130	99	38	22	11	8
Lough Corrib (Co. Galway)		121	78	47	23	11	20
Lough Bofin (Co. Galway)		88	84	31	13	10	
Lough Glore (Co. Westmeath)		139	78	38	30	20	14
Caragh Lake (Co. Kerry)		84	86	38	23	9	

Examination of Stomach Contents of Brown Trout

The stomach contents (fresh or preserved in formalin) should be put into a dish of water and a small amount of salt added to disperse the mucus.

A general picture of the stomach contents is obtained by sorting them into organisms taken at the surface, in mid-water, and off the bottom, a more detailed one by further analysis of these three categories (see tables 1, 2, 3, 4 below). Thus—surface organisms are the winged forms of various aquatic insects (mayflies, caddis flies, stoneflies etc.) or terrestrial insects which have fallen on to the water; mid-water organisms are those stages of aquatic insects which are on the way to the surface to emerge as winged forms (midge pupæ, late mayfly nymphs, etc.) or swimming insects (water boatmen, beetles) or fishes or, in lakes, zooplankton (water fleas); the bottom-living animals are larval forms of various aquatic insect groups (page 177) together with crustaceans, molluscs and aquatic worms and also non-aquatic animals such as earthworms.

This general method of stomach examination involves identifying the animals only into their main groups; this can be done from pictures of the invertebrates using a good hand lens. More detailed analysis of the stomach contents is sometimes required. Identification then involves the use of a compound microscope and technical reference books.

Tables 1, 2, 3 and 4 below illustrate the food of trout in still and running waters and the differences between that in lowland limestone waters (L. Inchiquin and R. Fergus) and upland, moorland non-limestone waters (Wise Een Tarn and upper Tees tributaries).

Table 1. Food of brown trout in Lough Inchiquin (Co. Clare), limestone water, based on 103 rod (fly) caught fish, April to September, average size 13 in., about 14 oz. (Data collected by the late R. Southern)

Organism	Percentage frequency of occurrence
Mayfly a.	2
Stonefly a.	1
Caddis fly a.	7
Diptera a. (aquatic origin)	8
Terrestrial insects	4
Caddis p.	5
Midge p.	17
Water boatmen	11
Beetles a.	2
Planktonic Cladocera (*Daphnia*, etc.)	53
Fish	5
Mayfly n.	7
Caddis l.	6
Midge l.	3
Diptera l.	2
Dragonfly n.	1
Shrimp	6
Water Slater	25
Weed-living Cladocera	6
Snails	11
Pea mussels	1

Table 2. Food of brown trout in River Fergus (Co. Clare), limestone water, based on 54 rod (fly) caught fish, April, May, June and September, average size 15 in., about $1\frac{1}{4}$ lb. (Data collected by the late R. Southern)

Organism	Percentage frequency of occurrence
Mayfly a.	39
Caddis fly a.	26
Diptera a. (aquatic origin)	17
Terrestrial insects	37
Caddis p.	17

Table 2. (*continued*)

Midge p.	13
Water boatmen	9
Beetle a.	15
Newts	2
Mayfly n.	35
Caddis fly l.	20
Diptera l (various)	11
Blackfly (*Simulium*) l.	17
Dragonfly n.	11
Shrimp	15
Water slater	17
Snails	20
Terrestrial (non-insects)	7

Table 3. Food of brown trout in Wise Een Tarn (near Windermere), moorland water, based on 166 rod (fly) caught fish, March to September, average size about 8 oz. (Data collected by W. E. Frost)

Organism	Percentage frequency of occurrence
Mayfly a.	13
Stonefly a.	+
Caddis fly a.	6
Diptera a (aquatic)	4
Dragonfly a.	2
Alderfly a.	1
Terrestrial insects	31
Midge p.	33
Water boatmen	+
Mayfly n.	30
Caddis l.	64
Midge l.	37
Phantom l.	8
Dragonfly n.	36
Alderfly l.	13
Beetle l.	7
Shrimp	3
Water slater	7
Weed-living Cladocera	38

Table 4.   Food of brown trout in upper River Tees tributaries, moorland non-limestone waters, based on 178 rod caught fish, March to September, average size about 3 oz. (Data from D. T. Crisp. Salm. Trout Mag. 167. 1963)

Organism	Percentage frequency of occurrence
Mayfly a.	25
Stonefly a.	27
Caddis fly a.	9
Midge a.	9
Terrestrial insects	73
Beetles a.	3
Mayfly n.	39
Stonefly n.	45
Caddis l.	39
Midge l.	59
Beetle l.	13
Fish (Bullhead)	11

Appendix VIII

List of Waters for which we have Data on Total Hardness (Shown in Map VI)

We are greatly indebted to Mr. R. C. S. Walters, B.SC., M.I.C.E., F.G.S., of Herbert Lapworth Partners, London, who gave us information about most of these waters.

1. R. Don, (Scot.) Bucksburn
2. R. North Esk, Montrose
3. R. Leven, Dumbarton
4. R. Clyde, Rutherglen
5. R. Irvine, Ayrshire
6. R. Eden, Berwickshire
7. R. Black Esk, Dumfries
8. R. Wiza, Wigton
9. R. Caldew, Dalston near Carlisle
10. R. Duddon, North Lancs.
11. R. Wharfe, Otley
12. R. Aire, Yorks.
13. R. Canon
14. R. Ouse, Selby, Yorks.
15. R. Roach, Littleborough near Rochdale
16. R. Calder, Wakefield
17. R. Hull, Westbeck
18. R. Tame, Oldham
19. R. Irwell
20. R. Don, Sheffield
21. R. Derwent, Derby
21. R. Derwent (supply to Sheffield Waterworks)
22. R. Dee, Wrexham
22. R. Dee, Chester
23. R. Wye, Buxton
24. R. Trent, Newark
25. R. Lymm, Spilsby
26. R. Dove, Sterndale Farm
27. R. Witham above Lincoln
28. R. Welland near Grantham
29. New River, Spalding
30. R. Avon, Ryton
31. R. Wissey, Norfolk
32. R. Ithom, Llandrindod Wells
33. R. Arrow, Hereford
34. R. Lugg, Hereford
35. R. Severn, Upton-on-Severn, Worcestershire
36. R. Stour, Long Marston, Warwick
37. R. Gt. Ouse, Stratford
37. R. Gt. Ouse, Bedford
38. R. Stour, Essex-Suffolk
39. Newbourne Stream, Suffolk
40. Bucklesham Stream, Suffolk
41. Llawddog, Carmarthen
41. R. Towy, Carmarthen
42. R. Llwchwr, Carmarthen
43. R. Caerfanel, Talybont, Newport
44. R. Chess, Bucks.
45. R. Coln, Herts.
46. R. Chelmer, Essex
47. R. Blackwater, Essex
48. R. Lee, Wittam
49. R. Avon, Colne, Wilts.
50. R. Thames, Slough
51. R. Thames, Staines
52. R. Mole, Surrey
53. R. Medway
54. R. Medway, Tonbridge
54. R. Medway, Maidstone
55. R. Brue, Somerset
56. R. Itchen, Hants.

57. Shell Brook, Ardingley, Sussex
58. R. Yeo, Yeovil, Somerset
59. R. Stour, Christchurch, Hants.
60. R. Avon, Hants.
61. R. Erme near Ivybridge
62. Mill Mehal S, St. Keverne
63. R. Annalee, Co. Monaghan
64. R. Suck, Roscommon
65. R. Shannon, Meelick
66. Mullingar R., Co. Westmeath
67. Boycetown R., Co. Meath
68. Tullamore R., Co. Offaly
69. R. Liffey, Straffan (Co. Kildare) *and* Ballysmuttan (Co. Wicklow)
70. Glencullen R., Co. Wicklow
71. R. Slaney, Tullow, Co. Wexford
72. R. Saw, Edenvale, Co. Wexford
73. R. Blackwater, Co. Cork

Lakes
Scotland
74. L. Borralie
75. L. Loyal
76. L. Watten
77. L. Assynt
78. L. Shin
79. L. Maree
80. L. Katrine
81. L. Leven

England
82. Ennerdale Water
83. Haweswater
84. Ullswater
85. Wastwater
86. Wise Een Tarn
87. Windermere

Wales
88. L. Llech Owain

Ireland
89. L. Neagh
90. L. Arrow
91. L. Sheelin
92. L. Ramor
93. L. Mask
94. L. Derravaragh
95. L. Corrib
96. L. Owel
97. L. Rea
98. L. Atorick
99. L. Derg

List of References

ALABASTER, J. S., HERBERT, D. W. M. & HEMENS, J. (1957). The survival of rainbow trout (*Salmo gairdneri* Richardson) and perch (*Perca fluviatilis* L.) at various concentrations of dissolved oxygen and carbon dioxide. *Ann. appl. Biol. 45*: 177-88.

ALLEN, K. R. (1938). Some observations on the biology of the trout (*Salmo trutta*) in Windermere. *J. Anim. Ecol. 7*: 333-49.

ALLEN, K. R. (1941). Studies on the biology of the early stages of the salmon (*Salmo salar*). 2. Feeding habits. *J. Anim. Ecol. 10*: 47-76.

ALLEN, K. R. (1951). The Horokiwi Stream. A study of a trout population. *Bull. Mar. Dept. N.Z. Fish. 10*: 1-238.

ALLEN, K. R. (1951). A New Zealand trout stream. *Bull. Mar. Dept. N.Z. Fish. 10a*: 1-70.

ALLPORT, M. (1870). Brief history of the introduction of salmon (*Salmo salar*) and other Salmonidæ to the waters of Tasmania. *Proc. Zool. Soc. Lond. 1870*: 14-30.

ALM, G. (1939). Investigations on the growth etc. by different forms of trout. *Medd. Undersökn. Anst. Sötvättensfisk. Stockh. 15*: 1-93.

ALM, G. (1949). Influence of heredity and environment on various forms of trout. *Rep. Inst. Freshw. Drottningholm 29*: 29-34.

ALM, G. (1959). Connection between maturity, size and age in fishes. *Rep. Inst. Freshw. Res. Drottningholm 40*: 5-145.

ASHBY, K. R. (1956). The early development of the reproductive system of the brown trout (*Salmo trutta* L.) *Proc. XIV Int. Congr. Zool. 1953*: 239-42.

BAINBRIDGE, R. (1958). The speed of swimming of fish as related to size and to the frequency and amplitude of the tail beat. *J. exp. Biol. 35*: 109-33.

BAINBRIDGE, R. (1962). Training, speed and stamina in trout. *J. exp. Biol. 39*: 537-55.

BALL, J. N. (1961). On the food of the brown trout of Llyn Tegid. *Proc. Zool. Soc. Lond. 137*: 599-622.

BALL, J. N. & JONES, J. W. (1961). On the movements of the brown trout of Llyn Tegid. *Proc. Zool. Soc. Lond. 138*: 205-24.

BALL, J. N. & JONES, J. W. (1960). On the growth of the brown trout of Llyn Tegid. *Proc. Zool. Soc. Lond. 134*: 1-41.

BERG, K. (1948). Biological studies on the River Susaa. *Folia limnol. scand.* 4: 1-318.

BERG, L. S. (1932). *Les poissons des eaux douces de l'U.R.S.S. et des pays limitrophes*. 3-e Edition, Partie 1. Leningrad, 1932.

BERG, L. S. (1932). Ubersicht der Verbreitung der Süsswasserfische Europas. *Zoogeografica Jena 1. 1932*. 107-208.

BERNERS, DAME JULIANA (1496). *The Treatyse of Fysshynge wyth an Angle*. Reprinted from the book of St. Albans. London. Pickering, 1827. 8°.

BERRY, J. (1932). The trapping of spawning trout. *Salm. Trout Mag.* 67: 119-24.

BERRY, J. (1936). The longtailed field mouse (*Apodemus sylvaticus*) as a destroyer of salmon ova. *Rep. Avon. Biol. Res.* 5: 67-9.

BHATIA, D. (1931). Production of annual zones in scales of rainbow trout. *J. exp. Zool.* 59: 45-59.

BHATIA, D. (1931). Critical study of scales of two specimens of starved and excessively fed trout. *J. Cons. int. Explor. Mer.* 6: 266-72.

BROCKWAY, D. R. (1950). Metabolic products and their effects. *Progr. Fish Cult.* 12: 127-9.

BROOK, A. J. & HOLDEN, A. V. (1957). Fertilisation experiments in Scottish freshwater lochs. 1. Loch Kinardochy. *Sci. Invest. Freshwat. Fish. Scot.* 17: 1-30.

BROWN, M. E. (1946). The growth of brown trout (*Salmo trutta* Linn.)
I. Factors influencing the growth of trout fry. *J. exp. Biol.* 22: 118-29.
II. The growth of two-year-old trout at a constant temperature of 11.5°C. *J. exp. Biol.* 22: 130-44.
III. The effect of temperature on the growth of two-year-old trout. *J. exp. Biol.* 22: 145-55.

BROWN, M. E. (1951). The growth of brown trout (*Salmo trutta* Linn.)
IV. The effect of food and temperature on the survival and growth of fry. *J. exp. Biol.* 28: 473-91.

BROWN, M. E. (1957). Ed. *The physiology of Fishes*. New York Academic Press. Vol. 1. *Metabolism*. Vol. 2. *Behaviour*.

BUSH, S. F. (1933). Trout problems in Natal. *Salm. Trout Mag.* 73: 359-80.

BUTCHER, R. W., PENTELOW, F. T. K. & WOODLEY, J. W. A. (1931). An investigation of the River Lark and the effect of beet-sugar pollution. *Fish. Invest. Lond.* Ser. 1. *3*. (3) 1-112.

CAMPBELL, R. N. (1961). The growth of brown trout in acid and alkaline waters. *Salm. Trout Mag. 161*: 47-52.

CARPENTER, K. E. (1928). *Life in inland waters*. London. Sidgwick & Jackson.

CATT, J. (1950). Some notes on brown trout with particular reference to their status in New Brunswick and Nova Scotia. *Canad. Fish. Cult. 7*: 25-7.

COPLEY, H. (1940). Trout in Kenya Colony. Part 1. Brown trout. Part 2. Rainbow trout. *E. Afr. agric. J. 5*: 1-24.

COPLEY, H. (1954). *Review of Kenya Fisheries*, 1953. Nairobi, Govt. Printer.

COSTON, D. T., PENTELOW, F. T. K. & BUTCHER, R. W. (1936). *River Management*. London. Seeley Service & Co. Ltd.

CRASS, R. S. (1960). Biological notes on the acclimatisation of trout in Natal. *S. Afr. J. Sci. 56*: 147-51.

CRISP, D. T. (1963). A preliminary survey of brown trout and bullheads in high altitude becks. *Salm. Trout Mag. 167*: 45-59.

DAHL, K. (1909). The assessment of age and growth in fish. *Int. Rev. Hydrobiol. 2*: 758-69.

DAHL, K. (1910). *Alder og vekst hos laks og ørret belyst ved studiet av deres skjael*. Kristiania. TRANSLATION: *The age and growth of salmon and trout in Norway as shown by their scales*. London. Salmon and Trout Association, 1910.

DAHL, K. (1916-17). Salmon and Trout: a handbook. *Salm. Trout Mag. 13*: 9-30, *14*: 55-60, *15*: 18-34.

DAHL, K. (1917). *Studier og forsøk over ørret og ørretvand*. Kristiania. TRANSLATION: Studies of trout and trout waters in Norway. *Salm. Trout Mag.* (1918). *17*: 58-79, 1919. *18*: 16-33.

DAHL, K. (1933). Are brown and sea trout interchangeable? *Salm. Trout Mag. 71*: 132-8.

DAVIS, H. S. (1934). Growth and heredity in trout. *Trans. Amer. Fish. Soc. 64*: 197-202.

DAVIS, H. S. (1956). *Culture and diseases of game fishes*. Berkeley. Univ. California Press.

DAY, F. (1887). *British and Irish Salmonidæ*. London. Williams & Norgate.

DOGIEL, V. A., PETRUSHEVSKI, G. K. & POLYANSKI, YU. I. (1958). (Translated by Kabata, Z., 1961.) *Parasitology of fishes*. Edinburgh. Oliver & Boyd.

DONALDSON, L. R. & OLSON, P. R. (1957). Development of rainbow brood stock by selective breeding. *Trans. Amer. Fish. Soc. 85*: 93-101.

DOWNING, K. M. & MERKENS, J. C. (1955). The influence of temperature on the survival of several species of fish in low tensions of dissolved oxygen. *Ann. appl. Biol. 45*: 243-6.

DYMOND, J. R. (1953). The introduction of foreign fishes in Canada. *Verh. int. Ver. Limnol. 12*: 543-53.

ED IN PISCATOR (1950). "Sixty years ago"— No. 1: The prologue of J. D. Ellis, June, 1890. *Piscator 4*: 14, 44-6. No. 2: The work of Ernest Latour, 1894-1896. *Piscator 4*: 15; 76-9.

EGGLISHAW, H. J. (1968). The quantitative relationship between bottom fauna and plant detritus in streams of different calcium concentrations. *J. appl. Biol. 5*: 731-40.

EGGLISHAW, H. J. (1969). The distribution of benthic invertebrates on substrata in fast flowing streams. *J. Anim. Ecol. 38*: 19-34.

ELLIOTT, J. M. (1965). Daily fluctuations of drift invertebrates in a Dartmoor stream. *Nature, 205*: 1127-9.

EMBODY, G. C. (1934). Relation of temperature to the incubation periods of four species of trout. *Trans. Amer. Fish. Soc. 64*: 281-92.

FORT, R. S. & BRAYSHAW, J. D. (1961). *Fishery Management*. London. Faber & Faber.

FROST, W. E. (1939). River Liffey Survey II. The food consumed by the brown trout (*Salmo trutta* Linn.) in acid and alkaline waters. *Proc. R. Irish Acad. 45B*: 139-206.

FROST, W. E. (1942). R. Liffey Survey IV. The fauna of submerged "mosses" in acid and alkaline waters. *Proc. R. Irish Acad. 47B*: 293-369.

FROST, W. E. (1945). R. Liffey Survey VI. Discussion on the results obtained from investigations on the food and growth of brown trout (*Salmo trutta* L.) in alkaline and acid waters. *Proc. R. Irish Acad. 50B*: 321-42.

FROST, W. E. (1945). On the food relationships of fish in Windermere. *Biol. Jaarb. 13*: 216-31.

FROST, W. E. (1946). Observations on the food of eels (*Anguilla anguilla*) from the Windermere catchment area. *J. Anim. Ecol. 15*: 43-53.

FROST, W. E. (1950). The growth and food of young salmon (*Salmo salar*) and trout (*Salmo trutta*) in the River Forss, Caithness. *J. Anim Ecol. 19*: 147-58.

FROST, W. E. (1954). The food of pike (*Esox lucius* L.) in Windermere. *J. Anim. Ecol. 23*: 339-60.

FROST, W. E. & SMYLY, W. J. P. (1952). The brown trout of a moorland fish pond. *J. Anim. Ecol. 21*: 62-86.

FROST, W. E. & WENT, A. E. J. (1940). R. Liffey Survey III. The growth and food of young salmon. *Proc. R. Irish Acad. 46B*: 53-80.

FRY, F. E. J. (1947). Effects of the environment on animal activity. *Univ. Toronto Stud. biol. 55. Publ. Ont. Fish. Res. Lab. 68*: 21-62.

FRY, F E. J. (1947). Temperature relations of Salmonids. *Proc. Nat. Com. Fish Cult. 10th Meeting*. Appendix D.

GENG, H. (1925). Die Futterwert der natürlichen Fischnahrung. *Z. Fisch. 23*: 137-65.

GERRISH, C. STRATTON (1935). Hatchery stock and trout streams. *Salm. Trout Mag. 81*: 331-44.

GERRISH, C. STRATTON (1936). The value of hatchery trout for stocking rivers. *Salm. Trout Mag. 84*: 245-54.

GERRISH, C. STRATTON (1940). The growth rate of trout, can it be acquired? *Salm. Trout Mag. 99*: 121-9.

GRAHAM, T. T. & JONES, J. W. (1962). The biology of Llyn Tegid trout 1960. *Proc. Zool. Soc. Lond. 139*: 657-83.

GRANT, D. K. S. (1933). Introduction of trout into Tanganyika Territory. *J. E. Afr. Ug. nat. Hist. Soc. 49-50*: 197-204

GRAY, J. (1926). The growth of fish. I. Relationship between embryo and yolk in *Salmo fario*. *J. exp. Biol. 4*: 215-25.

GRAY, J. (1928). The growth of fish. II. Growth rate of the embryo of *Salmo fario*. *J. exp. Biol. 6*: 110-24.

III. Effect of temperature on the development of the eggs of *Salmo fario*. *J. exp. Biol. 6*: 125-30.

GREELEY, J. R. (1932). The spawning habits of brook, brown and rainbow trout and the problem of egg predators. *Trans. Amer. Fish. Soc. 62*: 239-48.

GÜNTHER, A. C. L. G. (1866). *Catalogue of the fishes of the British Museum.* Vol. 6.

HARTLEY, P. H. T. (1940). The food of coarse fish. *Sci. Publ. Freshw Biol. Ass. 3*: 1-33.

HARTLEY, P. H. T. (1947). The natural history of some British freshwater fishes. *Proc. Zool. Soc. Lond. 117*: 129-206.

HARTLEY, P. H. T. (1948). Food and feeding relationships in a community of freshwater fishes. *J. Anim. Ecol. 17*: 1-14.

HARVEY, L. A. (1964). The ecology of some Dartmoor streams. *Dartmoor Essays* (Exeter). *Devonshire Ass. Advanc. Sci. Litt. Art.*

HAZZARD, A. Z. (1941). The effect of snow and ice on fish life. *Proc. cent. Snow. Conf. 1*: 90—.

HEWITT, E. R. (1943). Trout growth in America. *Salm. Trout Mag.* 108: 112-15.

HIGGS, A. (1942). Big trout from big eggs. *Salm. Trout Mag. 106*: 216-30.

HILLS, J. W. (1934). *River Keeper.* London. Methuen.

HOBBS, D. F. (1937). Natural reproduction of Quinnat salmon, brown and rainbow trout in certain New Zealand waters. *Fish. Bull. Wellington N.Z. 6*: 1-104.

HOFFBAUER, C. (1905). Weitere Beiträge zur alters- und Wachstumsbestimmung der Fische, spez des Karpfens. *Z. Fisch. 12*: 111-42.

HOLDEN, A. V. (1959). Fertilisation experiments in Scottish freshwater lochs. II. Sutherland, 1954. I. Chemical and botanical observations. *Sci. Invest. Freshwat. Fish. Scot. 24*: 1-42.

HOLMES, P. F. (1960). The brown trout of Malham Tarn, Yorkshire. *Salm. Trout Mag. 159*: 127-45.

HORTON, P. A. (1961). The bionomics of brown trout in a Dartmoor stream. *J. Anim. Ecol. 30*: 311-38.

HUET, M. (1954). Biologie profils en long et en travers des eaux courantes. *Bull. franç. Piscic. 175*: 41-53.

HUMPHRIES, C. F. (1936). An investigation of the profundal and sublittoral fauna of Windermere. *J. Anim. Ecol. 5*: 29-52.

HYNES, H. B. N. (1950). The food of freshwater sticklebacks (*Gasterosteus aculeatus* and *Pygosteus pungitius*) with a review of methods used in studies of the food of fishes. *J. Anim. Ecol. 19*: 35-58.

HYNES, H. B. N. (1960). *The biology of polluted waters*. Liverpool Univ. Press.

JONES, J. R. ERICHSEN (1948). The fauna of four streams in the "Black Mountain" district of South Wales. *J. Anim. Ecol. 17*: 51-65.

JONES, J. R. ERICHSEN (1951). An ecological study of the River Towy. *J. Anim. Ecol. 20*: 68-86.

JONES, J. W. (1947). Salmon and trout hybrids. *Proc. Zool. Soc. Lond. 117*: 708-15.

JONES, J. W. (1959). *The Salmon*. London. Collins, *New Nat.*

JONES, J. W. & BALL, J. N. (1954). The spawning behaviour of brown trout and salmon. *Brit. J. Anim. Behav. 2*: 103-14.

JONES, J. W. & EVANS, H. (1960). Eels may not be guilty after all. *Trout. Salm. 6 (64)*: 17-18.

KALLEBERG, H. (1958). Observations in a stream tank of territoriality and competition in juvenile salmon and trout. *Rep. Inst. Freshw. Res. Drottningholm 39*: 55-98.

KIPLING, C. (1962). The use of the scales of the brown trout (*Salmo trutta* L.) for the back-calculation of growth. *J. Cons. int. Explor. Mer. 27*: 304-15.

LANDGREBE, F. W. (1941). The role of the pituitary and thyroid in the development of teleosts. *J. exp. Biol. 18*: 162-9.

LE CREN, E. D. (1961). How many fish survive? *Yearb. Riv. Bds. Ass. 9*: 57-64.

MACAN, T. T. (1958). The temperature of a small stony stream. *Hydrobiologia 12*: 89-106.

MACAN, T. T. & WORTHINGTON, E. B. (1951). *Life in lakes and rivers*. London. Collins, *New Nat.*

MCCORMACK, J. C. (1962). The food of young trout (*Salmo trutta*) in two different becks. *J. Anim. Ecol. 31*: 305-16.

MAITLAND, P. S. (1965). The feeding relationships of salmon, trout, minnows, stone-loach and three-spined sticklebacks in the River Endrick, Scotland. *J. Anim. Ecol. 34*: 109-33.

MILLER, R. B. (1958). The role of competition in the mortality of hatchery trout. *J. Fish. Res. Bd. Can. 15*: 27-45.

MILLS, D. H. (1967). A study of trout and young salmon populations in forest streams with a view to management. Forestry. 40 (B). Supplement, 85-90.

MINOT, C. S. (1908). *The problem of age, growth and death.* London. Murray.

MOON, H. P. (1934). An investigation of the littoral region of Windermere. *J. Anim. Ecol. 3*: 8-28.

MUNRO, W. R. & BALMAIN, K. H. (1956). Observations on the spawning runs of brown trout in South Queich, Loch Leven. *Sci. Invest. Freshwat. Fish. Scot. 13*: 1-17.

MYERS, C. (1946). Trout foods. *Salm. Trout Mag. 118*: 212-18.

MYERS, C. (1950). Stocking. *J. Fly-Fish. Cl. 39*: 154, 41-5. 155, 62-7.

NALL, G. H. (1930). *The life of the sea trout.* London. Seeley Service & Co.

NEAVE, F. (1936). The development of the scales of *Salmo. Trans. roy. Soc. Can.* Ser. 3. *30*: 3, 55-72.

NEEDHAM, P. R. (1938). *Trout streams.* Ithaca, U.S.A. Comstock Publishing Co.

NEILL, R. M. (1938). The food and feeding of the brown trout (*Salmo trutta* L.) in relation to the organic environment. *Trans. roy. Soc. Edinb. 59*: 481-520.

NICHOLLS, A. G. (1957). The Tasmanian Trout Fishery I. *Aust. J. Mar. Freshw. Res. 8*: 451-75.

NICHOLLS, A. G. (1958). The Tasmanian Trout Fishery II. *Aust J. Mar. Freshw. Res. 9*: 19-59. The Tasmanian Trout Fishery III. *Aust. J. Mar. Freshw. Res. 9*: 167-90.

NICHOLLS, A. G. (1958). The population of a trout stream and the survival of released fish. *Aust. J. Mar. Freshw. Res. 9*: 319-50.

NICHOLLS, A. G. (1961). The Tasmanian Trout Fishery IV. *Aust. J. Mar. Freshw. Res. 12*: 17-53.

NICHOLS, W. R. (1882). *Acclimatisation of Salmonidæ at the Antipodes.*

NORDEN, C. R. (1961). Comparative osteology of representative salmonid fishes with particular reference to the grayling (*Thymallus thymallus*) and its phylogeny. *J. Fish. Res. Bd. Can. 18*: 679-791.

PARRY, G. (1960). The development of salinity tolerance in the salmon (*Salmo salar* L.) and some related species. *J. exp. Biol. 37*: 425-34.

PEART, L. R. (1938). *Fishing in the making.* London. A. & C. Black.

PEART, L. R. (1956). *Trout and Trout Waters.* London. Allen & Unwin.

PENTELOW, F. T. K. (1932). The food of the brown trout. (*Salmo trutta*). *J. Anim. Ecol. 1*: 101-7.

PENTELOW, F. T. K. (1939). The relation between growth and food consumption in the brown trout (*Salmo trutta*). *J. exp. Biol. 16*: 446-73.

PENTELOW, F. T. K. (1944). Nature of acid in soft water in relation to the growth of brown trout. *Nature, Lond. 153*: 464.

PERCIVAL, E. (1932). On the depreciation of trout fishing in the Oreti (or New River) Southland, with remarks on conditions in other parts of New Zealand. *Bull. Mar. Dept. N.Z. Fish. 5*: 1-48.

PERCIVAL, E. & WHITEHEAD, H. (1929). A quantitative study of the fauna of some types of stream bed. *J. Ecol. 17*: 238-314.

PYEFINCH, K. A. (1960). *Trout in Scotland. A story of brown trout research at Pitlochry.* Edinburgh, H.M. Stationery Office. 1-70.

REGAN, C. T. (1911). *The freshwater fishes of the British Isles.* London. Methuen.

ROGERS, A., SPENCE, J. A. & WEST, A. B. (1965). The Cottage River Experiment. *Rep. Salm. Res. Trust. Ireland.* Append. III, 27-40.

Salmon & Freshwater Fisheries Report for 1936 (1937). The growth of brown trout. 28-31.

Salmon & Freshwater Fisheries Report for 1937 (1938). The growth of brown trout. 31-4.

SAWYER, F. (1952). *Keeper of the Stream.* A. and C. Black. London.

SAWYER, R. E. (1944). Nature of the acid in soft water in relation to the growth of brown trout. *Nature, Lond. 153*: 55-6.

SKROCHOWSKA, ST. (1952). The rearing of sea trout (*Salmo trutta* L.) in artificial ponds. *Bull. int. Acad. Cracovie 1951 B, II*: 179-226.

SMITH, M. W. (1952). Fertilisation and predator control to improve trout production in Crecy lake, New Brunswick. *Canad. Fish Cult. 13*: 33-9.

SMYLY, W. J. P. (1955). On the biology of the stone-loach (*Nemacheilus barbatula* (L.)) *J. Anim. Ecol. 24*: 167-86.

SMYLY, W. J. P. (1957). The life history of the bullhead or Miller's Thumb (*Cottus gobio* L.) *Proc. Zool. Soc. Lond. 128*: 431-53.

SØMME, J. D. (1948). *Ørretboka*. Oslo, Jacob Dybwads Fonlag.

SØMME, S. (1930). En undersøkelse over vekst-og gykteforhold hos ørret og harr i Øyer. (Gudbrandsdalen) *Nyt. Mag. Naturv. 68*: 171-244.

SOUTHERN, H. N. ED. (1964). *The Handbook of British Mammals*. Blackwell Scientific Publications, Oxford.

SOUTHERN, R. (1932). The food and growth of brown trout. *Salm. Trout Mag. 67*: 168-76, *68*: 243-58, *69*: 339-44.

SOUTHERN, R. (1935). Reports from the Limnological Laboratory III. Food and growth of brown trout from Lough Derg and the River Shannon. *Proc. R. Irish Acad. 42B*: 87-172.

SPAAS, J. T. & HUETS, M. J. (1959). Contributions to the comparative physiology and genetics of the European Salmonidæ. II. Physiologie et genetique du developpement embryonnaire. *Hydrobiologia 12*: 1-26.

STEPHENS, M. (1957). *The Otter Report*. London Univ. Fed. Anim. Welfare.

STEVEN, D. M. (1948). Studies on animal carotenoids. I. Carotenoids of the brown trout (*Salmo trutta* Linn.). *J. exp. Biol. 25*: 369-87.

STEVEN, D. M. (1949). Studies on animal carotenoids. II. Carotenoids in the reproductive cycle of the brown trout. *J. exp. Biol. 26*: 295-303.

STUART, T. A. (1953). Spawning migration, reproduction and young stages of loch trout (*Salmo trutta* L.). *Sci. Invest. Freshwat. Fish. Scot. 5*: 1-39.

STUART, T. A. (1957). The migrations and homing behaviour of brown trout (*Salmo trutta* L.). *Sci. Invest. Freshwat. Scot. 18*: 1-27.

SWIFT, D. R. (1955). Seasonal variations in the growth rate, thyroid gland activity and food reserves of brown trout (*Salmo trutta* Linn.). *J. exp. Biol. 32*: 751-64.

SWIFT, D. R. (1960). Cyclical activity of the thyroid gland of fish in relation to environmental changes. *Symp. zool. Soc. Lond. 2*: 17-27.

SWIFT, D. R. (1961). The annual growth rate cycle in brown trout (*Salmo trutta* Linn.) and its cause. *J. exp. Biol. 38*: 595-604.

SWIFT, D. R. (1962). Evidence for the absence of an endogenous growth rate rhythm in brown trout (*Salmo trutta* Linn.). *Comp. Biochem. Physiol. 6*: 91-3.

THOMAS, J. D. (1962). The food and growth of brown trout (*Salmo trutta* L.) and its feeding relationships with the salmon parr (*Salmo salar* L.) and the eel (*Anguilla anguilla* (L.)) in the River Teifi, west Wales. *J. Anim. Ecol. 31*: 175-205.

TONER, E. D. (1959). Predation by pike (*Esox lucius* L.) in three Irish loughs. *Rep. Sea Inl. Fish. Ire. 1959*, Appendix 25, 1-7.

TREWAVAS, E. (1953). Sea trout and brown trout. *Salm. Trout Mag. 139*: 199-215.

TUCKER, D. S. (1958). The distribution of some freshwater invertebrates in ponds in relation to annual fluctuations in the chemical composition of the water. *J. Anim. Ecol. 27*: 105-23.

VAN SOMEREN, V. D. (1950). The "winter check" on trout scales in East Africa. *Nature, Lond. 165*: 473-4.

VAN SOMEREN, V. D. (1952). *The biology of trout in Kenya Colony*. Nairobi, Govt. Printer. 1-110.

WALLS, G. L. (1942). The vertebrate eye. *Cranbrook Institute of Science Bull. 19*: 1-785.

WALTON, IZAAK (1653). *The compleat angler.*

WENT, A. E. J. & FROST, W. E. (1942). River Liffey Survey v. Growth of brown trout (*Salmo trutta* L.) in alkaline and acid waters. *Proc. R. Irish Acad. 48B*: 67-84.

WHITEHEAD, H. (1935). An ecological study of the invertebrate fauna of a chalk stream near Great Driffield, Yorkshire. *J. Anim. Ecol. 4*: 58-78.

WILLOUGHBY, L. G. (1969). Salmon disease in Windermere and

the River Leven; the fungal aspect. *Salm. Trout Mag.* 186 : 124-9.

WINGFIELD, C. A. (1940). The effect of certain environmental factors on the growth of brown trout (*Salmo trutta* L.). *J. exp. Biol. 17* : 435-48.

WOOD, A. H. (1932). The effect of temperature on the growth and respiration of fish embryos (*Salmo fario*). *J. exp. Biol. 9* : 271-6.

Index

acid waters, 152-8, 162-75, 208
Africa—Kenya, 61-3, 71, 94, 139, 263
 other parts, 15, 50, 57-8, 60-3, 94
age—determination of, 86-93, 95-6
 and growth, 96-108
 and maturity, 106, 110-18
air bladder (swim bladder), 22-3, 42, 218, 237
alevin, 77-82, Plates 3 and 4
Allen, K. Radway, 19, 70, 79-80, 93, 128, 137, 187-8, 193, 214, 222, 247, 262-6
Alm, G., 110-20, 137
America—Canada and New-foundland, 16, 46-7, 48-9, 58, 63, 251
 South, 58, 63
 U.S.A., 16, 46-7, 48-9, 58, 63, 112-14
ammonia, 25, 31-4, 163, 165
angling, 15-19, 63, 186, 241-3, 258-9, 262, 268-9
Antipodes, 15, 58-60, 139, 141
 Australia, 58-60
 New Zealand (and see Horo-kiwi River), 19, 53, 58-60, 63-4, 77
 Tasmania, 58-60, 64, 255
aquarium experiments and ob-servations, 54-5, 139-40, 143-7, 162-6, 218, 221-2, 223
argentines, Argentina silus and A. sphyraena, 43
Asia, 50, 57

India and Kashmir, 15, 58, 60
Japan, 46
U.S.S.R., 44, 46, 57

Bainbridge, R., 23
Ball, J. N. and Jones, J. W., 93
Ballysmuttan, see River Liffey
behaviour—of alevins, 77-8
 of fry, 78-9, 82, 171, 182, 183-4, 186
 feeding, 178, 182-9
 homing, 83-4
 spawning, 69-77
 territorial, 218-25
Berg, K., 210
Berg, L. S., 57
Berners, Dame Juliana, 15, 176, 241-2, 268-9
Berry, J., 234-5
Bhatia, D., 94
birds—as competitors, 234
 as hosts for parasites, 236-8
 as predators, 235, 251
blood, 22, 27, 32-5, 77-8, 142, 164, 251
bogs and bog water, 54, 162, 164
Brachymystax, 44
bream, Abramis brama, 125, 133, 231
Buckland, F., 59
bullhead (Miller's thumb), Cottus gobio, 125, 127, 133, 194, 229
Butcher, R. W., Pentelow, F. T. K. and Woodley, J. W. A., and see Coston, D. T., 199

calcium—absorption of ions, 28
  calcium carbonate in solution,
  see hard waters, soft waters,
  Map VI (159)
Campbell, R. N., 149, 160, 168,
  171-3, 258
cannibalism, 195
carbon dioxide, 23-5, 33-4, 155,
  163, 165, 225
carp, *Cyprinus carpio*, 44, 90
Carpenter, K., 124
chalk streams, 17, 114-15, 129,
  260, 263
char, *Salvelinus alpinus*, 43-4,
  46-7, 132, 192, 194, 228-9, 233
chromosomes, 109-10, 122
chub, *Squalius cephalus*, 125,
  127, 231
colour-change, 34, 53-5
  diversity of pattern, 17, 46-56,
    60, 110-13, 121-3
  of flesh, 17, 28, 55
  of fry, 79
  of spawning trout, 73-4
competition—between   trout,
  218-24, 255-6 *and see* territory
  with other species of fish, 224-
  34
condition factor, K, 65, 86, 172
Conroy, D. H., 63
Copley, H., 266
Coston, D. T., Pentelow, F.
  T. K. and Butcher, R. W.,
  251-2
crop, 64, 247-68; *especially*,
  262-6
crustaceans, aquatic, 28, 55,
  216, 229-30
  crayfish, *Astacus*, 177, 192,
    212-13
  freshwater shrimp, *Gammar-
    us*, 131, 135, 137, 168, 170,
    177, 183-7, 199-202, 205-6,
    208-15, 225, 229, 231, 235-6,
    261
  lake shrimp, *Mysis*, 177
  Sphaeroma, 216

waterfleas (Cladocera and Copepoda), 135, 177, 193, 213,
  226, 228, 231
  Bosmina, 193-4
  Bythotrephes, 194
  Cyclops, 181, 193, 237
  Daphnia, 181, 193-4
  Diaptomus, 193, 237
  Eurycercus, 135, 194
  Leptodora, 194
water slater, *Asellus*, 131, 137,
  177, 181, 191, 199, 205, 212-
  13, 246
current, *see* floods *and* rivers
Cyprinidae (principal family of
  "coarse fish"), 127, 133-4,
  171, 232, 244-5; *see also*
  bream, carp, chub, dace,
  gudgeon, loach, minnow,
  roach, rudd, tench

dace, *Leuciscus leuciscus*, 23,
  125, 127, 231
Dahl, Knut, 18, 90-1, 120, 172,
  206
Davis, H. S., 78, 112
Day, Francis, 55-60
daylength, 69, 137-44, 149
death, 84, 107 *and see* mortality
diet, *see* food
Donaldson, L. R. and Olson,
  P. R., 112-13
Downing, K. M. and Merkens,
  J. C., 25
drift, 182, 201-2, 217

earthworm (Oligochaeta), 177,
  181, 185, 199, 205-6
eel, *Anguilla anguilla*, 72, 125,
  133-4, 229, 233-4, 257, 262
elver, 194, 262
eggs (ova), 42, 66-8, 75-6, 234-5,
  240, 251-2, 258
  development of, 77-8, 150,
    163-4
  number and size of, 118-21,
    174-5

elephant-snout fish (Mormyrid), 42

Elliot, J. M., 202

Embody, G. C., 78

England, *see* lakes, English *and* rivers, English

Europe (except British Isles), 44-7, 48, 50, 57 (*and see* lakes, foreign, *and* rivers, foreign)
  Denmark, 16, 200
  Germany, 62, 120
  Norway, 18, 43, 46, 52, 90, 120, 128, 172, 193, 206
  Poland, 122
  Sweden, 43, 83-4, 110-12, 120
  U.S.S.R., 46, 57

eyes, 36-40, 53-4, 140, 186-9

Falkland Islands, 53

fatness, 65, 68 (*and see* condition factor)

fauna (*see also* common names of fish; crustaceans; drift; insects; mites; molluscs; worms; zooplankton)
  bottom fauna compared with food, 184-93, 196, 215-16, 229
  making additions to, 260-1
  of lakes (still waters), 135-7, 203-8
  of polluted waters, 244-7
  of rivers (running waters), 126-31, 197-202
  seasonal changes in, 188-96
  and water hardness, 167-70, 208-12

feeding, 140, 146, 167, 176-217
  behaviour, 178, 182-9
  mechanics of, 26-7
  on drift, 182
  on fish, 194-6, 222, 229-31
  on zooplankton, 193, 223

fertilisation of eggs, 76-7

fertilisation of waters—by adding chemicals, 168-70, 175, 260
  by sewage effluents, 244-5

fins, 21-3, 42, 48, 56, 75, 110-12

floods, 71-2, 128, 138, 173, 193, 259

food (*see also* fauna, feeding)
  animals eaten, 26-8, 176-217, 224-7, 229
  drawings of, 179, 180, 181
  invertebrates, aquatic (*see also* crustaceans, insects, mites, molluscs, worms), 182-3 192-3, 201-3, 205, 210-12, 216, 225-6, 229-30, 232-4, 260
  invertebrates, terrestrial (*see also* earthworms, insects, slugs, spiders, woodlice), 182-3, 192, 225-6, 233
  vertebrates-amphibians (frogs, newts, tadpoles), 177, fish (*and see under common names*), 189, 194-6
  mammals (mice), 178
  conversion into fish flesh, 29-31
  in acid waters, 208
  in hard waters, 203-4, 207-16
  in lakes (still waters), 136-7, 197, 203-7
  in rivers (running waters), 129, 196-205
  in soft waters, 203-4, 207-16
  requirements in relation to growth, 27-31, 84, 144-6
  seasonal changes, 93, 150, 189-93, 196
  supply in relation to growth, 30-1, 63, 160, 167, 196, 218-20

forage ratio (availability factor, co-efficient of accessibility), 186-8, 195, 200, 212

Fort, R. S. and Brayshaw, J. D. *and see* Myers, C., 252

Francis, F., 59

Freshwater Biological Association, 19, 120, 138, 163, 169-70, 260

Freshwater Fisheries Laboratory, Pitlochry, 70, 160, 170, 210, 260

fry (O+ fish, fingerling), Plate 4—food of, 178, 182-3
  behaviour of, 78-9, 82, 178, 182-3, 186
  mortality (survival) of, 79-82

genetics, 109-23, 146
Geng, H., 212
geology, 151-60
Gerrish, G. S., 107, 115-16, 147
gills, 24, 31-3, 163, 236
goldfish, *Carassius auratus*, 23, 32
gonads, 35, 46, 65-70, 95, 140-1
grayling, *Thymallus thymallus*, 44, 125, 127, 229
Greeley, J. R., 74
growth (*see also* growth rate, length, weight)
  of newly introduced fish, 63, 240
  of parasitised fish, 239
growth rate, 96-102
  and age, 100-8; Appendix VI
  and food, 196-217
  and heredity, 110-23
  and light, 138-43
  and sexual maturity, 105-8, 114-18
  and temperature, 144-51
  and water chemistry, 152, 162-7, 169-75
  annual variation, 100, 138-9
gudgeon, *Gobio gobio*, 194, 231
gut, 22, 26-8, 42, 55-6, 163, 236-7, Appendix I
Günther, A. C. L. G., 42, 50, 54-5
gwyniad, *see* whitefish

hard waters, 152-8, 160-8, 171, 203, 207-13
Hartley, P. H. T., 231, 250, 258
Harvey, L. A., 212-13
hatcheries, 55, 60-2, 76-7, 110-11, 116-18, 120, 138, 163, 237

fry from compared with wild fish, 250-2
"hatching" of "flies", 188-9, 192, 201
Hebrides, 53
herrings, 42
Hewitt, E. R., 147
Higgs, A., 120
Hills, J. W., 251
Hobbs, D. F., 77
Hoffbauer, C., 90
Holmes, P. F., 239
hormones, 34-5, 139
  gonadial, 65, 68, 70
  pituitary, 34, 69
  thyroid, 34
Horokiwi, *see under* river, foreign
Horton, Mrs. P. A., 202, 266
Hucho, 44
Huet, M., 124
Humphries, C. F., 205
hybrids—brown trout × salmon, sea trout, rainbow trout, 122-3
  brown trout × speckled trout (gives zebra trout), 123
Hynes, H. B. N., 126, 208, 210, 245

India, *see* Asia
Inland Fisheries Trust (Ireland), 257
insects, aquatic, 229-30, 235
  alderflies (Neuroptera), *Sialis*, 131, 135, 177-8, 185, 199, 205, 226
  beetles (Coleoptera), 131, 135, 177-8, 185, 189, 198, 210-13, 226
  caddisflies (Trichoptera), 131, 135, 137, 179, 182-5, 187, 190-1, 198, 200-1, 205, 208-13, 226, 228
    Brachycentrus, 261
    Hydropsyche, 187
    Leptocerus, 192

Limnophilus, 192
Sericostoma, 261
dragonflies (Odonata), 131, 135, 177, 185
  Pyrrhosoma nymphula, 215
mayflies (Ephemeroptera), 131, 135, 177-9, 182-90, 198-205, 208-15, 226, 261
  Baëtis, 131, 179, 182, 187-8
  Caenis, 135, 179, 187, 200, 205
  Cloëon, 135, 169
  Ecdyonurus, 131, 135, 179
  Ephemera, 135, 179, 187-8, 192, 200, 234, 243, 261, 263
  Ephemerella, 131, 188, 193
  Heptagenia, 135
  Leptophlebia, 135, 234
  Rithrogena, 131
stoneflies (Plecoptera), 131, 135, 179-80, 185, 187, 190, 198, 202, 205, 208-14, 226
  Nemoura, 192
  Perla (creeper), 244
two-winged flies (Diptera), 178, 185, 190, 211, 213
non-biting midges (Chironomids), 131, 135, 177, 180, 187, 189, 192, 196, 202, 203-7, 208-15, 230, 246
  Chironomus thummi, 246
phantom larva, *Chaoborus*, 135, 178, 180, 202-3
reed smut (blackfly), *Simulium*, 131, 177-8, 184-5, 187-90, 199, 200-1, 210, 213
water boatmen (Hemiptera), Corixids, 131, 135, 177, 185
insects, terrestrial, 189, 226, 228
aphids and tree bugs (Hemiptera), 177
beetles (Coleoptera), 177
caterpillars (Lepidoptera), 193
flies (Diptera), 178
springtails (Collembola), 183
iodine, 164
Ireland, *see under* lakes, Irish and rivers, Irish

Japan, *see* Asia
Jones, J. R. E., 129, 210
Jones, J. W., 48
  and Ball, J. N., 74-5, 93
  and Evans, 233

K, *see* condition factor
Kalleberg, H., 219-22, 256
Kashmir, *see* Asia (India)
Kashmir box, 252
kidney, 31-2
Kipling, C., 91-2

lakes, including references to all still waters, 17, 46, 53-5, 70, 72-3, 82-3, 132-7, 149, 152, 155, 160, 197, 203-8, 223, 235-7, 243, 267
lakes, English (lakes, tarns and reservoirs), *and see* Appendix IV
  Abbeystead Lake, 70
  Blagdon Reservoir, 106, 160, 163, 193-4, 207, 231, 256, 267
  Buttermere, 133
  Cheddar Reservoir, 232
  Chew Valley Reservoir, 267
  Coniston Water, 228
  Ennerdale Water, 228
  Esthwaite Water, 230
  Eye Brook Reservoir, 195, 231, 256
  Hodson's Tarn, 215
  Ladybower Reservoir, 267
  Malham Tarn, 102, 106, 193, 239
  Norfolk Broads, 133
  Scale Tarn, 138, 174, 216, 261
  Sunbiggin Tarn, 209
  Sutton Bingham Reservoir, 267
  tarns near Windermere, 17, 71, 133, 143, 160, 224
  Three Dubs Tarn, 81-2, 107, 137, 169, 173-4, 184, 194, 197, 267
  Wastwater, 102, 133, 207-9

lakes, English [contd.]
Weir Wood Reservoir, 267
Windermere, 17-19, 70-1, 74,
  83, 92, 102, 107, 133, 136-9,
  140, 148, 173-4, 190-5, 205-9,
  228-37, 257, 263, 267
Wise Een Tarn, 123, 193-4,
  234, 253, 267
Yew Tree Tarn, 106, 172-3, 194
lakes, foreign
Brûlé, Canada, 62
Crecy, Canada, 257
Cultus, Canada, 257
Ellesmere, Tasmania, 266
Esrom, Denmark, 197, 210
Garda, Italy, 57
Gibson, Canada, 257
Gribsø, Denmark, 210
Paalsbu Fjord, Norway, 137
Tunhov Fjord, Norway, 137
lakes, Irish (loughs and reser-
  voirs), 53-5, 243, 257, and see
  Appendix IV
Atorick, 95, 102, 193, 209
Bofin, 106
in Co. Cavan, 133
Corrib, 106, 232
Derg, 17, 102, 106, 133, 209,
  263, Plate 9
Glore, 209
Inchiquin, 106, 193, 209
Mask, 133, 232
Melvin, 55
Neagh, 55
Owel, 223
Poulaphouca Reservoir, 70
Rea, 102, 209
Ree, 133
Sheelin, 232
lakes, Scottish (lochs, lochans
  and reservoirs), 160, 170, 257,
  and see Appendix IV
Boisdale, 209
Borralie, 173
an Daim, 70, 173
Daimh Mhor, 170
Dunalastair Reservoir, 70-1, 83

nan Ealachan, 173
Fincastle, 106, 173
Garry, 149
Glutt, 173
Granabhat, 209
Kinardochy, 170
Kinnaird Mill Dam, 267
Lanish, 173
Leven, 50, 55, 70-2, 74, 102,
  207-9, 267
Lomond, 133, 206
Moraig, 70, 73, 83
Rannoch, 133
Scourie lochs, 170
of Stennes, Orkney, 52
Strathkyle, 173, 209
Tummel, 195
Unnamed, 173-4
lakes, Welsh, and see Appendix
  IV
Reservoir near Cardiff, 236-7
Llyn Tegid (Bala Lake), 93,
  106, 133, 149, 197, 206, 209
Vyrnwy, 267

lamprey (Petromyzonti), 267
Latour, Ernest, 61
Le Cren, E. D., 70, 80-1, 219-20
leeches, see worms, aquatic and
  parasites
length (of brown trout), see also
  growth, growth rate, 63-4,
  85-8, 90-4, 169-70, 100-4, 110-
  41, 150-1, 167-8, 170, 172-5,
  184, 195, 202-5, 207-8, 209,
  213, 219-21, 227, 232-3, 266
  at three years old in British
    waters, 102-3, 158-60, Map V
    (157)
  at sexual maturity, 110, 118-19
  back-calculation of Appendix
    II, 91-3, 103-5
  back-calculated for British
    lakes, Appendix IV
  back-calculated for British
    rivers, Appendix III
length-weight relationship, see
  condition factor

"lies", 129-8, 130-2, 259-61
limits to angling—by bag and size, 257-8, 261-7
by close season, 263-7
by number of rod-days, 263-7
Linnaeus, C., 42, 50
liver—in diet, 26-7, 55
of trout, 27
loach (stoneloach), *Nemacheilus barbatula*, 127, 194, 230

Macan, T. T., 136, 148, 169, 215
and Worthington, E. B., 148
McCormack, Miss J., 149, 182-3
McIvor, Mr., 60
mackerel, *Scomber scomber*, 44
Maclean, Mr., 61
Maintenance requirement, 28-9, 144-6, 151, 163
Maitland, P. S., 225
mammals, as food (mice), 177-8
as predators (brown rat, mink, otter, water shrew), 235, 236-9, 257
management of waters, 15-17, 248-66
maturity, 105-8, 109-19, 121-3, 139-41, 173-5
metabolic rate, 128, 142-6
migration—of brown and sea trout, 50-2, 60, 62-3, 69-70, 82-4, 105, 166-8, 218
of hybrids, 122-3, 166
of other salmonids, 45-6, 48-50
Miller, R. B., 251
milt (sperm), 68-9, 75-6
minnow, *Phoxinus phoxinus*, 125, 127, 132-3, 172, 195, 223, 229-31, 233
Minot, C. S., 100
mites (Hydracarina), 131, 135, 185, 198, 211, 213
molluscs, aquatic, 55, 200, 208-10, 216, 225-6, 229
limpets, 181, 187, 198-200, 204, 211, 226-9

Acroloxus, 135
Ancylus, 131, 135, 215
pea mussels, 177, 181, 199-200, 205-6
Pisidium, 131, 135, 169, 187
Sphaerium, 135
snails, 28, 131, 135, 137, 168, 177, 181, 185, 190-2, 198, 200-2, 205, 211-12, 246, 261
Limnaea, 131, 135, 191, 236
Neritina (*Theodoxus*), 199
Planorbis, 135
Valvata, 131, 135
Vivipara, 261
Moon, H. P., 205-6
Morgan, N. C., 210
mortality, *and see* predators, of eggs, and alevins, 76-7, 79-82, 120-2, 128-9
of fry, 79-82, 121, 129-30, 171-2, 219-22, 249-51, 255
of older trout, 80-2, 84, 106-8, 118, 129, 236-9
Munro, W. R. and Balmain, K. H., 70
muscles, 21-3, 33, 41, 237, 251
Myers, C., 70, 147, 255, 256
and Bevins, J., 70
and Fort, R. S., 82

Nall, G. H., 52
Neave, F., 88
Neill, R. M., 185
nervous system and nerves, 21, 35-41
Newfoundland, *see* America
New Zealand, *see* Antipodes
Nicholls, A. G., 254, 256, 266
Norden, C. R., 45
Norway, *see* Europe

Oncorhynchus, *see* salmon, Pacific orography, Map II, 153
ovaries, 65-9 *and see* gonads
oxygen, 22-3, 33-4, 58-63, 124, 134, 143-4, 244-5

parasites, 85, 235-40, 261
flukes (Trematoda)
  Crepidostomum, 236
  Diplostomulum, 236
  Discocotyle, 236
  Gyrodactylus, 236
leech *Piscicola* (Hirundinea), 236
louse *Argulus* (Crustacea), 236
protozoans
  Chloromyxum, 237
  Ichthyophthirius (white spot or "ich"), 236-9
  Octomitis, 237
roundworms (Nemertoda), 235-7
  Agamonema, 237
  Cystidicola, 237
spiny-headed worms (Acanthocephala), 236
  Echinorhynchus, 237
  tapeworms (Cestoda), 236
  Diphyllobothrium, 237-9
  Eubothrium, 236-7
Pentelow, F. T. K., 147, 164-5, 171, 210 *and see* Butcher, R. W. *and* Coston, D. T.
perch, *Perca fluviatilis*, 25, 53, 125, 127, 133, 161, 194-5, 223, 228-30, 257
Percival, E. and Whitehead, H., 198
pH, 151-8, 168-75, 213 *and see* acid waters
pike, *Esox lucius*, 125, 127, 138-9, 161, 162, 229, 232-3, 257-8
plants, aquatic, 130-2, 134-6, 142-3, 162, 168, 197-203, 207-8, 213-16, 220, 244-5, 260
algae, 130-1, 209
  Cladophora (blanket weed), 198
  Nitella, 169
  Nostoc, 178
  phytoplankton, 135
  stonewort *Chara*, 135

bulrush, *Scirpus lacustris*, 131, 135
bur-reed, *Sparganium*, 131
Canadian pondweed, *Elodea canadensis*, 131, 135
common reed, *Phragmites communis*, 135
lakewort, *Littorella*, 135-6, 207
mare's tail, *Hippuris vulgaris*, 131, 200-1
mosses, 131, 135-6, 196, 200, 212-13, 215
pondweeds *Potamogeton* spp., 131, 135-6, 198, 200
quillwort, *Isoetes lacustris*, 135-6
reedmace, *Typha*, 135
sedge, *Carex* spp., 131, 135-6
water buttercup, *Ranunculus*, 200-1
celery, *Apium nodiflorum*, 131
cress, *Nasturtium officinale*, 131
crowfoot, *Ranunculus fluitans*, 131
lobelia, *Lobelia dortmanni*, 135
milfoil, *Myriophyllum* spp., 131, 135
parsnip, *Sium erectum*, 131, 200-1
starwort, *Callitriche stagnalis*, 131
poisons, 246-7, 251 *and see* pollution
pollan, *see* whitefish
populations, 63, 171-5, 216-25, 237-9
powan, *see* whitefish
Power, John Clarke, 61
predators, 84, 134, 231-5, 255-8, 262, 247-68, 258-62

Quebec, *see* America—Canada

rainfall, 71-2, 130, 138, 152
redd, described, 72-6 *and see* spawning
Regan, C. Tate, 50-6

reservoirs, 137, 230, 236-7, 243-4 *and see* lakes

respiration, 23-5, 142 *and see* oxygen

rhythms, 69, 93-5, 100, 138-41 *and see* seasonal changes

rivers, including references to all running waters, 17, 47, 49, 52-4, 69-74, 82-4, 123-4, 141, 148, 152-8, 160, 196-205, 218, 259-61, 263-7

rivers, English, *and see* Appendix III

Aire, 198

Avon (Bristol), 160

Avon (Wilts and Hants), 69, 106, 127-9, 204, 211, 264

Bela, 102, 204, 227

Black Brows Beck, 178, 182, 195, 219-20

Brathay, 182, 194, 230

Cam, 195, 230

Chess, 49

Dart, 102, 141, 150-1, 160, 204

Derwent (Derbys), 69, 160, 227

Driffield Beck, 69, 200-2, 208

Duddon, 129

Itchen, 151, 193, 204

Kingswell Beck, 92, 151, 183

Kennet, 102, 160, 204

Kennet Canal, 204

lakeland becks, 69, 129

Lambourn, 151

Lark, 199, 210

Leven, 194

Lune, 253

Misbourne, 49

Nidd, 197-8

Raise Beck, 102, 197, 204

Scandale Beck, 120

Severn, 152

Shepreth Brook, 195

Tamar, 141, 160

Tees, 150, 152, 193, 195, 210

Test, 106, 129, 148, 151, 204, 261

Thames, 160

Troutbeck, 70-1, 132

Walla Brook, 150, 160, 202, 213, 266

Wharfe, 197-8

Windrush, 204

Wye (Derbys), 49

Wye (Herefords and Mon), 160, 235

Wyre, 70, 82

Yarty, 213

rivers, foreign

Bushman's, Natal, 61

Danube, 44

of Gudbrandsdal, Norway, 128

Gura, Kenya, 61

Guysborough, Canada, 62

Horokiwi, North Island, New Zealand, 19, 128, 137, 214-16, 222, 253, 263, 266

Kiringa, Kenya, 267

Mooi, Natal, 61, 63

North Esk, Tasmania, 256, 266

Oxus, U.S.S.R., 57

Plenty (tributary of Derwent), Tasmania, 59-60

Sacramento, U.S.A., 48

Sagana, Kenya, 94, 267

Salmon, Canada, 62

Susaa, Denmark, 197, 200

Thego, Kenya, 267

Thiba, Kenya, 283

Tuel Aa, Denmark, 200

Umgeni, Natal, 61

Waiou, S.I. New Zealand, 60

rivers, Irish, *and see* Appendix III

Clare-Galway, 96-8, 100-2

Fergus, 102, 106, 193, 204

Liffey, 19, 70, 93, 96-7, 100-2, 140-2, 160, 189-93, 196, 204, 212, 215-17, Plate 11

Owenea, 119

Shannon, 160

rivers, Scottish, *and see* Appendix III

Don, 185

rivers, Scottish [contd.]
  Endrick, 225
  Forss, 102, 106, 141, 151, 182, 204, 225-8
  Gisla, 141
  Thurso, 69
  Tweed, 69, Plate 13
rivers, Welsh, *and see* Appendix III
  Afon Hirnant, 208-10
  Dee, 160, 211
  Rhydwen, 102, 106, 150, 197
  Teifi, 106, 225, 233
  Towy, 129
roach, *Rutilus rutilus*, 25, 125, 127, 162, 195, 231
rudd, *Scardinius erythrophthalmus*, 125, 133, 195, 231
Runnstrom, Dr., 83-4

salinity—effect on growth, 166-8; and osmo-regulation, 30-5, 43-4, 235-6
salmon, Atlantic, *Salmo salar*, 32, 42-8, 58-60, 122-6, 141, 187-9, 195, 225-8, 257-8
salmon, Pacific, *Oncorhynchus* spp., 45-6, 83
  pink (humpback), *O. gorbuscha*, 46
  quinnat (king), *O. tschawytscha*, 46
Salmonidae, 44-56
Salmonoidei, 42-4
Sandwith, Major, 62
Sawyer, Frank, 127, 234, 264, 257
scales, 22, 42, 44-5, 86-96, 102-3, 107, 115-16, 138-9, 169, Plates 6, 7, 8
  annulus, circulus and zones on, 89-96, 138, 151
  back-calculation from, 90-3, 102-4, Appendix II
  replacement, 95
  spawning marks and absorption (erosion), 95

schelly, *see* whitefish
Scotland, *see* lakes, Scottish, *and* rivers, Scottish
Seas—Aral, Black, Caspian, North and Mediterranean, 57
  Baltic, 57, 166-7
  White, 46
seasonal changes—in food, 93-4 149-50, 150-1, 185-6, 195-6
  in physical environment, 69-70, 137-44
  in trout growth, 91, 92-3, 100, 138, 149-50, 196
seawater, *see* salinity
senses, 35-41 *and see* eyes
shrimps, *see* crustaceans
silt, 125-6, 197-8, 199-200, 259-60
skeleton and skull, 21, 23, 44-51, 52, 54, 56
Skrochowska, St., 122, 166-7
smelt, *Osmerus eperlanus*, 43
Smith, Charles, 148
Smith, M. W., 257
Smyly, W. J. P., 230
  with Frost, W. E., 82, 170, 172, 184
snails, *see* molluscs
soft waters, 121, 152-8, 162-75, 204, 207-13
Sømme, I. D., 67
Sømme, S., 128
Southern, H. N., 235
Southern, Rowland, 18, 84, 152, 174, 193, 212
spawning, 18-19, 58-63, 66-8, 70-7, 83-4, 93-5, 105-7, 109-12, 124, 127-30, 133-4, 138-42, 172-5, 222-4, 228-9, 232-4, 244-5, 256-7
  grounds, 69-74, 126-7, 132-4, 222-3, 224-5, 229, 232, 234, 256-60
spiders (Arachnida), 178
springs, 129, 147-8, 151, 251
Stephens, M., 235
stickleback, *Gasterosteus acule-*

atus, 133, 194, 223, 229-32, 236

stock, 63-4, 247-68; especially, 257-8

values for, 263-7

stocking, 249-57

stoneloach, *see* loach

Straffan, *see* River Liffey

Stuart, T. A., 70-4, 78, 82-4

substratum, eroding & depositing, 124-38, 197-212, 220-1 *and see* silt, spawning grounds

Sweden *see* Europe

Swift, D. R., 138-141, 146-7, 149

swimming, 21-3

survival, *see* mortality

tail, 21-3, 48, 53-4, 75, 79

tarpon, *Megalops*, 42

Tasmania, *see* Antipodes

temperature, 24-6, 30, 52-3, 58-63, 71-2, 78-94, 103, 122, 124, 134, 137-51, 152, 196, 244, 259, Map III (154)

lethal limits for eggs, 77, 150

lethal limits for older fish, 142-4

and optimum growth, 144-8

of British waters, 138, 147-51

tench, *Tinca tinca*, 24-5

territories, 175, 218-25, 255

of fry, 79-80, 218-21

of yearlings, 82

testes, 68-70 *and see* gonads

Thomas, J. D., 225, 233

Toner, E. D., 232

topography, 124-37, 152

trees and bushes, 132-3, 136-7, 259-60

trout, brown, *Salmo trutta*, Plates 1, 2, 3, 4; Map I, 51

Linnaeus' and Günther's species, 42, 48-56

compared with salmon parr, 49

world distribution, 50, 57-64, Map I

trout, cut-throat, *Salmo clarkii*, 49-50, 63-4, 249-50

trout, rainbow, *Salmo gairdneri*, 24-5, 42, 48, 54, 58, 61-2, 112-15, 120, 250, 253, 267, Plate 4

trout, sea, *Salmo trutta*, 32, 34, 52, 121-3, 167, 176, 216, 224-5

trout, speckled (American brook trout), *Salvelinus fontinalis*, 26, 42, 44, 47, 63, 112, 141, 145, 174, 267

Tucker, D. S., 168

U.S.A., *see* America

U.S.S.R., *see* Asia *and* Europe

van Someren, V. D., 71, 94, 139

vendace, *see* whitefish

Vibert box, 252

vomerine teeth, 45

Wales, *see* lakes, Welsh *and* rivers, Welsh

Walls, G. L., 37-9

Walton, Izaak, 15, 18, 124, 269

weeds, *see* plants

Weerekoon, A. C. J., 206

weight (of brown trout), *see also* growth, growth rate, condition factor, 17-18, 59-62, 85-7, 95-6, 144, 166-8, 170-1, 173-4, 193-5, 222-4, 239, 248-50, 263-6

Went, A. E. J. and Frost, W. E., 226

whitefish (Coregoninae) gwyniad, pollan, powan, vendace (all *Coregonus* spp.), 44-5, 125-6, 228-9

ciscoes, 45

Prosopium, Stenodus, 44-5

Whitehead, H., 200-1

Wingfield, C. A., 146-7, 164

"winter kill", 143

woodlice (Crustacea), 177

worms, aquatic
  bristle (Oligochaeta, including
    Tubificidae), 131-2, 135-6,
    177, 181, 185, 187, 189-90,
    208-10, 213, 245-6
  flat (Turbellaria), 177, 200
  leeches (Hirudinea), 131, 135,
    177, 180, 185, 199-200, 205,
    245-6

  Erpobdella, 246
  threadworms (Nematoda), 213
worms, parasitic, *see* parasites

Youl, James Arundel, 58

zinc, 61, 246
zooplankton, 46, 135, 193, 228
  and see crustaceans, feeding

Fontana Books

Fontana is at present best known (outside the field of popular fiction) for its extensive list of books on history, philosophy and theology. Now, however, the list is expanding rapidly to include most main subjects, such as literature, politics, economics and sociology. At the same time, the number of paperback reprints of books already published in hardcover editions is being increased. Further information on Fontana's present list and future plans can be obtained from: The Non-Fiction Editor, Fontana Books, 14 St James's Place, London S.W.1.

All Fontana books are available at your bookshop or newsagent; or can be ordered direct. Just fill in the form below and list the titles you want.

FONTANA BOOKS, Cash Sales Department, P.O. Box 4, Godalming, Surrey. Please send purchase price plus 5p postage per book by cheque, postal or money order. No currency.

NAME (Block Letters) _____

ADDRESS _____

_____

_____

While every effort is made to keep prices low, it is sometimes necessary to increase prices at short notice. Fontana Books reserve the right to show new retail prices on covers which may differ from those previously advertised in the text or elsewhere.

Fontana Social Science

Books available include:

African Genesis   Robert Ardrey   **50p**

The Territorial Imperative   Robert Ardrey   **50p**

Racial Minorities   Michael Banton   **50p**

The Sociology of Modern Britain
Edited by Eric Butterworth and David Weir **60p**

Social Problems of Modern Britain
Edited by Eric Butterworth and David Weir **75p**

Strikes   Richard Hyman   **50p**

Memories, Dreams, Reflections   C. J. Jung   **60p**

Strike at Pilkingtons   Tony Lane and Kenneth Roberts   **50p**

Figuring Out Society   Ronald Meek   **45p**

Lectures on Economic Principles   Sir Dennis Robertson   **75p**

People and Cities   Stephen Verney   **37½p**

Fontana Politics

Books available include:

Battle for the Environment Tony Aldous **45p**

The English Constitution Walter Bagehot
Edited by R. H. S. Crossman **40p**

War in Modern Society Alastair Buchan **42½p**

At War With Asia Noam Chomsky **50p**

Problems of Knowledge and Freedom Noam Chomsky **30p**

Selected Writings of Mahatma Gandhi
Edited by Ronald Duncan **45p**

Marx and Engels: Basic Writings
Edited by Lewis S. Feuer **50p**

Governing Britain A. H. Hanson and Malcolm Walles **50p**

The Commons in Transition *Edited by* A. H. Hanson and
Bernard Crick **50p**

Sir Charles Dilke Roy Jenkins **52½p**

Europe Tomorrow *Edited by* Richard Mayne **60p**

Machiavelli: Selections *Edited by* John Plamenatz **60p**

Democracy in America Alexis de Tocqueville
Edited by J. P. Mayer and Max Lerner Vols I & II **75p** each

The Cabinet Patrick Gordon Walker **40p**

The Downfall of the Liberal Party 1914–1935
Trevor Wilson **60p**

Economics and Policy Donald Winch **80p**

Fontana Introduction to Modern Economics

General Editor: C. D. Harbury

Each of the seven books in the series introduces the reader to a major area or aspect of modern economics. Each stands on its own, but all fit together to form an introductory course which covers most A-Level and first year university syllabuses, and those of most professional bodies.

Already published

Income, Spending and the Price Level   A. G. Ford   **75p**

An Introduction to Economic Behaviour   C. D. Harbury   **60p**

International Trade and the Balance of Payments
H. Katrak   **50p**

Mathematics for Modern Economics   R. Morley   **£1**

Private and Public Finance   G. H. Peters   **60p**

Britain and the World Economy, 1919-1970
L. J. Williams   **50p**

For publication 1973

Economics of the Market   G. Hewitt